T0053431

BIBLICAL HEBREW VOCABULARY

BY

CONCEPTUAL CATEGORIES

BIBLICAL HEBREW VOCABULARY

by

CONCEPTUAL CATEGORIES

BIBLICAL HEBREW VOCABULARY BY CONCEPTUAL CATEGORIES

A STUDENT'S GUIDE TO NOUNS IN THE OLD TESTAMENT

J. David Pleins
with Jonathan Homrighausen

ZONDERVAN®

ZONDERVAN

Biblical Hebrew Vocabulary by Conceptual Categories
Copyright © 2017 by J. David Pleins

Requests for information should be addressed to:
Zondervan, 3900 *Sparks Dr. SE, Grand Rapids, Michigan 49546*

ISBN 978-0-310-53074-9

All Scripture quotations, unless otherwise indicated, are taken from The Holy Bible, New International Version®, NIV®. Copyright © 1973, 1978, 1984, 2011 by Biblica, Inc.® Used by permission of Zondervan. All rights reserved worldwide www.Zondervan.com. The "NIV" and "New International Version" are trademarks registered in the United States Patent and Trademark Office by Biblica, Inc.®

Any Internet addresses (websites, blogs, etc.) and telephone numbers in this book are offered as a resource. They are not intended in any way to be or imply an endorsement by Zondervan, nor does Zondervan vouch for the content of these sites and numbers for the life of this book.

All rights reserved. No part of this publication may be reproduced, stored in a retrieval system, or transmitted in any form or by any means – electronic, mechanical, photocopy, recording, or any other – except for brief quotations in printed reviews, without the prior permission of the publisher.

Cover design: Tobias Design: Outerwear for books
Cover photo: Adobe Stock
Interior design: Matthew Van Zomeren

Printed in the United States of America

HB 06.02.2022

J. D. P.: To Hoy Ledbetter†, who first inspired my interest
in biblical languages, his devoted wife Jary and, of course,
to Karen whose friendship, love, and support have brought such joy to my life.

כִּי-עַזָּה כַמָּוֶת אַהֲבָה קָשָׁה כִשְׁאוֹל קִנְאָה
Song of Solomon 8:6b

J. H.: To Michelle and April

אֵשֶׁת־חַיִל מִי יִמְצָא וְרָחֹק מִפְּנִינִים מִכְרָהּ
בָּטַח בָּהּ לֵב בַּעְלָהּ וְשָׁלָל לֹא יֶחְסָר
גְּמָלַתְהוּ טוֹב וְלֹא־רָע כֹּל יְמֵי חַיֶּיהָ
Proverbs 31:10–12

מוֹשִׁיבִי עֲקֶרֶת הַבַּיִת אֵם־הַבָּנִים שְׂמֵחָה הַלְלוּ־יָהּ
Psalm 113:9

BRIEF TABLE OF CONTENTS

Detailed Table of Contents 8
Abbreviations 15
Preface 16
Bibliography 22

I. The Created Order 27
Heavens and Earth 28
Metals, Stones, Gems, Minerals, and Pearls 37
Colors 41
Time 43
Animals 46
Flora 56
II. The Human Order 61
Human 62
Human Anatomy 65
Disease, Mortality, and Disability 71
Food and Spices 76
Clothing 84
III. The Social Order 91
Family and Kinship 92
Worship/Cultic 94
Law and Covenant 100
Professions and Occupations 103
Military 107
Maritime 115
Music 117
Education 120
IV. The Constructed Order 123
Buildings and Structures 124
Containers and Implements 132
Tools 136
Measurement 140

Appendix One: Guide to Further Reading 143
Appendix Two: Cluster Verses for Study 148
Hebrew Word Index 151
Scripture Index 165

DETAILED TABLE OF CONTENTS

Abbreviations 15
Preface 16
Bibliography 22

I. The Created Order 27

Heavens and Earth 28
Cosmology 28
Sky/Firmament 28
Stars 28
Sun 29
Moon 29
Earth 29
Clouds 31
Wind/Hurricane 32
Lightning 32
Fire 32
Rain/Storm 33
Water 33
Underworld 35
Compass/Directions 36

Metals, Stones, Gems, Minerals, and Pearls 37
Metals 37
General Terms: Stones, Gems 38
Stones 39
Gems 39
Minerals 40
Pearls 40

Colors 41
General Terms 41
Specific Colors 41
Spotted/Speckled 42

Time 43
Day: Morning to Night 43
General Terms: Days/Week 43
General Terms: Time 43

Month/Year 44
Calendar 45
Seasons 45

Animals 46
General Terms 46
Birds 46
Cattle 48
Sheep, Goats 48
Enclosures/Troughs 49
Animal Husbandry Tools 50
Pasturage 50
Horses, Mules, Asses 50
Large Mammals 51
Small Mammals 53
Lizards/Reptiles 53
Snakes 53
Fish/Aquatic 54
Mollusks 54
Arthropods: Insects, Worms, Etc. 54
Locusts 54
Snares and Traps 55

Flora 56
Trees: General and Specific 56
Grasses 57
Reeds 57
Flowers and Plants 57
Thorns, Thistles, Briars 58
Bushes and Shrubs 58
Parts of Trees and Plants 59
Gardens and Planting Places 60

II. The Human Order 61

Human 62
General Terms 62
Male and Female 62
Infant 62
Youth 63
Old Age 63
Friend 63
(For Enemy, see Military ➡ Enemy) 107
Slaves/Servants 64
Nations/Peoples 64

Human Anatomy 65
Head 65
Hair 65
Face 65
Neck 66
Throat 66
Upper Body 66
Arm/Hand 66
Bones 67
Abdomen 67
Kidney/Liver 68
Loins 68
Back 68
Buttocks/Hip/Anus 68
Excrement 68
Genitals 68
Leg 69
Foot 70
Body/Muscle 70
Body Fat 70
Corpse 70

Disease, Mortality, and Disability 71
Disease 71
Specific Diseases 71
Medical Tools, Herbs 71
Wound 73
Pain 73
Disabilities 73
Death, Burial, Mourning 74

Food and Spices 76
Food/Drink: General Terms 76
Taste 77
Grains 77
Threshing/Winnowing 78
Grain: Baked Goods/Dough/Leaven 78
Vine, Wine, Grapes (includes Strong Drink) 78
Dairy 80
Nuts 80
Fruits 80
Vegetables 81
Honey 82
Herbs and Spices, Ointments/Resins/Balms, Incense 82

Clothing 84
General Terms 84
Old Clothes 84
Outer Garment 84
Robe 85
Band 85
Tunic 85
Hem/Fringes 85
Cloak 85
Head Covering 86
Veils 86
Footwear 86
Jewelry 86
Fabric 87
Cosmetics 88

III. The Social Order 91

Family and Kinship 92
Immediate Family 92
In-Laws 93
Marriage/Divorce 93
Widowhood 93
Family/Clan 93

Worship/Cultic 94
Structures 94
Ark of the Covenant 94
Altars 94
Menorah/Lampstand 95
Personnel 95
Garb (Priestly) 95
Accoutrements 96
(For Bowls, etc., see Containers and Implements) 132
Vow 96
Sacrifices and Offerings 96
Idolatry 97
Divination 97
Dream/Vision/Oracle 98
Purity/Impurity 98
Assembly 99
Holidays/Festivals 99

Law and Covenant 100
Laws/Decrees 100

Oath/Blessing/Curse 100
Justice 100
Crime/Evil/Wrong 101
Freedom 101
Poor/Oppressed 102
Wealthy/Rich 102

Professions and Occupations 103
(For Religious Professions, see Worship/Cultic ➡ Personnel) 95
Government: Leaders 103
Foreign Rulers and Leaders 104
Royal Ornament: Scepters/Staffs/Crowns/Throne/Footstool 104
Government: Administration 104
Artisans 105
Merchants/Business/Banking 105
Food Production 106
Prostitute/Sex Worker 106

Military 107
War: General Terms 107
Enemy/Victory/Defeat 107
Army 107
Officers/Leaders 107
Soldiers 108
Weapons/Armor 108
Vehicles, Horses, and Travel 111
Formations/Groups 112
Flags/Standards 112
Fortifications 112
Spoils, Plunder, Booty 113
Captive/Exile 114
Chains/Bonds/Fetters 114

Maritime 115
Ships 115
Crew 115
Structures 115
Trade/Cargo 116

Music 117
General Terms and Types 117
Instruments 117
Dance 119

Education 120
Teachers and Students 120

Writing Tools and Implements 120
(For Writing on Paper/Stone, see Tools ➡ Artisanal Tools ➡ Carving/Writing) 137
IV. The Constructed Order 123
Buildings and Structures 124
Town and Village 124
Buildings 124
(For Roads, see Military ➡ Vehicles, Horses, and Travel ➡ Road) 111
(For Fortifications, see Military ➡ Fortifications) 112
Structural Features 126
Furniture 130
Containers and Implements 132
General Terms 132
Chest/Box 132
Cup 132
Crucible 132
Bowl, Basin 132
Jug, Jar 133
Pot, Kettle 133
Pans 133
Flask 134
Pottery 134
Oven 134
Hearth 134
Sacks, Bags, Skins 134
Basket 135
Cutting Instruments 135
Fork 135
Tools 136
(Many other categories contain "Tools" vocabulary as well:
for Animal Husbandry Tools, see Animals ➡ Animal Husbandry Tools 50
for Hunting Tools, see Animals ➡ Snares and Traps 55
for Medical Tools, see Disease, Mortality, and Disability ➡ Medical Tools, Herbs 71
for Harvesting Tools, see Foods and Spices ➡ Threshing/Winnowing 78
for Military Tools see Military ➡ Weapons/Armor 108
for Literacy, see Education ➡ Writing Tools and Implements) . . . 120
General Tools 136

Artisanal Tools 137
(For Writing Implements, see Education ➡ Writing Tools and Implements) 120
Agricultural Tools 138

Measurement 140
General Terms 140
Liquid 140
Dry 140
Width 140
Height 141
Length 141
Weight 141
Currency 142
Scales 142

Appendix One: Guide to Further Reading 143
Appendix Two: Cluster Verses for Study 148
Hebrew Word Index 151
Scripture Index 165

ABBREVIATIONS

CHB Shafer-Elliott, Cynthia. "Cooking in the Hebrew Bible." *Bible and Interpretation*, May 2013. http://www.bibleinterp.com/articles/2013/sha378013.shtml.

CT Brenner, Athalya. *Colour Terms in the Old Testament.* Journal for the Study of the Old Testament Supplement Series 21. Sheffield, UK: Sheffield Academic Press, 1982.

DCH Clines, David J. A, ed. *The Dictionary of Classical Hebrew.* Sheffield: Sheffield Phoenix Press, 1993–2011.

ELT Borowski, Oded. *Every Living Thing: Daily Use of Animals in Ancient Israel.* Walnut Creek, CA: AltaMira Press, 1999.

FAJ Shafer-Elliott, Cynthia. *Food in Ancient Judah: Domestic Cooking in the Time of the Hebrew Bible.* BibleWorld. Sheffield, UK: Routledge, 2013.

HALOT Holladay, William L., ed. *A Concise Hebrew and Aramaic Lexicon of the Old Testament.* Grand Rapids: Eerdmans, 1972.

HCW Stadelmann, Luis I. J. *The Hebrew Conception of the World: A Philological and Literary Study.* Analecta Biblica 39. Rome: Pontificial Biblical Institute, 1970.

MPTOT Scott, R. B. Y. "Meteorological Phenomena and Terminology in the Old Testament." *Zeitschrift für die Alttestamentliche Wissenschaft* 64, no. 1 (1952): 11–25.

SDBH United Bible Societies. *Semantic Dictionary of Biblical Hebrew.* 2000–2009. http://www.sdbh.org/dictionary/main.php?language=en.

UBS United Bible Societies. *Fauna and Flora of the Bible.* Helps for Translators. London: United Bible Societies, 1980.

כלי De Moore, Johannes, ed. כלי *Database: Utensils in the Hebrew Bible.* Het Oudtestamentisch Werkgezelschap, 2010–2016. http://www.otw-site.eu/KLY/kly.php.

PREFACE

A command of Hebrew vocabulary is the essential key to an enjoyable encounter with sacred Scripture. Yet beginners who master the basics soon realize that their limited word stock stands in the way of fluid reading and an intuitive grasp of the biblical text. What should be enjoyable exercises in reading Scripture, unmediated by translation, become tedious page-flipping exercises through lexicons. No one tool provides the answer to this frustration. The eager student needs many vocabulary-building resources: Biblical Hebrew word frequency books,[1] Hebrew-English lexicons, a copy of *A Reader's Hebrew Bible* with marginal glosses,[2] flash cards, and perhaps a biblical vocabulary app or two. What makes *Biblical Hebrew Vocabulary by Conceptual Categories* (*BHVCC*) unique among all these resources is that words are grouped into logical categories. This approach is crucial because the mind constructs its mental space for language by making connections between words. Without these associations, vocabulary building is reduced to rote memorization that all too often becomes an exercise in futility. Unfortunately, until this book was compiled there was no handy reference that brought together all the Hebrew words for items such as gems, trees, birds, weapons, idols, storms, and the like.[3] To be sure, there are a few volumes that cover specific word groups, such as the plants or animals of the Bible, but these books are often limited in scope, cumbersome to use, expensive, and usually only available to those who have access to a specialized theological library (some of the more important titles are listed in the bibliography here). Needless to say, the student requires a more comprehensive and user-friendly resource. At last, in one place, are gathered the words for the body's anatomy, soldiers, ships, musical instruments, celestial phenomena, and more.

Format of *BHVCC*

This work has been divided into four major sections:

- The Created Order
- The Human Order
- The Social Order
- The Constructed Order

---

1. Larry Mitchel, *A Student's Vocabulary for Biblical Hebrew and Aramaic, Updated Edition* (Grand Rapids: Zondervan, 2017); Miles V. Van Pelt and Gary D. Pratico, *The Vocabulary Guide to Biblical Hebrew* (Grand Rapids: Zondervan, 2003); George M. Landes, *Building Your Biblical Hebrew Vocabulary: Learning Words by Frequency and Cognate*, 2nd ed. (Atlanta: Society of Biblical Literature, 2001).
2. A. Philip Brown II and Bryan W. Smith, eds., *A Reader's Hebrew Bible* (Grand Rapids: Zondervan, 2008).
3. While there is a student handbook to New Testament Greek vocabulary by categories, there is no counterpart in English for Old Testament vocabulary. Mark Wilson and Jason Oden, *Mastering New Testament Greek Vocabulary Through Semantic Domains* (Grand Rapids: Kregel Academic, 2003).

Underneath each of these four orders are numerous categories and subcategories designed to group specific meanings and create logical connections. Thus, for example, under "The Created Order," the reader will find the category "Heavens and Earth" with many subcategories such as "Moon" and "Clouds." Under "The Social Order," one finds the category "Family and Kinship" with such subcategories as "Immediate Family" and "Widowhood." Elsewhere, under "The Constructed Order," the student finds, for example, the numerous types of "Containers and Implements," all subdivided into logical groupings such as "Cup," "Pans," and "Cutting Implements." In short, the entire book is carefully arranged to create sensible groupings of related terms.

Each entry contains several elements. Immediately after the Hebrew word stands the main gloss. The initial glosses were, in part, devised by Pleins based on his years of reading and teaching the Hebrew text. To obtain some "public domain" vocabulary, at times these words were researched in older lexicons, such as Gesenius and BDB. However, every effort has been made to avoid outmoded English words or obsolete definitions. After the initial gloss (or sometimes the gloss as such), we add alternative definitions reflecting the results of technical scholarly studies or major lexicons. These glosses will be marked by an abbreviated form of the author's name or lexicon placed in parentheses after the alternatives. The specific works we consulted for these additional meanings can be found in the bibliography. At times, these specialized studies and lexicons agree with our initial gloss, and so in many cases we are only adding further possible meanings as suggested by these works. The student may be perplexed at the wide array of proposed meanings. One of our objects is to alert the student to debates about the meanings of many words, especially those that are rare. Students will want to consult commentaries for further insight into these debates. Lastly, the entry contains a biblical verse for reference. While in some cases the choice simply provides an example of usage, many of these were selected with a view to presenting the word in a context in which the meaning is more readily apparent. The vivid nature of passages in Proverbs, for example, often makes the meaning of the Hebrew word much more memorable.

One of the unique features of this work is that the words are gathered in relatively short lists, allowing the student to build up a working vocabulary in manageable blocks. For long lists, we suggest dividing them into groups of seven for ease of memorization.[4] In fact, a general familiarity with a particular list can help jar a reader's thinking when encountering the same word in the biblical text. This is even the case when a particular word in the list has not yet been fully committed to memory. Rapid vocabulary review is likewise made easier through the shortness of the lists.

The lists are mainly alphabetized in Hebrew order. Sometimes there will be an arrangement that follows an underlying logic, as in the case of "Human Anatomy," which runs from head to toe. On rare occasions, as with "Trees," we use the English order to ease memorization. In general, if the word appears only in the plural form, we

4. Studies show that memorizing words in groups of up to seven is more effective. See Jeremy P. Thompson, "Word-List Size and Biblical Hebrew Vocabulary Learning," *Hebrew Higher Education* 14 (2012): 47–61.

print the plural form here. However, if a word is in a construct state or has a possessive suffix or a preposition, we remove those and provide the lexical form. Because of range of meaning and to keep some lists more complete, a few words appear in multiple lists, e.g. קִנָּמוֹן, "cinnamon," which appears in both "Herbs and Spices" and "Ointment/ Perfume." Lastly, words not appearing in the Old Testament are not included here.

We do not arrange words within lists by frequency. This is done out of a recognition that an ancient reader would have known most, if not all, of the words in a given category. To achieve such fluency, the student needs to be ready to recognize a word regardless of how "rare" it is. Lacking this level of familiarity, a student's reading of Scripture in the original language all too often becomes an act of decipherment. Inasmuch as this book does not arrange vocabulary by frequency, it is designed to complement, not replace, the books (mentioned in footnote 1) that do. Users may be interested to know, therefore, the nature of this complementarity in this connection. According to Andersen and Forbes' *Vocabulary of the Old Testament*, there are 9,980 unique words in the OT, only roughly 21 percent (2,148 words) of which occur ten times or more.[5] However, many of the words in our book occur fewer than ten times: low-frequency words.

Yet users can still gauge the relative frequency of words in our lists. As an aid to learners, we have marked all hapax legomena with an "H" and all words used less than ten times with an "R" for "rare."[6] This has two aims. First, students who wish to focus on high-frequency vocabulary within a list can do so. Second, given that the definitions of hapax legomena and rare words are more contested, the reader can be aware that the definitions of words marked "H" or "R" are more tentative. Phrases only appearing once are also marked with an "H" or an "R." Of course, not all such words are equally well understood or explained by the lexicographers, and so students should exercise caution in this regard, consulting the commentaries (or the bibliography of this volume) for the more obscure passages. Scholars will necessarily dispute some of the translations offered here, but we would suggest that for the learner it is useful to have a working definition for a word, even if one discovers through further study that a particular word's meaning is rather speculative. Thus, we have erred on the side of inclusivity in these lists, including words whose definitions might be highly contested.

Students who become familiar with the various lists in this book will find large tracts of Scripture open to them. This is the case not merely for the more popular biblical narratives but also for texts that at first blush seem more advanced. A student who tackles the worship and cultic terms gathered here, for example, will learn to

---

5. Francis I. Anderson and A. Dean Forbes, *The Vocabulary of the Old Testament* (Rome: Pontificial Biblical Institute, 1989), 8.
6. Vocabulary frequency data drawn from David J. A. Clines, ed., *The Concise Dictionary of Classical Hebrew* (Sheffield, UK: Sheffield Phoenix Press, 2009). Phrases in this book will not have "H" or "R" marked, but most of them are infrequent or *hapax*. A *hapax legomenon* ("spoken once" in Greek) is a word that only appears once in a text. The Old Testament has over 1,300 *hapax legomena*: Moisés Silva, *Biblical Words and Their Meaning: An Introduction to Lexical Semantics*, rev. and exp. ed. (Grand Rapids: Zondervan, 1995), 42; Frederick E. Greenspahn, *Hapax Legomena in Biblical Hebrew: A Study of the Phenomenon and Its Treatment since Antiquity with Special Reference to Verbal Forms* (1983; repr., Eugene, OR: Wipf and Stock, 2016).

appreciate the rhythm and poetic sensibilities of a book such as Leviticus. Too often such biblical texts remain closed worlds for students of Biblical Hebrew. It is hoped that this book will encourage the student to tackle the whole of Scripture and not merely favorite passages.

To this end, it is also recommended that students listen to the biblical text read aloud by a professional reader.[7] By treating biblical vocabulary in this immersive fashion, readers will find their reading of the Hebrew Bible to be a much more rewarding and enriching experience, stimulating the mind and nourishing the heart.

The choice in this book has been to focus on nouns over verbs. We occasionally note participle forms that are used as nouns, and we sometimes note verbs when they seem key to the semantic field as an assistance to the student. Too often "objects" are underplayed when teaching students biblical grammar. Understandably, biblical language instruction emphasizes the Hebrew verb, primarily due to its many stems and the seemingly endless numbers of weak verbs. Unfortunately, however, when elementary grammar study comes to a close, the lack of an extensive exposure to nouns quickly leads to frustration for the student reader and ends in many wasted hours leafing through the lexicon. Our philosophy is that an ancient child did not need a dictionary to learn to read Hebrew and neither should you. (Dictionaries are for reference, not for language acquisition.) This book tries to imitate something of the immersive quality of genuine language learning by gathering words that would normally occur together in a given lexical moment. A volume built on nouns can aid students in their acquisition of verbs. Certainly, because of the close tie between verbal roots and nouns in Biblical Hebrew, it is in principle possible to construct a topical book using verbs instead of nouns. But nouns, because they can be pictured, are generally the more memorable of the two. And verbal groupings tend to be less obvious because verbal associations are far more fluid than groupings of plants, spices, containers, tools, artisans, idols, and weights. We suggest that a solid command of Hebrew nouns will make the memorization of the related verbal forms much easier in the long run. Thus, it is much better to encourage students to work extensively on nouns after their basic grammar work has been completed. Another choice made in this volume is to focus on concrete nouns, rather than abstractions or qualities. Thus, though we have words for "teachers" and "students," we do not list terms for wisdom or for other abstract qualities such as fear or compassion. This includes the range of human emotions (which might be added to a future edition). Also, only in rare instances do we cite forms not appearing in the Hebrew Bible, such as from Sirach or the calendar of months (a future edition could easily delve into this territory).

How To Use *BHVCC*

These lists can be used as a springboard for many different types of activities designed to help intermediate Hebrew students learn how to use the language better. One such exercise, for instance, might capitalize on the fact that certain passages in Scrip-

7. The website haktuvim.co.il is a marvelous resource in this regard.

ture contain several words clustered together from one list. The teacher might ask students to examine these passages to try to determine how various items on the corresponding list relate to one another. This could be done as part of a lesson on semantics and biblical interpretation.[8] Examples of what we call "cluster verses" will be found in appendix two. These lists can also be used as sources for exploring the nuances of individual words or as exercises accompanying the presentation of information on the historical and sociolinguistic aspects of Biblical Hebrew.[9] For example, two words might have the same denotation yet vary stylistically: one poetic while the other prosaic. Alternatively, one word might be earlier and the other later in time, and students could examine passages that reveal the chronological development of words and word groups. For example, מְגִלָּה is a later term than סֵפֶר, though both refer to books or scrolls. These lists might also reveal pecularities of a particular book's style. For example, the usual biblical word for "witness" is עֵד, but Proverbs instead uses יָפִיחַ. Studying Hebrew using these lists could also reveal dialectical differences between words used in Israel and in Judah. Such exercises would give students a rich appreciation of the historical sweep of the texts brought together under one roof. Inasmuch as these lists contain so many rare words, these lists could be used as part of an exercise in figuring out the contextual meaning of infrequent words, especially hapax legomena. Even if a word will always defy easy definition, it is useful for students to know how scholars approach what sounds like a simple question: How do we know what a word means? Lastly, this book might be very useful for programs teaching Biblical Hebrew using communicative pedagogy, since these lists supply many terms used in daily life.[10]

In addition to the appendices providing bibliographies and cluster verses for each category, we have also included a master index of Hebrew words at the end of the book for the convenience of the student. In the index we do not distinguish between homonyms, words that are spelled the same but have different meanings. Readers should keep in mind the possibility that the words may indeed be true homonyms with varied histories and grammatical roots that have dovetailed in a particular form.

---

8. A good introduction to lexical semantics and biblical interpretation, though it focuses on Greek rather than Hebrew, is Moisés Silva, *Biblical Words and Their Meaning: An Introduction to Lexical Semantics*, rev. and exp. ed. (Grand Rapids: Zondervan, 1995). On Biblical Hebrew semantics, the writings of those associated with the Semantics of Ancient Hebrew Database (SAHD) and the Semantic Dictionary of Biblical Hebrew (SDBH) are useful. On SAHD, see T. Muraoka, *Studies in Ancient Hebrew Semantics*, Abr-Nahrain Supplement Series 4 (Louvain: Peeters, 1995); H. G. M. Williamson, "Semantics and Lexicography: A Methodological Conundrum," in *Biblical Lexicology: Hebrew and Greek: Semantics—Exegesis—Translation*, ed. Eberhard Bons, Jan Joosten, and Regine Hunziker-Rodewald, Beihefte zur Zeitschrift für die Alttestamentliche Wissenschaft 44 (Berlin: De Gruyter, 2015), 327–39. On SDBH, see Reinier de Blois, "Towards a New Dictionary of Biblical Hebrew Based on Semantic Domains," 2000, http://www.sdbh.org/documentation/Paper_SBL_2000.pdf; Enio R. Mueller, "The Semantics of Biblical Hebrew: Some Remarks From a Cognitive Perspective," http://www.sdbh.org/documentation/EnioRMueller_SemanticsBiblicalHebrew.pdf.
9. Joel Hoffman, *In the Beginning: A Short History of the Hebrew Language* (New York: New York University Press, 2006); William M. Schniedewind, *A Social History of Hebrew: Its Origins Through the Rabbinic Period* (New Haven: Yale University Press, 2013).
10. See, for example, Randall Buth's *Living Biblical Hebrew* and Paul Overland's *Learning Biblical Hebrew Interactively* curricula. See Paul Overland, "Can Communicative Methods Enhance Ancient Language Acquisition?," *Teaching Theology & Religion* 7, no. 1 (2004): 51–57.

Acknowledgments

Invariably, in such a compilation, there will be omissions (intended or not) and errors. In the interest of providing an accurate resource for students to build their vocabulary, the authors encourage readers to contact them regarding any additions and corrections that will help keep this book as useful as possible. The authors can be contacted at these e-mail addresses: jpleins@scu.edu and jdhomrighausen@gmail.com.

We hope that this book will open you to the promised land of a more satisfying experience of reading the Hebrew Bible. We also hope that this volume will aid in deepening your appreciation of Scripture, enliven your explorations of its wisdom, and open you at long last to the varied and vital vocabulary used by our spiritual forebearers.

Inasmuch as this work has proven to be a genuine collaboration, we would like to say a few words about the division of labor. David Pleins created the initial word lists from his research, teaching, and observation, and developed the schema of categories and subcategories. Jonathan Homrighausen consulted a number of specialized studies, and where these supplied new words or new nuances of words already on our lists, crediting the source in parentheses. (Appendix one indicates which ones were more useful to encourage further study of the rich resources available.) He also created the appendices and checked every word in the book against David Clines' Dictionary of Classical Hebrew, both to consult its definition and to mark words as either infrequent or hapax. Both authors contributed to this preface. Any oversights, of course, remain our own.

We are grateful to Dr. Nancy Erickson, Senior Editor of Biblical Languages, Textbooks, and Reference at Zondervan Academic, for her enthusiastic support of this book from the moment it crossed the transom. Jonathan Homrighausen would like to thank Rabbi Larry Moldo and Andrea Moldo, Catherine Murphy, Barbara Green, and David Pleins, who took the time to teach him Hebrew. In addition to his wife and mother, to whom he dedicates this book, he would like to thank his new family: Kate, Dave, Matt, Kelley, Laura, Pat, and Chet, who have taken him in as one of their own and never once complained when he brought work for this book to family gatherings. Because of this fruitful collaboration, David Pleins wishes to express his debt to and admiration of Jonathan Homrighausen, a graduate student and research assistant of unparalleled creativity, insight, and dedication to this project. He is grateful as well to his teachers and early mentors in Biblical Hebrew: Belinda Bicknell and Dr. Charles Krahmalkov, who valued exactitude over cleverness. He also wishes to express gratitude to Karen for her computer, her humor, her wisdom, and her love of life.

BIBLIOGRAPHY

Aitken, J. K. *The Semantics of Blessing and Cursing in Ancient Hebrew*. Ancient Near Eastern Studies Supplement 23. Louvain: Peeters, 2007.

———. "מַעֲגָל." In *Semantics of Ancient Hebrew*, edited by T. Muraoka, 79–85. Abr-Nahrain Supplement Series 6. Louvain: Peeters, 1998.

———. "מִשְׁעוֹל." In *Semantics of Ancient Hebrew*, edited by T. Muraoka, 86–88. Abr-Nahrain Supplement Series 6. Louvain: Peeters, 1998.

———. "נָקַב II." In *Semantics of Ancient Hebrew*, edited by T. Muraoka, 101–5. Abr-Nahrain Supplement Series 6. Louvain: Peeters, 1998.

Amzallag, Nissim. "Copper Metallurgy: A Hidden Fundament of the Theology of Ancient Israel?" *Scandinavian Journal of the Old Testament* 27, no. 2 (2013): 151–69.

———. "Furnace Remelting as the Expression of YHWH's Holiness: Evidence from the Meaning of Qannâ in the Divine Context." *Journal of Biblical Literature* 134, no. 2 (2015): 233–52.

Barr, James. *Biblical Words for Time*. Naperville, IL: A. R. Allenson, 1962.

Boer, Roland. "The Patriarch's Nuts: Concerning the Testicular Logic of Biblical Hebrew." *Journal of Men, Masculinities & Spirituality* 5, no. 2 (2011): 41–52.

Borowski, Oded. *Agriculture in Iron Age Israel*. Winona Lake, IN: Eisenbrauns, 1987.

———. *Daily Life in Biblical Times*. Archaeology and Biblical Studies 5. Atlanta: Society of Biblical Literature, 2003.

———. *Every Living Thing: Daily Use of Animals in Ancient Israel*. Walnut Creek, CA: AltaMira Press, 1999.

Bovati, Pietro. *Re-Establishing Justice: Legal Terms, Concepts and Procedures in the Hebrew Bible*. Translated by Michael J. Smith. Journal for the Study of the Old Testament Supplement Series 105. Sheffield, UK: Sheffield Academic Press, 1994.

Braun, Joachim. *Music in Ancient Israel/Palestine: Archaeological, Written and Comparative Sources*. Translated by Douglas W. Stott. Grand Rapids: Eerdmans, 2002.

Brenner, Athalya. *Colour Terms in the Old Testament*. Journal for the Study of the Old Testament Supplement Series 21. Sheffield, UK: Sheffield Academic Press, 1982.

———. "The Food of Love: Gendered Food and Food Imagery in the Song of Songs." *Semeia* 86 (1999): 101–12.

Bridge, Edward J. "The Metaphoric Use of Slave Terms in the Hebrew Bible." *Bulletin for Biblical Research* 23, no. 1 (2013): 13–28.

Burgh, Theodore W. *Listening to the Artifacts: Music Culture in Ancient Palestine*. New York: T&T Clark, 2006.

Clines, David J. A, ed. *The Dictionary of Classical Hebrew*. Sheffield: Sheffield Phoenix Press, 1993–2011.

Clines, David J. A. "Misapprehensions, Ancient and Modern, about Lions (Nahum 2.13)." Accessed May 31, 2016. https://www.academia.edu/7385702/Misapprehensions_Ancient_and_Modern_about_Lions_Nahum_2.13_.

De Moore, Johannes, ed. כלי *Database: Utensils in the Hebrew Bible.* Het Oudtestamentisch Werkgezelschap, 2010–2016. http://www.otw-site.eu/KLY/kly.php.

Eichler, Raanan. "The Meaning of Pa'am in the Context of Furniture." *Journal of Semitic Studies* 60, no. 1 (2015): 1–18.

———. "The Meaning of Zēr." *Vetus Testamentum* 64, no. 2 (2014): 196–210.

Eng, Milton. *The Days of Our Years: A Lexical Semantic Study of the Life Cycle in Biblical Israel.* The Library of Hebrew Bible/Old Testament Studies 464. New York: Bloomsbury T&T Clark, 2011.

Grzybowski, Andrzej, and Malgorzata Nita. "Leprosy in the Bible." *Clinics in Dermatology* 34 (2016): 3–7.

Guillaume, A. "Metallurgy in the Old Testament." *Palestine Exploration Quarterly* 94, no. 2 (December 1, 1962): 129–32.

Harrison, Roland K. *Healing Herbs of the Bible.* Leiden: Brill, 1966.

Hartley, John E. *The Semantics of Ancient Hebrew Colour Lexemes.* Ancient Near Eastern Studies Supplement 33. Louvain: Peeters, 2011.

Holladay, William L., ed. *A Concise Hebrew and Aramaic Lexicon of the Old Testament.* Grand Rapids: Eerdmans, 1972.

Hobbins, John. "The Human Anatomy in Ancient Hebrew: Advanced Level." *Ancient Hebrew Poetry*, November 26, 2007. http://ancienthebrewpoetry.typepad.com/ancient_hebrew_poetry/2007/11/the-human-ana-2.html.

Hobbs, T. R. *A Time for War: A Study of Warfare in the Old Testament.* Old Testament Studies 3. Wilmington, DE: Michael Glazier, 1989.

Hope, Edward R. *All Creatures Great and Small: Living Things in the Bible.* Helps for Translators. New York: United Bible Societies, 2003.

Hurvitz, Avi. *A Concise Lexicon of Late Biblical Hebrew: Linguistic Innovations in the Writings of the Second Temple Period.* Vetus Testamentum Supplements 160. Leiden: Brill, 2014.

Jordan, David John. "An Offering of Wine: An Introductory Exploration of the Role of Wine in the Hebrew Bible and Ancient Judaism Through the Examination of the Semantics of Some Keywords." PhD diss., University of Sydney, 2002. https://ses.library.usyd.edu.au/handle/2123/482.

Kelso, James L., and W. F. Albright. "The Ceramic Vocabulary of the Old Testament." *Bulletin of the American Schools of Oriental Research Supplementary Studies*, no. 5/6 (1948): 1–48.

Koller, Aaron J. *The Semantic Field of Cutting Tools in Biblical Hebrew: The Interface of Philological, Semantic, and Archaeological Evidence.* Catholic Biblical Quarterly Monograph Series 49. Washington, DC: Catholic Biblical Association of America, 2012.

Kolyada, Yelena. *A Compendium of Musical Instruments and Instrumental Terminology in the Bible.* BibleWorld. London: Routledge, 2014.

Koops, Robert, and Donald Slager. *Each According to Its Kind: Plants and Trees in the Bible.* Helps for Translators. New York: United Bible Societies, 2012.

Kottek, Samuel S. "Hygiene and Health Care in the Bible." In *Health and Disease in the Holy Land: Studies in the History and Sociology of Medicine from Ancient Times to the Present,* edited by Manfred Waserman and Samuel S. Kottek, 37–66. Lewiston, NY: Edwin Mellen, 1996.

MacDonald, Nathan. *What Did the Ancient Israelites Eat? Diet in Biblical Times.* Grand Rapids: Eerdmans, 2008.

Massey-Gillespie, Kevin. "A New Approach to Basic Hebrew Colour Terms." *Journal of Northwest Semitic Languages* 20, no. 1 (1994): 1–11.

Miano, David. *Shadow on the Steps: Time Measurement in Ancient Israel.* Resources for Biblical Study. Atlanta: Society of Biblical Literature, 2010.

Mitchell, T. C. "The Music of the Old Testament Reconsidered." *Palestine Exploration Quarterly* 124, no. 2 (1992): 124–43.

Montagu, Jeremy. *Musical Instruments of the Bible.* Lanham, MD: Scarecrow Press, 2002.

Muraoka, T., ed. *Semantics of Ancient Hebrew.* Abr-Nahrain Supplement Series 6. Louvain: Peeters, 1998.

Nielsen, Kjeld. *Incense in Ancient Israel.* Vetus Testamentum Supplements 38. Leiden: Brill, 1986.

Noonan, Benjamin J. "There and Back Again: 'Tin' or 'Lead' in Amos 7:7–9?" *Vetus Testamentum* 63, no. 2 (2013): 299–307.

———. "Zion's Foundation: The Meaning of בֹּחַן in Isaiah 28,16." *Zeitschrift für die Alttestamentliche Wissenschaft* 125, no. 2 (2013): 314–19.

Notebaart, Cor. "Metallurgical Metaphors in the Hebrew Bible." PhD diss., Protestant Theological University, 2010.

Olyan, Saul M. *Disability in the Hebrew Bible: Interpreting Mental and Physical Differences.* Cambridge: Cambridge University Press, 2008.

Parker, Julie Faith. *Valuable and Vulnerable: Children in the Hebrew Bible, Especially the Elisha Cycle.* Brown Judaic Studies 355. Providence, RI: Brown University Press, 2013.

Patai, Raphael. *The Children of Noah: Jewish Seafaring in Ancient Times.* Princeton, NJ: Princeton University Press, 1999.

Peters, Kurtis. *Hebrew Lexical Semantics and Daily Life in Ancient Israel: What's Cooking in Biblical Hebrew?* Biblical Interpretation Series 146. Leiden: Brill, 2016.

Platt, Elizabeth. "Jewelry of Bible Times and the Catalog of Isaiah 3:18–23: Part I." *Andrews University Seminary Studies* 17, no. 1 (1979): 71–84.

———. "Jewelry of Bible Times and the Catalog of Isaiah 3:18–23: Part II." *Andrews University Seminary Studies* 17, no. 2 (1979): 189–201.

Pritz, Ray. *The Works of Their Hands: Man-Made Things in the Bible.* Helps for Translators. New York: United Bible Societies, 2009.

Rattray, S. "Marriage Rules, Kinship Terms and Family Structure in the Bible." In *1987 Seminar Papers: One Hundred Twenty-Third Annual Meeting, December 5–8, 1987*, edited by Kent Harold Richards. Atlanta: Scholars Press, 1987.

Rollston, Christopher A. *Writing and Literacy in the World of Ancient Israel: Epigraphic Evidence from the Iron Age*. Archaeology and Biblical Studies 11. Atlanta: Society of Biblical Literature, 2010.

Salvesen, Alison. "Esther 1:11; 2:17; 6:8: 'Something to Do with a Camel'?" *Journal of Semitic Studies* 44, no. 1 (1999): 35–46.

———. "The Trappings of Royalty in Ancient Hebrew." In *King and Messiah in Israel and the Ancient Near East: Proceedings of the Oxford Old Testament Seminar*, edited by John Day, 119–40. Journal for the Study of the Old Testament Supplement Series 270. Sheffield: Sheffield Academic Press, 1998.

———. "הֲדֹם." In *Semantics of Ancient Hebrew*, edited by T. Muraoka, 38–43. Abr-Nahrain Supplement Series 6. Louvain: Peeters, 1998.

———. "עֲטָרָה." In *Semantics of Ancient Hebrew*, edited by T. Muraoka, 106–13. Abr-Nahrain Supplement Series 6. Louvain: Peeters, 1998.

———. "שֵׁבֶט." In *Semantics of Ancient Hebrew*, edited by T. Muraoka, 122–36. Abr-Nahrain Supplement Series 6. Louvain: Peeters, 1998.

Scott, R. B. Y. "Meteorological Phenomena and Terminology in the Old Testament." *Zeitschrift Für Die Alttestamentliche Wissenschaft* 64, no. 1 (1952): 11–25.

———. "Weights and Measures of the Bible." *The Biblical Archaeologist* 22, no. 2 (1959): 22–40.

Seevers, Boyd. *Warfare in the Old Testament: The Organization, Weapons, and Tactics of Ancient Near Eastern Armies*. Grand Rapids: Kregel Academic, 2013.

Shafer-Elliott, Cynthia. "Food in the Hebrew Bible." *Biblical Interpretation*, May 2013. http://www.bibleinterp.com/articles/2013/sha378013.shtml.

———. *Food in Ancient Judah: Domestic Cooking in the Time of the Hebrew Bible*. BibleWorld. Sheffield, UK: Routledge, 2013.

Sherwin, Simon J. "In Search of Trees: Isaiah XLIV 14 and Its Implications." *Vetus Testamentum* 53, no. 4 (2003): 514–29.

Smith, John Arthur. *Music in Ancient Judaism and Early Christianity*. Burlington, VT: Ashgate Publishing, 2011.

Stadelmann, Luis I. J. *The Hebrew Conception of the World: A Philological and Literary Study*. Analecta Biblica 39. Rome: Pontificial Biblical Institute, 1970.

Steiner, Richard C. *Stockmen from Tekoa, Sycomores from Sheba: A Study of Amos' Occupations*. Catholic Biblical Quarterly Monograph Series 36. Washington, DC: Catholic Biblical Association, 2003.

Stewart, David Tabb. "Sexual Disabilities in the Hebrew Bible." In *Disability Studies and Biblical Literature*, edited by Candida Moss and Jeremy Schipper, 67–88. New York: Palgrave Macmillan, 2011.

Stieglitz, Robert R. "Hebrew Seafaring in the Biblical Period." In *Seafaring and the Jews*, edited by Nadav Kashtan, 5–15. London: Frank Cass, 2001.

Toorn, Karel Van der. *Scribal Culture and the Making of the Hebrew Bible.* Cambridge, MA: Harvard University Press, 2009.

United Bible Societies. *Semantic Dictionary of Biblical Hebrew.* 2000–2009. http://www.sdbh.org/dictionary/main.php?language=en.

United Bible Societies. *Fauna and Flora of the Bible.* Helps for Translators. London: United Bible Societies, 1980.

Walsh, Carey. *The Fruit of the Vine: Viticulture in Ancient Israel.* Harvard Semitic Monographs 60. Winona Lake, IN: Eisenbrauns, 2000.

Way, Kenneth C. "Donkey Domain: Zechariah 9:9 and Lexical Semantics." *Journal of Biblical Literature* 129, no. 1 (2010): 105–14.

Widder, Wendy. *"To Teach" in Ancient Israel: A Cognitive Linguistic Study of a Biblical Hebrew Lexical Set.* Beihefte Zur Zeitschrift Für Die Alttestamentliche Wissenschaft 456. Boston: De Gruyter, 2014.

Wiggins, Steve A. *Weathering the Psalms: A Meteorotheological Survey.* Eugene, OR: Cascade Books, 2014.

Wilkinson, John. "The Body in the Old Testament." *Evangelical Quarterly* 63 (1991): 195–210.

Williams, Gillian Patricia. "A Talmudic Perspective on Old Testament Diseases, Physicians and Remedies." MA thesis, University of South Africa, 2009. http://uir.unisa.ac.za/handle/10500/3318.

Zatelli, Ida. "Astrology and the Worship of the Stars in the Bible." *Zeitschrift Für Die Alttestamentliche Wissenschaft* 103, no. 1 (2009): 86–99.

Zhakevich, Philip. "The Tools of an Israelite Scribe: A Semantic Study of the Terms Signifying the Tools and Materials of Writing in Biblical Hebrew." PhD diss., University of Texas, Austin, 2015. https://repositories.lib.utexas.edu/handle/2152/31558.

PART I

THE CREATED ORDER

HEAVENS AND EARTH

Cosmology

אַרְבַּע כַּנְפוֹת הָאָרֶץ four corners of the earth (HCW) (Isa 11:12)
טַבּוּר הָאָרֶץ navel, center of the earth = Jerusalem (HCW) (Ezek 38:12)
יַרְכְּתֵי־אָרֶץ remote parts of the earth (HCW) (Jer 6:22)
הָכֹל the universe (HCW) (Ps 119:91)
עוֹלָם world, creation, created order (DCH) (Eccl 3:11)
קַצְוֵי־אָרֶץ ends of the earth, boundaries of the firmament (HCW) (Ps 48:11)

Sky/Firmament

אֲגֻדָּה vault (holding up the sky) (Amos 9:6 R)
אֲרֻבֹּת הַשָּׁמַיִם "the windows of heaven," holes in the firmament through which rain comes (HCW) (Gen 7:11)
דְּלָתַיִם doors of the firmament, through which rain comes (HCW) (Job 38:8)
חוּג הָאָרֶץ horizon; boundary between earth and heaven (HCW) (Isa 40:22)
חוּג שָׁמַיִם horizon; boundary between earth and heaven (HCW); firmament (SDBH) (Job 22:14)
מַבּוּל waters above the firmament (HCW) (Gen 6:17)
עָרִיפִים skies, clouds, mists (Isa 5:30 H)
רָקִיעַ sky-dome, firmament (Ezek 1:22–23)
שָׁמַיִם sky, heaven (Gen 7:9)

Stars

אוֹר luminary (Gen 1:3)
הֵילֵל the morning-star (Venus) (Isa 14:12 H)
כּוֹכָב star (Job 25:5)
כִּיּוּן Saturn (HCW) (Amos 5:26 H)
כִּימָה Pleiades, cluster of stars (Amos 5:8 R)
כְּסִיל Orion, constellation (Job 9:9 R)
מַזָּלוֹת planets, Zodiac signs ("inn" of sun); Mazzaroth, a star or constellation (DCH) (2 Kgs 23:5 H)
מַזָּרוֹת twelve stations of the sun during its yearly orbit (Zatelli); Mazzaroth, a star or constellation (DCH) (Job 38:32 H)
עֵז she-goat; goat hair, the She-goat (constellation) (DCH) (Amos 5:9)
עַיִשׁ / עָשׁ Great Bear (Ursa Major); Aldebaran or Arcturus, the Great Bear (Job 38:32 H)
שׁוֹר Taurus (in Zodiac) (DCH); single head of cattle, bullock; ox (ELT) (Amos 5:9)

Sun

חַמָּה sun, heat (Ps 19:7 R)
חֳרָבוֹן dryness, heat of summer (Wiggins) (Ps 32:4 H)
חֶרֶס sun (SDBH) (Judg 14:18 R)
צַח sunny, bright (Isa 18:4 R)
שֶׁמֶשׁ sun (Gen 15:12)

Moon

חֹדֶשׁ new moon (HCW) (Num 10:10)
יָרֵחַ moon (Josh 10:12–13)
כֶּסֶא full moon (Prov 7:20 R)
לְבָנָה moon; white (Song 6:10 R)

Earth

General

אִי island (Isa 23:2)
אֶרֶץ earth, land; dry native clay (Kelso and Albright) (Ps 12:7)
חֶבֶל הַיָּם coastal plain (HCW) (Zeph 2:5–6)
חֶדֶל era, age, lifetime, space of the world (HCW) (Isa 38:11 R)
חֶלֶד world, duration (Ps 17:14)
חוֹחַ hole, crevice (SDBH) (1 Sam 13:6 H)
יַבָּשָׁה dry land (Gen 1:9)
יְשִׁימוֹן wilderness; Jeshimon (SDBH) (Num 21:20)
מִמְכָּר mortgaged land, land sold; merchandise; ancestral land (DCH) (Deut 18:8 R)
מַעֲנָה furrow (SDBH) (1 Sam 14:14 R)
מַשְׁקֶה well-irrigated land (HCW) (Gen 13:10 R)
עָקֹב steep ground (HCW) (Isa 40:4 H)
שָׁרָב hot ground reflecting mirage (MPTOT); parched ground (DCH) (Isa 35:7 R)
שָׂדֶה field (Stadelmann); countryside, bush, uninhabited land (SDBH) (Gen 2:5)
תֵּבֵל earth, globe, land (1 Sam 2:8)
תֵּל tell, mound (HCW) (Josh 8:28 R)

Soil

אָבָק dusty soil, stirred up by wind (HCW) (Exod 9:9 R)
אֲדָמָה land, soil (Gen 2:5); topsoil, humus (HCW); dry native clay (Kelso and Albright) (Isa 45:9)
בֹּץ wet mire near bodies of water (Zhakevich) (Jer 38:22 H)
דֻּכָּא dust (SDBH) (Ps 90:3)
חוֹל sand (HCW) (Gen 32:13)
חֹמֶר clay (HCW); worked clay (Kelso and Albright); mud, clay, mortar (SDBH) (Isa 10:6)

טִיט mud, mire, silt, clay (HCW) (Job 41:22)
יָוֵן mud, mire (Zhakevich) (Ps 40:3 R)
מָעָה grain of sand (SDBH) (Isa 48:19 H)
נִיר untilled soil (Jer 4:3 R)
עָפָר dust, raw clay (Kelso and Albright) (Job 10:9)
רֶגֶב clod of earth (SDBH) (Job 21:33 R)
רֶפֶשׁ mud, mire, foam (Zhakevich) (Isa 57:20 H)

Mountain

General

הַר mountain, range (Gen 22:2)
הָרָר mountain (Deut 33:15)
מַדְרֵגָה mountain escarpment, cliff (HCW) (Ezek 38:20 R)
מַעֲלֵה pass between mountains or hills (HCW) (Josh 15:7)

Top/Rock/Height

אָמִיר summit; branch (of tree) DCH) (Isa 17:6 R)
רֹאשׁ top of mountain (HCW) (Gen 8:5)
רֶכֶס mountain ridge, rugged place (Isa 40:4 H)
שֵׁן peak of mountain (HCW); tooth, crag of rock (DCH) (Job 39:28)
שְׁפִי bare mountain, height (Num 23:3)

Slope/Terrace/Ridge

אֶשֶׁד slope (Josh 10:40 R)
אַשְׁדֹּת slopes of a mountain (HCW) (Deut 3:17 R)
גַּבְנֻנִּים peaks, ridges of a mountain (HCW) (Ps 68:16 R)
גְּדוּד ridge; barrier, wall (SDBH) (2 Sam 22:30 R)
כֶּתֶף slope of mountain (HCW) (Num 34:11)
מוֹרָד slope of mountain (HCW) (Josh 7:5 R)
צֵלָע terrace cut in the side of a mountain (HCW); side, mountain slope (DCH) (2 Sam 16:13)

Foot/Base

מוֹסְדֵי הָרִים foundations of mountains (HCW) (Deut 32:22 H)
תַּחְתִּית foot of a mountain (HCW) (Exod 19:17)

Hill

גִּבְעָה hillock (Isa 40:4)
נָפָת hill (?) (SDBH); height, hill-country (DCH) (Josh 17:11 R)
קֶרֶן hill (SDBH) (Isa 5:1 H)
רְכָסִים hillocks (HCW); rough place, uneven ground (DCH) (Isa 40:4 H)
שְׁפִי bare hill, plain (Isa 49:9)

Valley

בִּקְעָה valley (Amos 1:5)
גַּיְא valley (HCW) (Isa 22:1)
כִּכָּר valley, circle; district (DCH) (Gen 13:10)
מִישֹׁר plain, plateau (HCW) (Isa 40:4)
עֵמֶק valley, lowland (1 Chr 12:16)
שְׁפֵלָה lowland (HCW) (Deut 1:7)

Desert/Steppe

חָרְבָּה desolation, desert (HCW) (Isa 44:26)
חֲרֵרִים dry places, parched places (SDBH) (Jer 17:6 H)
יְשִׁימוֹן desert waste (Ps 107:4)
מִדְבָּר desert, wilderness, pasture; also steppe (HCW) (Gen 4:20)
מְלֵחָה saltness, barrenness, salt flat (HCW) (Job 39:6 R)
נָוֶה steppe (HCW) (Jer 9:9)
עֲרָבָה desert plain, steppe (Deut 1:1)
צִיָּה dryness, desert land (HCW) (Isa 35:1)
צִיּוֹן dryness, parched ground (HCW) (Isa 25:5 R)
צִמָּאוֹן thirsty ground (HCW) (Isa 35:7 R)
שַׁמָּה devastation, waste (HCW) (Jer 51:43)

Cave

מְעָרָה cave (Gen 19:3)

Rock/Stone/Pebble

אֶבֶן stone (Gen 35:14)
חַלָּמִישׁ flint (HCW) (Deut 8:15 R)
חָצָץ gravel (HCW) (Prov 20:17 R)
כֵּף rock (Jer 4:29 R)
אֶבֶן מַעֲמָסָה heavy stone (SDBH); stone of burden (DCH) (Zech 12:3)
מַסָּע quarry; missile, dart (1 Kgs 6:7 R)
מַקֶּבֶת quarry (SDBH) (Isa 51:1 H)
סֶלַע rock, crag, cliff (Amos 6:12)
פּוּר small pebble or potsherd used to make decisions = lot (SDBH) (Esth 3:7 R)
צוּר rock (Deut 8:15)
צַר / צֹר flint (HCW) (Isa 5:28 R)
צְרוֹר pebble (HCW); tiny grain (SDBH) (2 Sam 17:13 R)
שְׁבָרִים stone quarries (SDBH); Shebarim (DCH) (Josh 7:5 H)

Clouds

חֲזִיז raincloud, thundercloud (MPTOT); thunderstorm (DCH) (Zech 10:1 R)

נָשִׂיא clouds, mist, vapor; ruler (Jer 10:13 R)
עָב dark cloud; rain cloud, thundercloud (MPTOT); cumulus clouds (Wiggins) (Judg 5:4)
עָנָן cloud, fog, mist, morning fog (MPTOT); "pillar of cloud" (Ps 78:14)
עֲנַן בֹּקֶר morning fog (MPTOT) (Hos 6:4)
עֲנָנָה cloud, cloudy (Job 3:5 H)
עֲרָפֶל dark threatening cloud, thundercloud (MPTOT) (1 Kgs 8:12)
קִיטוֹר dense cloud (MPTOT); smoke (DCH) (Ps 148:8 R)
שַׁחַק dust, cloud; cirrus clouds (Wiggins) (Ps 89:7)

Wind/Hurricane

גַּלְגַּל / גִּלְגָּל whirlwind; wheel (Ps 77:19)
מְזָרִים north winds, scatterers (Job 37:9)
סוּפָה hurricane, storm-wind (Job 37:9)
סַעַר / שַׂעַר / סְעָרָה hurricane, tempest; wind-storm, gale (MPTOT) (Ps 55:9 R)
רוּחַ wind; spirit (Ps 1:4)
רוּחַ מִדְבָּר desert wind (HCW) (Jer 13:24)

Lightning

אֵשׁ fire, lightning (Wiggins) (Ps 11:6)
בָּזָק flash of lightning (Ezek 1:14 H)
בָּרָק lightning; flashing sword (Ps 18:15)
גַּחֶלֶת coal of fire, (metaphorically) lightning (Wiggins) (Isa 47:14)
חֲזִיז flash of lightning (Job 28:26 R)
חֲנָמֵל lightning (Wiggins); frost, flood (DCH) (Ps 78:47 H)
רַעַם thunder (Wiggins) (Ps 77:19 R)
רֶשֶׁף flames, (metaphorically) lightning (Wiggins) (Ps 78:48)

Fire

אוּר fire, eastern country (SDBH) (Isa 31:9 R)
אֵפֶר ashes (SDBH) (Gen 18:27)
אֵשׁ fire (SDBH) (Gen 15:17)
יָקוּד hearth (CHB); glowing fire (כלי) (Isa 30:14 H)
כִּידוֹד spark of flame (SDBH) (Job 41:11 H)
לַהַב flame (SDBH) (Judg 13:20)
מוֹקֵד fire, burning (of God's judgment) (SDBH) (Isa 33:14 R)
נִיצוֹץ spark (SDBH) (Isa 1:31 H)
שְׂרֵפָה burning, fire, incineration, funeral pyre (Gen 11:3)

Rain/Storm

General

בַּצֹּרֶת drought (DCH) (Jer 14:1 R)
גֶּשֶׁם/גֶּשֶׁם shower, rain; winter rain (Wiggins) (1 Kgs 18:45)
הַוּוֹת storm (?) (Wiggins); wind, bluster, boast (DCH) (Ps 57:2)
זִרְזִיף pouring rain (Ps 72:6 H)
זֶרֶם thunderstorm, gush of water, storm; rain-storm, downpour (HCW) (Isa 4:6 R)
מָטַר/מָטָר rain (Deut 11:11)
מַיִם waters, rain (Wiggins) (Ps 77:18)
נָפָץ driving storm; cloudburst (DCH) (Isa 30:30 H)
סַגְרִיר steady, pouring rain (Prov 27:15 H)
קֶשֶׁת rainbow (Gen 9:13)
רְבִיבִים heavy rains; showers (DCH); spring rains (MPTOT) (Deut 32:2 R)
שָׁעִיר a shower, small rain (Deut 32:2 H)
שַׂעַר tempest; terror (Isa 28:2 R)
שׁוֹאָה/שׁוֹא tempest; ruin; sudden destructive storm (MPTOT) (Ps 35:8)

Spring Rain

מַלְקוֹשׁ spring rain (later) (Deut 11:14 R)
רְבִיבִים heavy rains; showers (DCH); spring rains (MPTOT) (Deut 32:2 R)

Autumn Rain

יוֹרֶה autumn rain (early) (Deut 11:14 R)
מוֹרֶה autumn rain (MPTOT) (Joel 2:23 R)

Hail

אֶבֶן hailstone (SDBH) (Josh 10:11)
אֶלְגָּבִישׁ hail; hailstone (SDBH) (Ezek 13:11 R)
בָּרָד hail (MPTOT) (Ezra 10:9)

Water

General

בְּאֵר well, watering place, spring (SDBH) (Gen 16:14); tar pit, bitumen pit (Gen 14:10)
בּוֹר pit; cistern (Gen 37:20) (SDBH)
בְּרֵכָה pool (2 Sam 2:13) (SDBH)
גֵּב/גֶּבָא pool, puddle (SDBH); trench, cistern (DCH) (2 Kgs 3:16 R)
מַיִם water (Gen 21:14)
מִפְרָץ bay (HCW); wadi (DCH) (Judg 5:17 H)

Swamp

אֲגַם swamp, marsh, reedy pool (HCW); pool, swamp (DCH) (Exod 7:19 R)

בְּצָה swamp, marsh (SDBH) (Job 8:11 R)

Sea/Ocean

אֲפִקֵי יָם channels on the bottom of the sea (HCW) (2 Sam 22:16 R)

גַּל wave of sea (HCW) (Isa 48:18)

חֵקֶר תְּהוֹם recesses of the deep (poetic for "depths of sea") (HCW) (Job 38:16)

יָם sea; west (Gen 49:13)

מִבְּכִי נְהָרוֹת sources of the rivers (HCW) (Job 28:11)

מַעֲמַקֵּי־יָם depths of the sea (HCW) (Isa 51:10)

מְצֻלֹּת יָם depths of the sea (HCW) (Mic 7:19)

מִשְׁבָּר wave breaking against shore (HCW) (Ps 93:4 R)

נִבְכֵי־יָם springs of the sea (poetic) (HCW) (Job 38:16)

קַרְקַע הַיָּם sea-bed; floor; bottom of the sea (HCW) (Amos 9:3)

תְּהוֹם abyss, deep; ocean, great deep (SDBH) (Amos 7:4)

Dew

אֶגְלֵי־טָל drops of dew (HCW) (Job 38:28 H)

טַל dew, mist (Ps 110:3)

רְסִיסֵי לָיְלָה nighttime dew (HCW) (Song 5:2)

Spring/Source

בְּאֵר / בֵּיר tar pit, bitumen pit; well, watering place, spring (SDBH) (Gen 16:14)

גֻּלָּה spring (SDBH) (Josh 15:19)

מַבּוּעַ fountain, spring (Isa 35:7 R)

מַעְיָן fountain, source (Isa 41:18)

מָקוֹר spring, source, well (Jer 2:13)

נֵבֶךְ fountain, spring (Job 38:16 H)

עַיִן spring; eye (Exod 15:27)

Flood

יְבוּל / יְבָל flood (HCW) (Job 20:28)

מַבּוּל flood; the Flood; deluge, frost, sleet (SDBH) (Ps 29:10)

נְזָלִים floods, streams (HCW) (Exod 15:8)

שֶׁטֶף flood, downpour (Nah 1:8 R)

שׁוֹט outburst of water (DCH) (Isa 28:15 R)

River/Stream

אַרְבָּעָה רָאשִׁים four branch streams, head streams (HCW) (Gen 2:10)

גְּדָיָה/גְּדָה riverbank (Isa 8:7 R)
יְאֹר channel (Job 28:10), the Nile (Gen 41:1), later the Tigris (Dan 12:5–7) (HCW); stream (SDBH)
יוּבָל/אוּבָל/יָבָל stream, watercourse (Isa 30:25 R)
מִיכָל little stream (2 Sam 17:20 H)
נָהָר river, stream (Isa 44:27); the Euphrates (HCW) (Gen 31:21)
פֶּלֶג / פְּלַגּוֹת river, stream; water channel (HCW) (Isa 30:25 R)
שִׁבֹּלֶת flowing stream, flood (HCW) (Isa 27:12 R)

Valley/Ravine

אָפִיק ravine, stream, tube; wadi, watercourse (SDBH) (Job 6:15)
אֲשֵׁדָה ravine, slope (Josh 12:8 R)
בִּתָּה ravine (SDBH) (Isa 7:19 H)
גַּיְא gorge, valley (Isa 40:4)
נַחַל wadi, stream, valley, torrent (Gen 26:19)
עֲרוּץ holes in ground caused by erosion of gullies (HCW) (Job 30:6 H)
שׁוּחָה gorge, pits; pit (SDBH); pit, ravine (DCH) (Prov 22:14 R)

Channel/Canal

אוּבָל canal (SDBH) (Dan 8:2 R)
יְאֹר channel, canal, Nile (Exod 7:19)
פֶּלֶג / פְּלַגּוֹת river, stream; water-channel (HCW) (Isa 30:25 R)
שֶׁלַח water-conduit (man-made) (SDBH) (Neh 3:15 R)
תְּעָלָה channel, watercourse; bandage (Job 38:25 R)

Cold/Ice

כְּפוֹר hoar-frost (Job 38:29 R)
קָרָה cold (Ps 147:17 R)
קֶרַח ice; frost (DCH) (Gen 31:40 R)
שֶׁלֶג / שֶׁלֶג snow (Ps 51:9)

Underworld

אֶרֶץ תַּחְתִּיּוֹת / אֶרֶץ תַּחְתִּית / אֶרֶץ תַּחְתִּיּוֹת land of the lowest parts, underworld (HCW) (Ezek 26:20)
אֲבַדּוֹן place of destruction, underworld (HCW); Abaddon, world of the dead (SDBH) (Ps 88:12 R)
בּוֹר pit, underworld (poetic) (HCW) (Ezek 31:14)
בּוֹר שָׁאוֹן pit of Destruction (HCW) (Ps 40:3)
בּוֹר תַּחְתִּיּוֹת pit of the lowest part, underworld (poetic) (HCW) (Lam 3:55)
יַרְכְּתֵי־בוֹר recesses of the pit, underworld (poetic) (HCW) (Isa 14:15)
עָפָר dust, underworld (poetic) (HCW) (Ps 22:30)

קֶבֶר grave, world of the dead (SDBH) (Ps 88:12)
שְׁאוֹל Sheol, realm of the dead (HCW) (Gen 37:35)
שַׁחַת pit, pitfall, netherworld (Isa 38:17)

Compass/Directions

North

צָפוֹן north; north wind (HCW) (Song 4:16)
שְׂמֹאל left side, north (HCW) (Gen 14:15)
צָפֹנָה northward (DCH) (Num 2:25 R)

South

דָּרוֹם south, south-wind (Deut 33:23)
נֶגֶב south (Exod 26:18)
תֵּימָן south; south wind (HCW, SDBH) (Ps 78:26)
תֵּימָנָה southward (HCW) (Exod 26:18 R)

East

אוּר eastern country; fire (SDBH) (Isa 24:15 R)
מוֹצָא place of sunrise, east (HCW) (Ps 75:7)
מִזְרָח east, place of sunrise (HCW) (Josh 4:19)
קָדִים east; East-wind, Scirocco (MPTOT) (Ps 48:8)
קֶדֶם east (Gen 25:6)
קַדְמוֹנִי eastern (Ezek 11:1)

West

אָחוֹר west; behind (2 Sam 1:22)
יָם west; sea (Deut 11:24)
מָבוֹא west, sunset (Deut 11:30)
מַעֲרָב place of sunset, the west (HCW) (Ps 75:7)

METALS, STONES, GEMS, MINERALS, AND PEARLS

Metals

Gold

בֶּצֶר precious ore (Guillame); gold (DCH, Notebaart) (Job 22:25 R)

זָהָב gold (Gen 2:11)

טָהוֹר זָהָב pure or purified gold (cultic context) (Notebaart) (Exod 25:11)

מְזֻקָּק זָהָב washed gold (Notebaart); refined, purified gold (DCH) (1 Chr 28:18)

סְגוּר זָהָב pure or purified gold (Notebaart); refined gold (DCH) (1 Kgs 6:20)

זָהָב מִכְלוֹת completely purified gold (Notebaart); perfect gold (DCH) (2 Chr 4:21)

חָרוּץ gold (Prov 8:10 R)

יְרַקְרַק חָרוּץ degraded, alloyed gold (Notebaart); greenness of gold (DCH) (Ps 68:14)

נִבְחָר חָרוּץ best quality gold (Notebaart); refined gold (DCH) (Prov 8:10)

כֶּתֶם gold (Song 5:11 R)

פָּז gold (Notebaart); pure gold (DCH) (Song 5:11 R)

Silver

כֶּסֶף silver; silver money, silver ore (DCH) (Job 28:1)

Lead

אֶבֶן הַבְּדִיל plumb-line (Pritz) (Zech 4:10)

אֲנָךְ lead, plumb-line (DCH) (Amos 7:8 R)

מִשְׁקֹלֶת / מִשְׁקָלֶת plumb-line (Pritz) (Isa 28:17 R)

עֹפֶרֶת lead, ore (Amzallag "Copper Metallurgy"); lead oxide (HALOT) (Num 31:22 R)

Iron

בַּרְזֶל iron (Job 28:2)

מְטִיל בַּרְזֶל iron bar (DCH) (Job 40:18 H)

Copper

נְחוּשָׁה / נְחֹשֶׁת copper, bronze; perhaps money (DCH) (Job 6:12 H)

Other Metals

בְּדִיל tin; antimony (DCH) (Isa 1:25 R)

חַשְׁמָל brass, electrum, metal; amber or bronze (DCH); "the intense pale yellow light radiated by metal in a molten state" (Amzallag "Copper Metallurgy") (Ezek 1:27 R)

Metallurgical Terms

בָּחוֹן assayer (Guillame) (Jer 6:27 H)

בֹּחַן graywacke (Noonan "Zion's Foundation"); testing, granite (DCH) (Isaiah 28:16 R)

גָּפְרִית brimstone (Amzallag "Copper Metallurgy"); sulphur (HALOT) (Job 18:15 R)

חֶלְאָה corrosion (Amzallag "Copper Metallurgy"); rust (DCH) (Ezek 24:6 R)

כִּבְשָׁן smelting furnace, kiln (Pritz) (Gen 19:28 R)

כּוּר smelting pot (for gold); smelting pot, furnace, crucible (DCH) (Prov 27:21 R)

מַפֶּחַ bellows (Notebaart, DCH) (Jer 6:29 H)

מַצְרֵף refiner, crucible (for silver); crucible (Guillame, DCH) (Prov 27:21 R)

סִיג / סוּג dross (Amzallag "Copper Metallurgy") (Ezek 22:18 R)

עֲלִיל crucible (Guillame) (Ps 12:7 H)

פַּעַם anvil (Pritz) (Isa 41:7)

צָרוֹף metal smelter, refiner (DCH) (Jer 6:29 H)

צֹרֵף goldsmith (Notebaart); metal smelter, refiner (DCH) (Isa 41:7)

קַנָּא rust (Amzallag "Furnace Remelting"); jealous (DCH) (Exod 20:25 R)

רָקִיעַ metallic firmament, plate (Amzallag "Copper Metallurgy") (Gen 1:17)

General Terms: Stones, Gems

אֶבֶן small stone, large stone for building, stele marking or commemorating things (Zhakevich) (Gen 11:3)

אֶבֶן יְקָרָה precious stone (Ezek 27:22)

אֶבֶן מַעֲמָסָה heavy stone (SDBH); stone of burden (DCH) (Zech 12:3)

אֶקְדָּח precious stone; beryl, red granite (DCH) (Isa 54:12 H)

גָּזִית cutting, hewn stone (DCH); ashlar (HALOT) (Exod 20:25)

מַצֵּבָה pillar, memorial stone (DCH) (Gen 28:18)

מִשְׁבְּצָה setting (for gem); setting of stones, chequer-work, plaiting (DCH) (Exod 28:13 R)

סֹחֶרֶת stone, mineral, costly stone (Esth 1:6 H)

Stones

בַּהַט white marble, alabaster (CT); porphyry, marble (SDBH) (Esth 1:6 H)

דַּר alabaster; mother-of-pearl (Esth 1:6 H)

חַלָּמִישׁ flint, hard stone (Ps 114:8 R)

חָצָץ gravel (SDBH) (Prov 20:17 R)

טְחוֹן millstone; hand-mill (Lam 5:13 H)

יַהֲלֹם onyx (black); diamond (?) (SDBH) (Ezek 28:13 R)

יָשְׁפֵה jasper (deep orange-red); jasper, quartz (DCH) (Exod 28:20 R)

כֵּף rock (SDBH); rock or mountain top (DCH) (Job 30:6 R)

סֹחֶרֶת stone tile, used in paving (Esth 1:6 H)

פּוּר lot, small pebble used to decide questions, Purim (SDBH) (Esth 3:7 R)

פֶּלַח millstone, mill (Pritz) (Judg 9:53 R)

צוּר rock (SDBH); rock, cliff, rocky mountain, stone monument, rock (as metaphor) (DCH) (2 Sam 21:10)

צֹר / צַר flint (SDBH); pebble, flint, flint knife (HALOT) (Isa 5:28 R)

צְרוֹר pebble (HCW); tiny grain (SDBH) (Amos 9:9 R)

רֵחַיִם millstones (dual); hand-mill (dual) (DCH) (Exod 11:5 R)

רֶכֶב millstone (Pritz) (Deut 24:6 R)

שְׁבוֹ agate (multicolor inside); red gem, perhaps beryl or agate (CT) (Exod 28:19 R)

שַׁיִשׁ / שֵׁשׁ marble (CT); white alabaster (SDBH) (1 Chr 29:2 R)

שַׁיִת white marble; thistles (not marble) (DCH) (Isa 9:17 R)

Gems

אֹדֶם garnet (yellow-red); carnelian (brown-red); red ruby (CT); chalcedony (Zhakevich); ruby, carnelian (SDBH); sardius (DCH) (Ezek 28:13 R)

אַחְלָמָה amethyst (violet); amethyst, reddish-brown or wine color (CT); jasper (Zhakevich) (Exod 28:19 R)

בָּרְקַת emerald (deep green); green stone, possibly emerald, malachite, or green beryl (CT) (Ezek 28:13 H)

גָּבִישׁ crystal (SDBH); rock crystal (DCH) (Job 28:18 H)

יָשְׁפֵה jade (nephrite; jadeite) (Zhakevich); jasper (SDBH); jasper, or perhaps a kind of quartz (DCH) (Exod 28:20 R)

כַּדְכֹּד red ruby; agate (DCH) (Isa 54:12 R)

לֶשֶׁם jacinth (red-orange) (Exod 28:19 R)

נֹפֶךְ red ruby, carbuncle; emerald; dark gem, possibly onyx or dark jasper (CT); malachite or turquoise (Zhakevich); garnet (DCH) (Exod 28:18 R)

סָפִיר sapphire (blue); lapis lazuli (CT, DCH) (Lam 4:7)

פִּטְדָה topaz (yellow); yellow topaz or chrysolite (CT) (Exod 28:17 R)

רָאמוֹת black corals, or perhaps sea shells (plural) (DCH) (Job 28:18 R)

שֹׁהַם beryl (turquoise green); carnelian (Zhakevich); onyx (SDBH, DCH) (Gen 2:12)

שָׁמִיר gem, diamond; thorn (Isa 7:24 R)

תַּרְשִׁישׁ chrysolite (bright green); turqoise or another blue stone (CT); jasper (?), diamond (?) (Zhakevich); beryl (SDBH); topaz, beryl, or chrysolite (DCH) (Exod 28:20 R)

Minerals

בְּאֵר well, watering place, spring (SDBH) (Gen 16:14); tar pit, bitumen pit (Gen 14:10)

בֹּרִית potash, lye; alkali (HALOT) (Mal 3:2 R)

מְלֵחָה saltness, barrenness, salt flat (HCW) (Job 39:6 R)

נְצִיב pillar of salt (SDBH) (Gen 19:26)

נֶתֶר natron (Prov 25:20 R)

Pearls

בְּדֹלַח pearl (?), bdellium resin (DCH) (Num 11:7 R)

חָרוּז pearl bead; necklace (DCH) (Song 1:10 H)

פְּנִינִים pearls; rubies (DCH); corals (HALOT) (Lam 4:7 R)

COLORS

General Terms

כֵּהֶה colorless, dull; dim (of eyes) (DCH) (Lev 13:39 R)

רִקְמָה variegated color; embroidered cloth (SBDH) (Ezek 16:13)

Specific Colors

Black/Brown

אָמֹץ chestnut (Hartley); piebald (of horses) (HALOT) (Zech 6:3, 6:7 R)

חוּם swarthy, sunburnt; brown (color of sheep) (DCH) (Gen 30:32 R)

פּוּךְ black powder used as eye makeup (SDBH); antimony, malachite (DCH) (Jer 4:30 R)

קָדַר dressed in mourning attire (HALOT); be dark in mourning (DCH) (Jer 4:28)

קַדְרוּת darkness of clouds (Hartley); darkness of mourning (Hartley) (Isa 50:3 H)

שְׁחוֹר black; soot, blackness (HALOT) (Lam 4:8 H)

שׁחר to become dark, charred, blackened, sooty (Hartley) (Job 30:30 H)

שְׁחַרְחֹר swarthy, black (Song 1:6 H)

White

חור to grow pale (SBDH); be white, pale (DCH) (Isa 29:22 H)

חֹר white, pure, noble (Jer 39:6)

יֶרֶקוֹן paleness (of human complexion) (SDBH); rust, mildew (DCH) (Jer 30:6 R)

לָבָן white, light-colored, bare (Lev 13:4)

לֹבֶן whiteness (Hartley) (not in Hebrew Bible, only in Sir 43:18)

צַח bright, sunny; glowing, shimmering (Hartley) (Jer 4:11 R)

צחח to be bright, brilliant, glowing, radiant (Hartley) (Lam 4:7 H)

צַחֲר whiteness (of wool), sheen (Ezek 27:18 H)

Red

אדם to become orange, red, brown, copper-colored (Hartley); to be red (DCH) (Lam 4:7)

אָדוֹם/אָדֹם rosy, red, ruddy; reddish brown (Num 19:2, Zech 1:8, 6:2), brown (Gen 25:30) (Hartley) (R)

אֲדַמְדַּם reddish, bright red (Hartley R)

חַכְלִילִי red wine color (CT) (Gen 49:12 H)

חַכְלִלוּת redness of eyes (CT); dullness of eyes (DCH) (Prov 23:29 H)
חָמוּץ violent, glaring red; blood color (CT) (Isa 63:1 H)
חמר to be flushed red (CT); to ferment (DCH) (Job 16:16 R)
כַּרְמִיל carmine, deep-red; scarlet, crimson (CT) (2 Chr 2:6 R)
לָבָן אֲדַמְדַּם pink of skin diseases (CT) (Lev 13:19 R)
לַהַב aflame, enflamed red (Isa 13:8) (SDBH); point/flash of spear (Job 39:23) (DCH)
פָּארוּר flushed red in health (of face) (SDBH); pinkish color of human complexion (Hartley) (Joel 2:6 R)
צָחֹר tawny, yellowish-red (HALOT) (Judg 5:10 H)
שָׁנִי crimson red (Exod 25:41)
שָׂרֹק yellow-red, tawny (CT) (Zech 1:8 R)
שֵׁשֵׁר red ochre, vermillion (bright red) (Ezek 23:14 R)

Purple

אַרְגָּוָן/אַרְגָּמָן purple, red-purple; dye made from various mollusk species (Hartley) (Exod 25:4)
תְּכֵלֶת violet, cerulean purple; dye from shellfish purpura hyacinthea (Hartley) (Exod 25:4)

Green

יָרָק green, yellow (CT); herbage, vegetables (DCH) (Deut 11:10 R)
יֶרֶק greenness, yellowness (CT) (Ps 37:2 R)

Yellow

יְרַקְרַק yellowish, greenish; yellow gold (HALOT) (Lev 14:37 R)
צָהֹב golden, yellow, blonde (Hartley); shiny (CT); red (DCH) (Lev 13:30 R)
צהב to be bright, shine, polish, burnish (Hartley); to gleam (of copper) (DCH); to shine like gold (SDBH) (Ezra 8:27 H)
צהל to cause something to shine by rubbing it with oil (of human face; association of happiness) (SDBH) (Ps 104:15 H)

Blue

כָּחֹל dark blue (Hartley) (Ezek 23:40 H)

Spotted/Speckled

בָּרֹד mottled, blotched (Zech 6:3 R)
טָלָא spottled, colorful (Ezek 16:16 R)
צָבוּעַ speckled (of animals); hyena (?), bird of prey (?) (DCH) (Jer 12:9 H)
נָקֹד speckled (Gen 30:32 R)
עָקֹד striped, streaked (Gen 30:35 R)

TIME

Day: Morning to Night

Morning/Noon

אַשְׁמֹרֶת הַבֹּקֶר morning watch (Miano) (Exod 14:24)
בֹּקֶר morning, dawn (Gen 1:5)
בִּתְרוֹן morning (SDBH) (2 Sam 2:29 H)
מִשְׁחָר dawn (Ps 110:3 H)
נְהָרָה daylight (Job 3:4 H)
צָהֳרַיִם noon, midday (1 Kgs 18:29)
שַׁחַר dawn (Gen 19:15)

Evening

אֶמֶשׁ twilight, evening (SDBH) (Job 30:3 R)
מָבוֹא sunset, west (Josh 1:4)
נֶשֶׁף twilight (Ps 119:147)
עֲלָטָה dusk, twilight (Gen 15:17 R)
עֶרֶב evening (Gen 1:5)

Night

אַשְׁמוּרָה night watch (SDBH) (Exod 14:24 R)
אַשְׁמֹרֶת הַתִּיכוֹנָה middle watch (Miano) (Judg 7:19)
לַיְלָה/לַיִל night (Exod 12:42)

General Terms: Days/Week

אֶמֶשׁ yesterday; evening (DCH); last night (SDBH) (Gen 19:34)
אֶתְמוֹל/תְּמוֹל yesterday, ago (Exod 5:14)
יוֹם day; 24-hour span (Miano) (Gen 1:5)
יוֹמָם daily (Jer 15:9)
מָחָר tomorrow (Gen 30:33)
מָחֳרָת tomorrow, next day (Num 11:32)
שָׁבוּעַ week (Gen 29:27)
שָׁבַע week; seven (DCH) (Gen 5:7)
שִׁלְשׁוֹם day before yesterday (Prov 22:20)

General Terms: Time

Past

אֶשׁוּן starting time; period of time (SDBH); beginning (DCH) (Prov 20:20 H)
דּוֹר generation; roughly 28 years (Miano) (Isa 51:9)
יָשָׁן old (SDBH) (Lev 25:22 R)
כְּבָר formerly (Eccl 1:10 R)

קְדוּמִים ancient (SDBH) (Judg 5:21 H)
קַדְמֹנִי former, past, old (SDBH) (1 Sam 24:14)
רֵאשִׁית first, beginning (Gen 1:1)

Now

אֵפוֹא / אֵפוֹ now, then, here (Gen 27:37)
אֹפֶן right time, right moment (SDBH); occasion (DCH) (Prov 25:11 H)
זְמָן set time, appointment (Eccl 3:1 R)
עֵת time, now, when (Neh 9:28)
עַתָּה now, at this time (2 Sam 24:16)
עִתִּי timely; ready (DCH) (Lev 16:21 H)
פִּתְאֹם / פִּתְאוֹם instantly; suddenness (DCH) (2 Chr 29:36)
פֶּתַע moment, wink, instant (Num 6:9 R)
רֶגַע wink, short space of time (Ps 30:6)

Future

אַחֲרִית future (Prov 23:18)
יֶתֶר rest of time (SDBH) (Isa 38:10)
מוֹעֵד appointment, fixed time (Jer 8:7)
נְצַח duration, ever, everlasting rest (Jer 15:18)
עוֹלָם everlasting, eternity; perpetuity (Barr) (Isa 44:7)
צְפִירָה moment of doom (SDBH); doom, cycle, climax (DCH) (Ezek 7:7 R)

Month/Year

חַג feast, festival (SDBH) (Exod 10:9)
חַג הָאָסִף Feast of the Harvest (Borowski *Agriculture*) (Exod 23:16)
חַג הַמַּצּוֹת Feast of Unleavened Bread, Passover (Borowski *Agriculture*) (Exod 23:15)
חַג סֻכּוֹת Festival of Sukkoth; Feast of Booths (Borowski *Agriculture*) (Lev 23:34)
חַג שָׁבֻעֹת Feast of Weeks (Borowski *Agriculture*) (Exod 34:22)
חֹדֶשׁ month, New Moon Festival (SDBH) (Gen 7:11)
יָרֵחַ month (Exod 2:2)
כֶּסֶא full moon (Prov 7:20 R)
פּוּרִים Purim Festival (SDBH) (Esth 9:26 R)
פֶּסַח Passover (Exod 12:11)
צֵאת הַשָּׁנָה "exit of the year," end of the liturgical year (Miano) (Exod 23:16)
שָׁנָה year (Gen 5:4)
תְּקוּפָה circuit; end (of year) (SDBH) (Exod 34:22 R)

תְּקוּפַת הַשָּׁנָה "at the coming round of the year," the end of the civil year (Miano) (Exod 34:22)

Calendar

נִיסָן Nisan (1); March/April (SDBH) (Neh 2:1 R)
זִו Ziv (2), April/May (SDBH) (1 Kgs 6:1 R)
סִיוָן Sivan (3); May/June (SDBH) (Esth 8:9 H)
תַּמּוּז [Tammuz] (4)
אָב / אָבִיב Ab (5); July/August (SDBH) (Exod 13:4 R)
אֱלוּל Elul (6); August/September (SDBH) (Neh 6:15 H)
אֵיתָנִים Ethanim (7); September/October (SDBH) (1 Kgs 8:2 H)
בּוּל Bul (8); October/November (SDBH) (1 Kgs 6:38 H)
כִּסְלֵו Kislev (9); November/December (SDBH) (Neh 1:1 R)
טֵבֵת Teveth (10); mid-December to mid-January (SDBH) (Esth 2:16 H)
שְׁבָט Shevat (11); January/February (SDBH) (Zech 1:7 H)
אֲדָר Adar (12); February/March (SDBH) (Esth 3:7 R)

Seasons

דַּיִשׁ threshing time (Lev 26:5 H)
חָרִישׁ season of ploughing (Gen 45:6 R)
חֹרֶף autumn, harvest time; winter (SDBH); winter (DCH) (Gen 8:22 R)
סְתָיו winter (Song 2:11 H)
קַיִץ harvest; summer (SDBH) (Gen 8:22)
קָצִיר harvest (DCH) (Jer 8:20)

ANIMALS

General Terms

בְּהֵמָה animal (Gen 1:26)

חַי/חַיָּה living-creature, beast (Ezek 1:5)

טָרֵף/טְרֵפָה devoured, eaten (of animals) (ELT); savaged beast, one torn apart by other beasts (DCH) (Exod 22:30)

נְבֵלָה carcass, corpse (of animals) (ELT); corpse of animal, human, or idol (DCH) (Deut 28:26)

פַּרְסָה hoof (Exod 10:26)

רֶמֶשׂ creeping things, crawling; small, unclean creatures, esp. reptiles (Hope); esp. insects and reptiles (DCH) (Ps 148:10)

שֶׁרֶץ swarming things, teem; small, swarming mammals, reptiles, or flying insects (DCH) (Gen 7:21)

Birds

General

אֶבְרָה wing of bird (DCH) (Deut 32:11 R)

אֶפְרֹחַ nestling (SDBH); young bird (HALOT) (Deut 22:6 R)

בֵּיצָה egg (of bird) (DCH) (Deut 22:6 R)

עוֹף birds, fowl; flying birds or insects (DCH) (Lev 11:20)

עַיִט bird of prey, hawk (Jer 12:9 R)

קֵן bird's nest; nestlings, brood (DCH) (Obad 4)

תֻּכִּיִּים exotic birds, parrots (ELT); peacocks, or perhaps poultry, or apes (DCH) (1 Kgs 10:22 R)

Specific Birds (Listed in English Order)

Various B–C

קִפּוֹד bittern, bustard; porcupine (?); hedgehog, porcupine, or owl (DCH) (Isa 34:11 R)

שָׂכְוִי cock, rooster (Job 38:36 H)

זַרְזִיר cock, hen, chicken; "girt of loins"; strong, girded, perhaps greyhound or cockerel (DCH) (Prov 30:31 H)

שָׁלָךְ cormorant (DCH); osprey (Hope); owl (ELT) (Lev 11:17 R)

עָגוּר crane, swallow (Jer 8:7 R)

Doves/Geese

יוֹנָה dove, pigeon (Gen 8:11)

תֹּר/תּוֹר dove, ring-dove; turtledove (DCH) (Jer 8:7)

גּוֹזָל young-dove; nestling of any bird species (Hope); chick (ELT) (Gen 15:9 R)

בַּרְבָּרִים geese; cuckoos, young chickens (HALOT) (1 Kgs 5:3 H)

Hawks/Falcons

נֵץ kestrel; falcon (HALOT); sparrow, hawk (Hope) (Lev 11:16 R)

אַיָּה falcon, buzzard, harrier (screamer) (Lev 11:14 R)

אֲנָפָה heron; un-kosher bird, plover or cormorant (HALOT) (Lev 11:19 R)

דָּאָה / רָאָה kite, hawk; falcon (ELT) (Lev 11:14 H)

דַּיָּה kite, hawk, falcon, vulture (Deut 14:13 R)

רָחָם osprey, fisher-hawk; Egyptian vulture (Hope, ELT); carrion-vulture or osprey (DCH) (Lev 11:18 R)

Various H

דּוּכִיפַת hoopoe (orange crown) (Deut 14:18 R)

Ostriches

יָעֵן ostrich (Lam 4:3 H)

בַּת־הַיַּעֲנָה ostrich; eagle owl (Hope); literally "daughter of the desert" (DCH) (Lev 11:16 R)

רְנָנִים ostriches; female ostriches (HALOT) (Job 39:13 H)

Owls

תַּחְמָס short-eared owl; falcon (ELT); perhaps nighthawk or male ostrich (DCH) (Lev 11:16 R)

כּוֹס tawny owl, little owl; little owl (UBS); screech-owl, little owl (HALOT) (Deut 14:16 R)

יַנְשׁוּף great owl; tawny owl (Hope); eagle owl, long-eared owl, bee-eater (UBS); screech owl, unclean bird (DCH) (Isa 34:11 R)

תִּנְשֶׁמֶת barn owl (Hope); white owl, or perhaps little owl or water hen, or chameleon (DCH) (Lev 11:30 R)

לִילִית night-hag, screech owl (?); tawny owl (unclear) (Hope); Lilith, or perhaps nightjar (DCH) (Isa 34:14 H)

Various P–S

קוֹרֵא / קֹרֵא partridge (caller) (Jer 17:11 R)

קָאַת pelican; jackdaw, owl (Hope); pelican, also perhaps hawk or vulture (DCH) (Zeph 2:14 R)

שְׂלָו quail (Exod 16:13 R)

עֹרֵב raven; rook (DCH) (1 Kgs 17:6)

שַׁחַף sea gull; tern; wood owl or gull (ELT); also possibly bat (HALOT) (Lev 11:16 R)

צִפּוֹר sparrow, little bird; general term for small birds about the size of a sparrow (Hope); (Job 40:29)

חֲסִידָה stork (the "kind" bird); "considered to be affectionate to its young, in contrast to the ostrich" (UBS); possibly heron (HALOT) (Zech 5:9 R)

דְּרוֹר swallow; dove; swallow, martin (Hope) (Ps 84:4 R)

סוּס / סִיס swift; possibly golden oriole (DCH) (Jer 8:7 R)

Vultures/Eagles

נֶשֶׁר eagle; general term for large bird of prey but also specifically large vulture, large eagle (Hope) (Exod 19:4)

פֶּרֶס Arrians vulture; eagle, bearded vulture (Hope) (Deut 14:12 R)

עָזְנִיָּה bearded vulture; eagle; black vulture (Hope); or osprey (DCH) (Lev 11:13 R)

Cattle

אַבִּיר "strong, mighty" bull; stallion (SDBH) (1 Sam 21:8)

אַלּוּף/אֶלֶף bullock; cattle, oxen (DCH) (Ps 144:14 R)

בְּהֵמָה cattle, animal; domestic animals, livestock (SDBH) (Ps 104:14)

בְּעִיר cattle, livestock; beasts of burden (DCH) (Gen 45:17 R)

בָּקָר ox, cattle, herd; usually cattle but may include sheep or goats (Hope); large cattle (ELT) (1 Kgs 7:25)

מִקְנָה livestock, cattle; usually cows and sheep but also camels, horses, asses (DCH) (Exod 9:3)

מְרִיא fattened calf, fatling; stall-fed calf, reserved for sacrifice (Hope) (Isa 1:11 R)

עֵגֶל calf; male calf, young bull (DCH) (Lev 9:2)

עֶגְלָה heifer (Deut 21:3)

פַּר/פָּר young bull, bullock; young bull reserved for sacrifice (Hope); bull, irrespective of age, offered for sacrifice (DCH) (Ps 22:13)

פָּרָה cow; young bull reserved for sacrifice (Hope) (Num 19:2)

רְאֵם wild ox (Job 39:9 R)

שׁוֹר single head of cattle, bullock; ox (ELT); Taurus (in Zodiac) (DCH) (Lev 4:10)

תְּאוֹ wild bull; antelope (DCH); oryx (Hope); water buffalo (ELT) (Deut 14:5 R)

תּוֹעֲפוֹת (bull) horns (pl.) (Num 23:22 R)

Sheep, Goats

Sheep

אַיִל ram; leader of nation (DCH) (Lev 23:18)

אֵיל הַמִּלֻּאִים fattened ram (ELT) (Lev 8:29)

אַלְיָה sheep's tail; fat tail of sacrificial ram (DCH); fat tail of sheep (HALOT) (Exod 29:22 R)

טָלֶה lamb; very young, unweaned lamb (Hope) (1 Sam 7:9 R)

יוֹבֵל ram's horn, ram (Josh 6:5)

כֶּבֶשׂ lamb (male); sheep (ELT); young ram, usually sacrificial animal (HALOT) (Lev 4:32)

כִּבְשָׂה ewe-lamb (female) (Lev 14:10 R)

כַּר ram; ram, pasture (ELT); young ram, battering ram (DCH) (Amos 6:4)

מֵחִים fattened ram (ELT); fatling of sheep (Isa 5:17 R)

עֵדֶר flock (sheep, goats); "a combination of flocks of domestic animals" (Hope) (Song 4:1)

צֹאן/צֹנֶה flock; a group within an עֵדֶר (Hope); small cattle (ELT) (Gen 30:32)

רָחֵל ewe (female adult) (Song 6:6 R)

שֶׂה member of flock, sheep, goat; young lamb (ELT); small livestock beast (DCH) (Gen 30:32)

Goats

אַקּוֹ wild goat, ibex, slender; mountain goat (SDBH) (Deut 14:5 H)

גְּדִי kid-goat; female kid-goat גְּדִיָּה (Hope) (Judg 6:19)

זֶמֶר mountain goat, mountain sheep (leap); wild ungulate (ELT) (Deut 14:5 H)

יָעֵל male wild-goat, ibex; mountain goat (SDBH) (Ps 104:18 R)

יַעֲלָה female wild-goat, ibex (Prov 5:19 H)

עֵז she-goat; goat hair, the She-goat (constellation) (DCH) (Gen 27:9)

עַתּוּד he-goat; dominant male goat in flock (Hope); ram (ELT); male goat, usually as sacrifice (DCH) (Gen 31:10)

צָפִיר/צְפִיר he-goat; possibly castrated male (Hope); kid goat (ELT) (2 Chr 29:21 R)

שָׂעִיר hairy goat (shaggy); young goat (ELT); he-goat, or hairy demon in shape of he-goat (Isa 13:21)

שְׂעִירָה hairy she-goat (Lev 4:28 R)

תַּיִשׁ he-goat, billy-goat; lit. "the one that butts" (Hope) (Gen 32:15 R)

Enclosures/Troughs

אֵבוּס feeding trough, manger, stall, crib (Prov 14:4 R)

אֶבְרָה manger, crib, stall; wing (DCH) (Job 39:13 R)

אֶרְוָה manger, crib, stall; herding place; stable (HALOT) (1 Kgs 5:6 R)

בָּצָרָה enclosure for sheep or goats (DCH) (Mic 2:12)

גִּדְרֹת צֹאן pens, enclosures (ELT) (Num 32:16)

מִכְלָא sheepfold, enclosure; pen for sheep and goats (HALOT) (Ps 78:70 R)

מְלוּנָה watchman's hut (in field) (Isa 24:20 R)

מִרְבָּה stall; fattening (DCH) (Sir 38:26 R)

מִרְבֵּץ fold for sheep, lair for wild animals (HALOT) (Ezek 25:5 R)

רְהָטִים troughs (ELT) (Gen 30:38 R)

רֶפֶת stable, stall for cattle (Hab 3:17 H)

שִׁקְתוֹת הַמָּיִם watering troughs (ELT) (Gen 30:38)

Animal Husbandry Tools

דָּרְבָן goad (Borowski *Agriculture*) (1 Sam 13:21 R)
חָח nose hook (ELT (2 Kgs 19:28 R)
יַלְקוּט bag/pouch of a shepherd (Pritz) (1 Sam 17:40 H)
כְּלֵי הַבָּקָר yoke (Borowski *Agriculture*) (2 Sam 24:22)
כְּלִי הָרֹעִים bag/pouch of a shepherd (Pritz) (1 Sam 17:40)
כַּר הַגָּמָל saddle for camel (ELT) (Gen 31:34)
מוֹטָה yoke (Borowski *Agriculture*); bar of yoke, yoke (DCH) (Nah 1:13)
מוֹסֵר rein, fetter (ELT) (Jer 5:5 R)
מַחְסוֹם muzzle (Pritz) (Ps 39:1 H)
מִשְׁעֶנֶת rod, club, shepherd's staff (Pritz) (Exod 21:19)
מַלְמָד goad (Borowski *Agriculture*) (Judg 3:31 H)
מַקֵּל rod, club, shepherd's staff (Pritz) (Gen 32:10)
מֶתֶג bridle (ELT); muzzle (DCH) (Ps 32:9 R)
עֲבֹת / עֲבוֹת reins (ELT); cord, branch (DCH) (Isa 5:18)
עֹל yoke (Deut 21:3)
צְרוֹר bundle, parcel, pouch; money pouch, purse (כלי) (Song 1:13 R)
רֶסֶן bit (ELT); halter for horse or mule (DCH) (Isa 30:28 R)
שֵׁבֶט rod, club, shepherd's staff (Pritz) (Exod 21:20)
שׁוֹט whip, scourge (Pritz) (Josh 23:13 H)

Pasturage

דֹּבֶר pasture (Mic 2:12 R)
מִדְבָּר מַדְבָּר pasturage, wilderness; desert (Exod 3:1)
מִרְעֶה feeding place, pasture; haunt (of wild animals); steppe, wilderness, desert, place of wild animals and birds (DCH) (Joel 1:18)
מִרְעִית pasturage; flock; shepherding (Jer 23:1)
נָאֶה pasture, meadow, abode; pleasant place, oasis (DCH) (Ps 65:13)
נַהֲלֹל pasture, watering-place (Isa 7:19 H)
נָוֶה abode of flocks, meadow, habitation (Exod 15:13)

Horses, Mules, Asses

Horses

אַבִּיר "mighty" (horse) (+bull); possibly war-horses, so "charger" or "steed" (Hope) (Judg 5:22)
סוּס horse (Exod 14:23)
עִקְּבֵי־סוּס horses' hooves (ELT) (Judg 5:22)

פָּרָשׁ horse, horseman; warhorse and rider as a unit, cavalry (Hope); charioteer (DCH) (Jer 4:29)

רֶכֶשׁ horses, charioting; fast, swift horse (Hope); draft horse (ELT); steeds (DCH); team of horses, post horses (HALOT) (Esth 8:10 R)

Mules

פֶּרֶד mule; mule (*Equus hemionus*) (Way) (Isa 66:20)

פִּרְדָּה she-mule; mule (*Equus hemionus*) (Way) (1 Kgs 1:38 R)

Asses

אָתוֹן she-ass; female donkey, "jenny" (Way) (1 Sam 9:3)

חֲמוֹר male-ass (red, tawny); general term for donkey (Way) (Gen 22:3)

עַיִר (male) young ass, ass colt, foal; male equid (Way); young donkey (ELT) (Isa 30:24 R)

עָרוֹד wild ass, onager; Nubian wild ass (Hope) (Job 39:5 H)

פֶּרֶא wild ass, onager; onager (Hope); less probably zebra (DCH) (Hos 8:9)

Large Mammals

Various

בְּהֵמוֹת hippo; elephant, Behemoth (SDBH); less probably hippopotamus (DCH) (Job 40:15)

דֹּב bear; Syrian brown bear (SDBH) (Lam 3:10)

דִּישׁוֹן antelope (leaper); addax, waterbuck, defassa, kob (SDBH); wild ungulate (ELT); ibex, or perhaps pygarg (DCH); bison (HALOT) (Deut 14:5 H)

חֲזִיר swine, pig; wild pig (SDBH); can be either domestic or wild pig (Hope); wild boar (Hope, HALOT) (Lev 11:7 R)

נָמֵר leopard; panther (HALOT) (Isa 11:6 R)

צְבִי/צְבִיָּה gazelle; doe (ELT); deer (DCH) (Song 4:5 R)

Camel

בֶּכֶר young camel (male) (Isa 60:6 H)

בִּכְרָה young she-camel; young she-camel in heat (Hope) (Jer 2:23 H)

גָּמָל camel (1 Sam 15:3)

כִּרְכָּרָה riding camel, a dromedary; fast-running female camel (HALOT) (Isa 66:20 H)

Primate

קוֹף monkey, ape, baboon (1 Kgs 10:22 R)

תֻּכִּיִּים baboon, monkey; vervet monkey (SDBH); peacocks, or perhaps poultry or apes (DCH); baboon (HALOT) (2 Chr 9:21 R)

Deer

אַיָּל deer (fallow, large); roe deer (ELT) (1 Kgs 5:3)

אַיָּלָה / אַיָּלֶת hind, doe (Hab 3:19)

אֵמֶר fawn (?) (SDBH) (Gen 49:21 H)

יַחְמוּר roe-deer; Red Hartebeest (antelope); Bubal Hartebeest (Hope); fallow deer (UBS); roebuck (DCH) (Deut 14:5 R)

עֹפֶר young hart, stag (Song of Solomon); young deer, fawn stag, or perhaps ibex (DCH) (Song 4:5 R)

Hyena

צָבוּעַ hyena; bird of prey (DCH) (Jer 12:9 H)

צִיִּים hyenas (?) (Hope) (Jer 50:39 R)

Lions

אֲרִי lion; male lion (Clines "Misapprehensions"); African lion (HALOT) (2 Kgs 17:25)

אַרְיֵה lion; female lion (Hope) (Gen 49:9)

גּוֹר / גּוּר cub (of lion) (Ezek 19:3 R)

כְּפִיר young lion (DCH, HALOT); not specifically young, but still male lion (Clines); hunting/killing lion (Hope) (Ezek 19:2)

לָבָא male lion (Clines "Misapprehensions") (Ps 57:5 H)

לְבָאֹת female lions (DCH) (Nah 2:13 H)

לָבִיא male lion (Clines "Misapprehensions") (Nah 2:12)

לְבִיָּה female lion (Nah 2:13 R)

לַיִשׁ lion, old lion; strong lion (SDBH); male lion (Clines "Misapprehensions"); lion in its prime, not old lion (Hope) (Isa 30:6 R)

שַׁחַל lion; male lion (Hope); lion-cub (HALOT) (Job 28:8 R)

Dog-Like

אֹחַ animal that produces sounds symbolizing death and destruction, jackal (?) (SDBH); owl (DCH) (Isa 13:21 H)

אִי jackal, howler (Isa 13:22 R)

זְאֵב wolf (Gen 49:27 R)

כֶּלֶב dog (1 Kgs 14:11)

נָבַח to bark (Isa 56:10 H)

כַּלְבֵי צֹאן sheep dog (ELT) (Job 30:1 R)

שׁוּעָל fox, jackal (Lam 5:18 R)

תַּן / תַּנָּה fox, jackal; a type of snake or dragon/sea monster in early Hebrew but became term for jackal in later Hebrew (Hope); jackal (HALOT) (Deut 32:33)

Small Mammals

אַרְנֶבֶת hare (Lev 11:6 R)
חֹלֶד weasel, mole; mongoose (Hope) (Lev 11:29 H)
חֲפָרְפַּרָה mole; mole rat (Hope); mole, shrew, perhaps bat (DCH) (Isa 2:20 H)
עֲטַלֵּף bat (Lev 11:19 R)
עַכְבָּר mouse; rat (Hope); jerboa (HALOT) (Isa 66:17 R)
שָׁפָן rock badger, hyrax (Lev 11:5 R)

Lizards/Reptiles

אֶנְקָה gecko; reptile (ELT) (Ps 79:11 R)
חֹמֶט skink (desert brown lizard) (Lev 11:30 H)
כַּח land crocodile; monitor lizard (Hope) (Lev 11:30 H)
לְטָאָה lizard; reptile (ELT); lacertid lizard (SDBH); gecko (HALOT) (Lev 11:30 H)
צַב horn-tailed lizard; thorn-tailed lizard (DCH) (Lev 11:29 H)
צְפַרְדֵּעַ / צְפַדֵּעַ frog; (plague of) frogs (SDBH) (Exod 8:5)
שַׁחַל lizard, usually lion (DCH) (Ps 91:13)
תִּנְשֶׁמֶת chameleon; white owl, little owl, water hen, perhaps chameleon (DCH) (Lev 11:18 R)

Snakes

אֶפְעֶה carpet viper (hissing) (Isa 59:5 R)
בֵּיצָה egg (of viper) (DCH) (Isa 59:5 R)
לִוְיָתָן Leviathan; mythical crocodile monster (?) (Hope); giant crocodile, giant sea monster (SDBH) (Ps 104:26 R)
נָחָשׁ snake; serpent, perhaps Leviathan (DCH) (Gen 3:1)
פֶּתֶן asp, cobra (Ps 58:5 R)
צֶפַע cat snake (ailurophis vivax); cobra (Hope); poisonous snake (DCH) (Isa 14:29 H)
קִפּוֹד arrow-snake (leaps); hedgehog, porcupine, or owl (DCH) (Is 34:11 R)
קִפּוֹז arrow snake, dart snake (Isa 34:15 H)
שְׁפִיפֹן horned adder; viper (Hope); horned viper (DCH); horned snake (HALOT) (Gen 49:17 H)
שָׂרָף poisonous snake; viper (Hope); carpet viper (SDBH); venomous snake, cobra (DCH) (Num 21:6 R)
תַּנִּין serpent; sea monster (Ezek 29:3)

Fish/Aquatic

דָּג/דָּגָה fish; fish (collective) (ELT) (Jonah 2:2)
תַּחַשׁ manatee (dugong), dolphin (?); crocodile (?) (ELT); dolphin, porpoise (DCH) (Num 4:6)

Mollusks

שַׁבְלוּל snail (Ps 58:9 H)
שְׁחֵלֶת onycha (mollusk) (aromatic) (Exod 30:34 H)

Arthropods: Insects, Worms, Etc.

דְּבוֹרָה bee (Deut 1:44 R)
זְבוּב fly (Eccl 10:1 R)
כִּן/כִּנִּם gnat, mosquito; lice (ELT); louse, maggot (DCH) (Isa 51:6 R)
נְמָלָה ant (Prov 6:6 R)
סָס moth (Isa 51:8 H)
עַכָּבִישׁ spider (Job 8:14 R)
עֲלוּקָה leech (Prov 30:15 H)
עַקְרָב scorpion (Deut 8:15 R)
עָרוֹב flier, swarm; swarms of flies (DCH) (Exod 8:20 R)
עָשׁ moth (Isa 50:9 R)
פַּרְעֹשׁ flea (1 Sam 26:20 R)
צִרְעָה hornet (Exod 23:28 R)
קֶרֶץ gadfly (Jer 46:20 H)
רִמָּה maggot; worm (DCH) (Exod 16:24 R)
שְׁמָמִית spider; gecko (SDBH); lizard (DCH) (Prov 30:28 H)
תּוֹלַע worm (Lam 4:5 R)

Locusts

אַרְבֶּה locust (winged stage) (Exod 10:14)
גֹּבַי locust; swarm of locusts (DCH) (Amos 7:1 R)
גָּזָם cutter, locust, caterpillar; locust grub (DCH) (Joel 1:4 R)
חָגָב locust, crawling nymph, caterpillar; grasshopper (Hope) (2 Chr 7:13 R)
חָסִיל hopper locust, ravager; cockroach; grasshopper (Hope) (1 Kgs 8:37 R)
חָרְגֹּל locust, leaping insect (Lev 11:22 H)
יֶלֶק grub (unwinged stage) (Ps 105:34 R)
סְלְעָם locust; perhaps long-headed locust or bald locust (DCH) (Lev 11:22 H)
צְלָצַל whirring locust; cricket; onomatopoeic word representing the sound of an insect swarm (Hope) (Deut 28:42 H)

Snares and Traps

General

חֶבֶל rope, noose (Pritz) (Job 18:10)
יָקוּשׁ trap, snare (Pritz); game hunter (DCH) (Ps 91:3 R)
כְּלוּב bird trap; basket; basket for fruit, bird-cage (DCH) (Jer 5:27 R)
מוֹקֵשׁ snare, noose; striker, bait, decoy (DCH) (Amos 3:5)
מָזוֹר trap, snare (Pritz) (Obad 7 H)
מִכְמָר/מִכְמֹר hunter's net, snare (Isa 51:20 R)
מָלְכֹדֶת snare, trap (Job 18:10 H)
מָצוֹד snare, net (Eccl 7:26 R)
סוּגַר cage, wooden collar (Pritz); neck collar (DCH) (Ezek 19:9 H)
פַּח net, snare; trap (DCH) (Isa 24:17)
פַּחַת pit, trap; ravine (DCH) (2 Sam 17:9)
צַמִּים snares (Pritz) (Job 18:9 R)
רֶשֶׁת net, trap (Prov 1:17)
שְׁבָכָה pitfall, pit trap (Pritz); network, toils, window-lattice or architectural ornamentation (DCH) (Job 18:8)
שׁוּחָה / שַׁחַת / שִׁיחָה trap, snare (Pritz) (Prov 22:14 R)

Fishing Equipment

חַכָּה fishing implement (ELT); fish-hook (DCH) (Isa 19:8 R)
חֵרֶם hunter's net; fishing net (ELT) (Eccl 7:26 R)
מִכְמֶרֶת fishing-net, dragnet (Hab 1:15 R)
מַסָּע fishing spear, harpoon (Pritz); missile, dart, arrow, or other weapon (DCH) (Job 41:26 R)
סִיר דּוּגָה (fish) hook (Pritz) (Amos 4:2 R)
צְלָצַל דָּגִים fishing harpoon, fishing spear (ELT) (Job 40:31 H)
צִנּוֹת (fish) hooks (Pritz) (Amos 4:2 H)
שֶׁכּוֹת fishing spears, harpoons (Pritz) (Job 41:7 H)

FLORA

Trees: General and Specific

General

אֶזְרָח native tree (SDBH); cedar (Koops) (Ps 37:35 H)
חֹרֶשׁ forest, wood (Ezek 31:3 R)
יַעַר wood, forest, thicket (2 Sam 18:8)
עֵץ tree (Exod 15:25)

Specific Trees

אַלָּה/אֵלָה terebinth (Isa 1:29 H)
אֵלוֹן/אַלּוֹן oak; terebinth (DCH) (Isa 44:14 R)
אַלְמֻגִּים/אַלְגּוּמִּים sandlewood, algum/almug (timber); juniper tree (SDBH); sandalwood (Koops) (1 Kgs 10:11 R)
אֶרֶז cedar; Phoenician juniper (Koops) (Lev 14:4)
אֹרֶן laurel (bay-tree) (not pine!); pine tree; fir tree; cedar; laurel (SDBH); pine (Sherwin) (Isa 44:14 H)
אֵשֶׁל tamarisk (Gen 21:33 R)
אֲשֻׁרִים/תַּאַשּׁוּר box tree (Ezek 27:6)
בָּכָא poplar; balsam tree, aspen tree, poplar (SDBH) (2 Sam 5:23–24 R)
בְּרוֹת/בְּרוֹשׁ cypress, fir, juniper; Grecian juniper (Koops) (2 Sam 6:5 H)
גֹּפֶר gopher; cypress (Koops) (Gen 6:14 H)
הֻבְנִים/הוֹבְנִים/הָבְנִי ebony (Ezek 27:15 H)
הֲדַס myrtle (Neh 8:15 R)
לִבְנָה styrax (white flower); white poplar (SDBH); styrax (Koops) (Gen 30:37 R)
נַחַל palm-tree; date palm (DCH) (Num 24:6 R)
עֵץ שֶׁמֶן "trees of oil," e.g., olive oil, hence "olive tree" (DCH); Aleppo pine (Neh 8:15 H)
עֲרָבִים poplar; willow (pl. only) (Ps 137:2 R)
עָרִיץ laurel (?) (Koops); terrifying (DCH) (Ps 37:35 H)
עֶרְמוֹן plane tree (Gen 30:37)
עָרֹעֵר/עַרְעָר juniper, tamarisk (DCH) (Jer 17:6 H)
צַפְצָפָה willow (Ezek 17:5 H)
קִדָּה cassia bark (aromatic) (Exod 30:24 R)
קָנֶה calamus reed (Harrison); sweet cane, ginger grass (Koops) (Ezek 27:19)
קָנֶה הַטּוֹב calamus reed, sweet cane, ginger grass (Koops) (Jer 6:20)
קָנֶה־בֹשֶׂם calamus reed, sweet cane, ginger grass (Koops) (Exod 30:23)
קְצִיעוֹת/קְצִיעָה cassia (Ps 45:9 H)
רֹתֶם broom tree (SDBH) (1 Kgs 19:4 R)

שִׁטָּה acacia (Exod 25:5)
שֶׁמֶן oil tree; wild olive; oleaster (SDBH) (1 Kgs 6:23)
שֶׁמֶן שָׂשׂוֹן "oil of gladness," possibly cassia, Indian orris, or Sausurea lappa (Harrison) (Ps 45:8)
שִׁקְמָה sycamore (1 Kgs 10:27 R)
תְּאַשּׁוּר cypress; fir; juniper (SDBH) (Isa 41:19 R)
תִּדְהָר Brutian pine; Laurustinus shrub; cypress (Koops) (Isa 41:19 R)
תִּרְזָה stone pine; holm tree; a type of oak (Sherwin); holm tree (DCH) (Isa 44:14 H)

Grasses

דֶּשֶׁא sprout, grass; green vegetation, grass (SDBH) (Gen 1:11)
חָצִיר grass; leek (Num 11:5 H)
חָשַׁשׁ dry grass (Isa 5:24 R)
מִרְעֶה grass, pasture (Koops) (Gen 47:4)
עֵשֶׂב grass (Gen 1:11–12)

Reeds

אֵבֶה papyrus; reeds (SDBH) (Job 9:26 H)
אַגְמוֹן cattail, bulrush (Job 41:12 R)
אָחוּ reed, marshy grass (Gen 41:2 R)
גֹּמֶא bulrush, papyrus (Exod 2:3 R)
סוּף (sea of) reeds; cattails, bulrushes (SDBH) (Exod 2:3)
קָנֶה reed, stem, rod (1 Kgs 14:15)

Flowers and Plants

בָּאֻשָׁה weed, stinky weed (Koops) (Job 31:40 H)
גַּלְגַּל tumbleweed (Ps 83:14)
גֶּפֶן סְדֹם "vine of Sodom" = colocynth, a poisonous plant (Koops) (Deut 32:32)
חֲבַצֶּלֶת narcissus, "rose"; "rose of Sharon," mountain tulip (Koops) (Song 2:1)
חַלְמוּת purslane; juice of purslane / mallows (SDBH) (Job 6:6 H)
יָרוֹק green (leaves, plants) (SDBH); "greens," vegetables (Job 39:8 H)
יֶרֶק grass, green (Koops) (Gen 1:30 R)
לַעֲנָה wormwood (Deut 29:17 R)
מַלּוּחַ saltbush; saltwort; mallow (SDBH) (Job 30:4 H)
פַּקֻּעֹת colocynths (Koops); gourds (DCH) (2 Kgs 4:39 H)
פִּשְׁתָּה flax (for linen, wicks); wick of a lamp, made of flax (כלי) (Exod 9:31 R)

צֶאֱלִים lotus plants (SDBH) (Job 40:21 R)
רֹאשׁ hemlock, poison; gall (Harrison) (Deut 29:17)
שׁוּשַׁן lily (Song 2:1)

Thorns, Thistles, Briars

אָטָד thorn-tree; bramble, thorn, thornbush (SDBH); boxthorn (Koops) (Judg 9:14 R)
חוֹחַ thorn; nose-ring (1 Sam 13:6)
חָרוּל weeds, nettles (SDBH) (Prov 24:31 R)
סִיר / סִירָה thorn; hook; pot (Eccl 7:6 R)
צִנִּנִים thorn, pricks (Num 33:55 R)
קוֹץ thorn (Gen 3:18)
שָׁמִיר thorn; gem, diamond; briers (SDBH) (Isa 5:6 R)

Thistle/Briar

בַּרְקָנִים briars; threshing-sledges (Judg 8:7 R)
דַּרְדַּר thistle; thistles (DCH) (Hos 10:8 R)
שֵׁךְ briar; thorn (DCH) (Num 33:55 H)

Thicket/Hedge/Shrub

מְשׂוּכָה / מְסוּכָה hedge (thorns) (Prov 15:19 H)
נַעֲצוּץ thorny thicket; thorn, thistle, brier (SDBH) (Isa 7:19 R)
סְבַךְ thicket (SDBH) (Gen 22:13 R)
עֵב thicket (SDBH) (Jer 4:29 H)
צֵן cactus hedge; barb (Job 5:5 R)
שַׂיִת wild growth, scrub (Isa 5:6 R)

Nettle/Prickle

חֵדֶק prickly plant; thorns; brier, nightshade (DCH) (Prov 15:19 R)
חָרוּל nettles (Koops) (Job 30:7 R)
סִלּוֹן prickle (Ezek 2:6 R)
סָרָבִים nettles (Koops) (Ezek 2:6 H)
סִרְפַּד nettle (Isa 55:13 H)
קִמּוֹשׂ prickly plant; weed, thistle, nettle (Prov 24:31 R)
שֵׁךְ prick (Koops); thorn (DCH) (Num 33:55 H)

Bushes and Shrubs

אֵזוֹב hyssop; marjoram (Koops) (Exod 12:22)
בְּדֹלַח bdellium (gum) (Gen 2:12 R)
כֹּפֶר henna (Song 4:13 R)
מַלּוּחַ mallow; sea-purslain (salt marsh plant) (Job 30:4 H)
מָן manna (Exod 16:15)

סְנֶה blackberry bush, bramble; generic word for bush, shrub (SDBH); burning bush (Koops) (Exod 3:2 R)
עֲרֹעֵר/עַרְעָר juniper, tamarisk (DCH) (Jer 17:6 H)
רֹתֶם broom; broom tree (SDBH) (1 Kgs 19:4 R)
שְׁחֵלֶת onycha, used for incense (DCH) (Exod 30:34 H)
שִׂיחַ bush, plant, shrub, shoot (Gen 2:5 R)

Parts of Trees and Plants

Root

שֹׁרֶשׁ root (Job 14:8)

Stump

גֵּזַע trunk, stump (Isa 11:1 R)

Shoot

יְנִיקָה sucker, sapling (Ezek 17:4 H)
נֵצֶר shoot (Isa 11:1 R)
שֶׁלַח shoot (Song 4:13 R)

Sprout

יוֹנֶקֶת sprout (Ezek 17:22)
צֶמַח sprout (Hos 8:7)

Tendril

נְטִישָׁה tendril (Isa 18:5 R)
שָׂרִיג tendril, branch (Joel 1:7 R)

Twig

זַלְזַל twig; tremulous (Isa 18:5 H)
זָמִיר twig; pruning (DCH) (Song 2:12 H)
עָנָף twigs, branches, bow (Lev 23:40 R)

Branch

אָמִיר branch (of tree); summit (DCH) (Isa 17:6 R)
חֹטֶר branch, rod, twig (Isa 11:1 R)
כִּפָּה palm frond or leaf; branch of tree (DCH) (Lev 23:40 R)
מַטֶּה branch, tribe, rod (Isa 10:15)
סַנְסִנָּה palm branches, date tree stalk (Song 7:9 H)
סָעִיף branches, boughs; cleft, branch, crutch (בלי) (Isa 2:21 R)
סְעַפָּה/סַרְעַפָּה branch (Ezek 31:8 R)
עָנָף branching; full of branches (DCH) (Ezek 19:10 H)
שׂוֹבֶךְ interlaced boughs, thicket (2 Sam 18:9 H)
שׂוֹךְ branch (Judg 9:49 H)
שֶׁלַח branch; spear (Neh 4:17 R)

Bud/Bloom/Blossom

נִצָּה blossom (Gen 40:10 R)
נִצָּן blossom (Song 2:12 H)
סְמָדַר vine blossom (Song 2:13 R)
פָּטוּר opened bud (1 Kgs 6:18 R)
פֶּרַח bloom; bud, flower (DCH) (Isa 18:5)

Flower

נֵץ flower; kestrel (hawk) (Gen 40:10 H)
צִיץ flower; glistening (Isa 28:4)

Foliage/Leaf

דָּלִית foliage, branch, bough (Jer 11:16 R)
טָרָף leaf, fresh shoot (Gen 8:11 R)
עֲבֹת foliage (Ezek 31:3 R)
עָלֶה leaf; foliage (Jer 17:8)
פֹּאֵרָה foliage, bough, branch, shoot (Ezek 31:5 R)
צַמֶּרֶת foliage, top branch ("wool-like"); tree-top (DCH) (Ezek 31:3 R)
רַעֲנָן leafy, luxuriant (Deut 12:2)

Gardens and Planting Places

גַּן garden (Song 4:12)
גַּנָּה / גִּנָּה garden (Isa 1:30)
גֹּרֶן threshing floor (Hos 9:2)
דִּיֹּשׁ threshing (Lev 26:5 H)
כֶּרֶם garden, vineyard (1 Kgs 21:1)
כַּרְמֶל planted field; orchard (DCH) (Isa 10:18)
מַטָּע place of planting; act/thing planted (Ezek 17:7 R)
מִקְשָׁה cucumber field; muskmellon, cantalope (Koops) (Jer 10:5 R)
עֲרוּגָה garden (Song 5:13 R)
פַּרְדֵּס park; orchard, forest (DCH) (Song 4:13 R)
שׁוּרָה row of plants in garden (SDBH) (Job 24:11 R)

PART II

THE HUMAN ORDER

HUMAN

General Terms

אָדָם man, human; human, humankind (SDBH) (Gen 1:26)
אֱנוֹשׁ man, mortal (Deut 32:26)
יָתוֹם orphan (Parker), fatherless (SDBH) (Job 24:9)
נֶפֶשׁ self, life, person; throat (Jer 31:12)
עִי a ruined person (SDBH) (Job 30:24 R)
שְׁאֵר male kindred, flesh (Lev 18:12)
שַׁאֲרָה female kindred (Lev 18:17)

Male and Female

Male

אִישׁ man, individual, husband; ages 25–60 (Eng) (Exod 1:1)
גֶּבֶר adult man, ages 25–60 (Eng) (Jer 31:22)
זָכָר male (Gen 17:14)
זָקֵן leading citizen; elder (Ezek 27:9)
מַת adult, man (Deut 33:6)

Female

אִשָּׁה woman, wife (Gen 2:22)
בַּעֲלָה lady, mistress of a house (DCH) (1 Kgs 17:17 R)
נְקֵבָה female (Num 5:3)
שָׂרָה noblewoman, princess (Isa 49:23 R)

Infant

בְּכוֹר firstborn (Gen 36:15)
בְּכוֹרָה birthright
גָּמוּל weaned child (Isa 11:8)
גמל to wean (Parker) (Gen 21:8)
טַף little one, child; dependent, vulnerable (Parker) (Deut 1:39)
יוֹנֵק infant, suckling (Lam 2:11 R)
ינק to suck (a mother's breast) (Parker) (Exod 2:9)
עָוִיל child, infant (Job 19:18 R)
עוּל infant, sucking, child (Isa 49:15 R)
עוֹלֵל child, infant, little one; small child, in a situation of danger (Parker) (1 Sam 22:19)
פִּטְרָה/פֶּטֶר firstborn (Num 8:16 H)
שִׁלְיָה fetus, afterbirth (Deut 28:57 H)

Youth

General

בְּחוּרוֹת / בְּחוּרִים period of youth nearing adulthood (Parker) (Eccl 11:9 R)
יַלְדָּה / יֶלֶד lad, offspring, child/girl; ages 0–3 years (Eng) (Exod 1:17)
נְעוּרִים youth, childhood (Parker) (Gen 46:34)
עֶלֶם adolescent; young man (DCH) (1 Sam 17:56)
עֲלוּמִים period of older youth (Parker) (Isa 54:4)
צְעִירָה young childhood (Parker) (Gen 43:33 R)

Male Youth

בָּחוּר young man, warrior (Deut 32:25)
וָלָד boy; child, fetus (DCH) (Gen 11:30 H)
יַלְדוּת boyhood (Eccl 11:9 R)
נַעַר boy, servant, retainer; ages 3–25 years (Eng) (Gen 21:12)
נֹעַר boyhood (Job 36:14 R)
נַעַר קָטֹן young boy, ages 3–13 years (Eng) (1 Kgs 3:7)
עֶלֶם male youth (Parker) (1 Sam 17:56 R)

Female Youth

בְּתוּלָה young woman, connotation of sexual maturity (Parker) (Deut 32:25)
בְּתוּלִים virginity (SDBH); young womanhood (DCH) (Lev 21:13)
יַלְדָּה young girl (Parker) (Gen 34:4 R)
נַעֲרָה girl (Gen 24:14)
עַלְמָה sexually mature female youth (Parker) (Isa 7:14 R)

Old Age

בָּאִים בַּיָּמִים advanced in years after a full life, ages 70+ (Eng) (Gen 18:11)
זֹקֶן old age (Gen 48:10 H)
זָקֵן old; ages 60+ (Eng) (Judg 19:16)
זָקֵן מְאֹד advanced old age, ages 70+ (Eng) (1 Sam 2:22)
זִקְנָה old age (1 Kgs 11:4 R)
זִקֻנִים son born in old age (Gen 44:20 R)
יָשִׁישׁ old man; aged (SDBH) (Job 12:12 R)
שֵׂיבָה old age, gray hair, hoary head (Hos 7:9)
שֵׂיבָה טוֹבָה advanced old age, ages 70+ (Eng) (Gen 15:15)

Friend

(For Enemy, see Military ➡ Enemy)

אַלּוּף friend, familiar; chieftain (Ps 55:14)
חָבֵר fellow, friend, partner (SDBH) (Judg 20:11)
יָדִיד loved one, dear one, special friend (SDBH) (Deut 33:12 R)

כְּנָת colleague; associate (SDBH) (Ezra 4:7 H)
מֹדָע / מוֹדַע acquaintance (Ruth 2:1 R)
מַכָּר acquaintance (SDBH) (2 Kgs 12:6 R)
עָמִית comrade, kindred (Lev 25:15)
רֵעַ friend, associate (Job 30:29)
רֵעֶה companion (2 Sam 15:37 R)
רֵעָה female associate (Judg 11:37 R)
רְעוּת female associate (Exod 11:2 R)
רַעְיָה female associate (Judg 11:37)

Slaves/Servants

אָדוֹן slavemaster, lord (Bridge) (Gen 44:8)
אָמָה maidservant, female slave (Exod 20:10)
יָלִיד slave born in the house; one who is born (DCH) (Gen 14:14)
עֶבֶד male slave; slave, servant, officer, official, subject, vassal (SDBH) (Gen 14:15)
פִּילֶגֶשׁ concubine (Gen 22:24)
שָׂכִיר hireling, day-laborer (Exod 12:45)
שִׁפְחָה female slave (Gen 33:1)

Nations, Peoples

אֲגֻדָּה group, band (SDBH) (2 Sam 2:25 R)
אֶזְרָח citizen, native (Exod 12:19)
אֶלֶף clan (SDBH) (Num 1:16)
אֻמָּה community; tribe, people (SDBH) (Gen 25:16 R)
אָמוֹן throng (Jer 52:15 H)
אֲסַפְסֻף group of foreigners, connotation of "riffraff" or "rabble" (SDBH) (Num 11:4 H)
גּוֹי foreign nation (Gen 35:11)
גֵּר guest, foreigner (Gen 15:13)
דּוֹר generation (SDBH) (Gen 6:9)
זָר foreigner (Exod 29:33)
לְאֹם community, people, nation (Isa 51:4)
מַטֶּה tribe (SDBH) (Exod 31:2)
מַלְכֻּת kingdom (Hurvitz) (Num 24:7)
מַקְהֵל assembly (SDBH) (Ps 26:12 R)
נָכְרִי foreigner (Judg 19:12)
עַם people, nation, army (Gen 11:6)
עֵרֶב / עֶרֶב mixed people; mixed rabble, foreigners (SDBH) (Exod 12:38 R)
שֵׁבֶט / שַׁרְבִיט tribe (SDBH) (Gen 49:16)
תּוֹשָׁב resident alien (Exod 12:45)

HUMAN ANATOMY

Head

גִּבֵּחַ/גִּבַּחַת bald forehead, receding hairline (Lev 13:55 R)
גֻּלְגֹּלֶת skull, head (Judg 9:53)
מֵצַח forehead, brow (Isa 48:4)
פֵּאָה hairline; corner (Lev 13:41)
פְּאַת רֹאשׁ temple (Hobbins) (Lev 19:27 H)
פֵּת/פֵּאָה/פֵּאָתַיִם temple (Hobbins) (Isa 3:17 R)
קָדְקֹד crown of head, pate (Deut 28:35)
קֵרַח/קָרַחַת/קָרְחָה bald spot (back of head) (Jer 47:5)
רֹאשׁ head (Hobbins) (Gen 48:14)
רַקָּה temple of head (Hobbins) (Song 4:3 R)

Hair

גְּדֵרָה coiffure (Lam 4:7 R)
דַּלָּה hair (DCH); tresses (Hobbins) (Song 7:6 R)
זָקָן beard (Hobbins) (Lev 13:29)
פְּאַת זָקָן sidegrowth of beard (Lev 19:27 R)
פֶּרַע long hair (Judg 5:2 R)
צִיצִת lock of hair, tassel (Num 15:38 R)
קְוֻצּוֹת locks (Hobbins) (Song 5:2 R)
שֵׂיבָה gray hair, hoary; old age (Hos 7:9)
שֵׂעָר hair (Lev 13:3)
שָׂפָם moustache (2 Sam 19:24 R)

Face

אֹזֶן/אוֹזֶן/אָזְנַיִם ear (Exod 29:20)
אָחוֹר back of head (Hobbins) (Ezek 8:16)
אִישׁוֹן pupil (Deut 32:10 R)
אַף nostril, nose (Amos 4:10)
בָּבָה pupil (Zech 2:12 H)
בְּדַל־אֹזֶן earlobe (Amos 3:12)
גַּב brow, eyebrow (Lev 14:9)
דַּל שְׂפָתַיִם door of the lips (poetic) (Hobbins) (Ps 141:3 H)
דִּמְעָה tears (SDBH) (2 Kgs 20:5)
חֵךְ palate (Ps 119:103)
לְחִי/לְחָיַיִם jaw-bone, cheek (Judg 15:15)
לָשׁוֹן tongue, language (Exod 4:10)
מִדְבָּר mouth (poetic) (Hobbins) (Song 4:3 H)
מַלְקוֹחַיִם jaws (Ps 22:16 H)

מְתַלְּעוֹת/מַלְתְּעוֹת tooth, biter, molar (Joel 1:6 R)
עַיִן/עֵינַיִם eye (Gen 46:4)
עַפְעַפַּיִם eyelash; eyelids (Hobbins) (Prov 4:25)
פְּאַת פָּנִים corner or side of the face, temple (Hobbins) (Lev 13:41 R)
פֶּה mouth (Neh 9:20)
פָּנִים face (Lev 13:41)
שְׁמֻרוֹת עֵינַיִם eyelids (Hobbins) (Ps 77:5 H)
שֵׁן tooth (Deut 19:21)
שָׂפָה/שְׂפָתַיִם lip, language; edge, brink, shore (Exod 6:12)
תְּנוּךְ earlobe (Exod 29:20 R)

Neck

גַּרְגְּרוֹת neck, outside of neck (Prov 1:9 R)
מַפְרֶקֶת vertebra of neck (1 Sam 4:18 H)
עֹרֶף back of neck; nape of neck (Hobbins) (Isa 48:4)
צַוָּאר neck, back of neck (Gen 27:40)

Throat

גָּרוֹן throat; windpipe (Ps 5:10 R)
לֹעַ throat, gullet (Prov 23:2 H)
נֶפֶשׁ throat; self (Prov 3:22)

Upper Body

דַּד breast (Prov 5:19 R)
דַּד nipples (Hobbins) (Ezek 23:3 R)
דָּם blood (Gen 9:4)
זִיז teat (Hobbins) (Isa 66:11 H)
זֵעָה perspiration, sweat (SDBH) (Gen 3:19 H)
חָזֶה chest (Lev 7:31)
כָּתֵף shoulder (Num 7:9)
לֵב/לֵבָב heart; "mind" (Isa 40:2)
נֶפֶשׁ life-breath (Hobbins) (Gen 35:18)
נֵצַח juice, blood (Hobbins) (Isa 63:3 R)
נִשְׁמָה breath (Wilkinson) (Gen 2:7)
סְגוֹר לֵב pericardium, membrane enclosing the heart (Hos 13:8 H)
רוּחַ air (Hobbins) (Exod 15:8)
שַׁד/שָׁדַיִם breast; (female) breast (DCH) (Ezek 16:7)

Arm/Hand

אֶצְבַּע finger, toe (Exod 29:12)
אַצִּיל knuckle; joint (Jer 38:12 R)

אַצִּילוֹת יָד armpits (Hobbins) (Jer 38:12 H)
אַצִּילֵי יָד elbows (Hobbins) (Ezek 13:18 H)
בֹּהֶן thumb; big toe (Judg 1:6)
זְרוֹעַ arm (2 Sam 1:10)
חֹפֶן hollow (of hand) (Ezek 10:2 R)
יָד / יָדַיִם hand; penis (euphemism) (Gen 3:22)
שְׂמֹאל left hand (Hobbins) (Song 2:6)
כַּף palm (of hand); sole (of foot) (1 Sam 5:4)
יָמִין right hand (Hobbins) (Gen 48:13)
צִפֹּרֶן fingernail (Deut 21:12 R)
קָטָן little finger; little one, in reference to finger or penis (DCH) (1 Kgs 12:10 R)
קָנֶה humerus bone (Hobbins) (Job 31:22)
שְׁעָלִים hollows of hands (Isa 40:12 R)

Bones

גֶּרֶם bone, self; bone, strength (DCH) (Gen 49:14 R)
מֹחַ bone marrow (Wilkinson) (Job 21:24 H)
עָצָה spine; sacrum (DCH) (Lev 3:9 H)
עֶצֶם bone, self (Lam 4:7)
צֵלָע spine; rib (Gen 2:22)

Abdomen

אוּל paunch (Hobbins); belly (DCH) (Ps 73:4 H)
בֶּטֶן belly, womb (Ps 31:9)
גָּחוֹן belly, stomach, abdomen (Gen 3:14 R)
גֹּלֶם embryo (Wilkinson) (Ps 139:16 H)
חַדְרֵי־בָטֶן "inner room of the abdomen" (Wilkinson); innards of body (DCH) (Prov 18:8 R)
חֵיק lap, bosom (Exod 4:6)
חֹמֶשׁ stomach (Hobbins) (2 Sam 2:23 R)
טַבּוּר navel (Judg 9:37 R)
כְּרֵשׂ belly; stomach (Hobbins) (Jer 51:34 H)
מֵעֶה / מֵעִים abdomen, intestines (2 Sam 20:10)
מַשְׁבֵּר orifice of womb; mouth of the womb (Hobbins); mouth of cervix (DCH) (Hos 13:13 H)
קִבָּה belly (Hobbins) (Deut 18:3 R)
קִיא to vomit, to throw up (SDBH) (Jer 25:27 R)
קֶרֶב entrails, bowels, heart, mind; inward parts (Hobbins); trunk of body (Wilkinson) (Exod 29:17)
רֶחֶם womb, belly (Jer 20:17)

שֹׁר navel, umbilical cord; vulva (Wilkinson) (Song 7:3 R)

Kidney/Liver

טֻחוֹת inward parts, kidneys (Job 38:36 R)
כָּבֵד liver (Lam 2:11 H)
כִּלְיָה kidney; "conscience" (Ps 139:13)
מְרֹרָה gall bladder (Hobbins); bile or gall (Wilkinson) (Job 20:14 R)

Loins

חֲלָצַיִם loins (Job 31:20)
כֶּסֶל / כְּסָלִים loins (Hobbins); thighs (DCH) (Ps 38:8 R)
מָתְנַיִם hips, loins (Exod 12:11)

Back

בָּמוֹת back (Hobbins) (Isa 2:22 R)
גַּב back (Ps 129:3)
גַּו/גֵּו/גֻּוָּה back, self (Ezek 40:13 R)
שְׁכֶם / שִׁכְמָה back (Hobbins); shoulder (DCH) (Exod 12:34)

Buttocks/Hip/Anus

כַּף הַיָּרֵךְ hip-socket (Hobbins) (Gen 32:33 H)
מִפְשָׁעָה buttocks, hip (1 Chr 19:4 H)
נָשֶׁה sciatic nerve (Hobbins) (Gen 32:33 H)
קֵבָה anus; vulva; abdomen (Num 25:8 H)
שֵׁתָה / שָׁתוֹת / שֵׁת buttocks (2 Sam 10:4 R)

Excrement

דֹּמֶן dung (SDBH) (2 Kgs 9:37 R)
חֲרָאִים dung, excrement (SDBH) (2 Kgs 6:25 R)
מַדְמֵנָה dung-pit (DCH) (Isa 25:10 H)
פֶּרֶשׁ dung, offal (SDBH); intestines, excrement (DCH) (Exod 29:14 R)
צֵאָה / צֹאָה excrement, dung (SDBH) (Deut 23:14 R)
מֵימֵי רֶגֶל urine, literally "penis water" (Wilkinson) (Isa 36:12)
שֵׁין urine (SDBH) (2 Kgs 18:27 R)

Genitals

General

יָרֵךְ vulva (Wilkinson) (Song 7:2)
כֶּסֶל / כְּסָלִים loins, genitalia (Hobbins) (Lev 3:4 R)
עֶרְוָה genitals (male, female); nakedness (Gen 9:22)

Male

אֶשֶׁךְ testicle (Lev 21:20 H)
בָּשָׂר flesh, penis (Hobbins) (Exod 28:42)
זִרְמָה phallus, semen; emission of sperm (SDBH) (Ezek 23:20 R)
חֲלָצַיִם testicles (Boer) (Gen 35:11 R)
יָד / יָדַיִם penis (euphemism); hand (Jer 5:31)
יָרֵךְ male genitals (Gen 24:2), vagina (Boer)
מְבוּשִׁים male genitals (Gen 24:2), vagina (Boer)
מָבֵשׁ male genitals (Deut 25:11 H)
מַקֵּל staff, club, penis (DCH) (Hos 4:12)
מַשְׁכִּים testicles (Boer) (Jer 5:8 H)
מָתְנַיִם testicles (Boer) (Job 40:16 R)
עָרְלָה foreskin (Deut 10:16)
פַּחַד testicle (Job 40:17 H)
קֹטֶן little finger; little one, in reference to finger or penis (DCH) (1 Kgs 12:10 R)
רֶגֶל / רַגְלַיִם penis, genitals (euphemism); leg, foot (Judg 3:24)
שָׁפְכָה penis, urethra (Deut 23:2 H)

Female

בְּשַׂר עֶרְוָה flesh of nakedness, female genitalia (Lev 28:42 R)
דוה to menstruate (SDBH) (Lev 12:2 H)
יָרֵךְ vagina (Song 7:2), male genitals (Boer)
מְבוּשִׁים shameful things, female genitalia (Hobbins); male genitalia (DCH) (Deut 25:11 H)
מַעַר nakedness, female genitalia (Hobbins) (Nah 3:5 R)
נַבְלוּת shamelessness, female genitalia (Hobbins) (Hos 2:12 H)
עֶרְוָה nakedness, female genitalia (Hobbins) (Gen 9:22)
שׁוּחָה possibly vagina (DCH); gorge, pits; pit (SDBH) (Prov 23:27 R)
שֹׁר navel, umbilical cord; vulva (Wilkinson) (Song 7:3 R)

Leg

בֶּרֶךְ / בִּרְכַּיִם knee (1 Kgs 19:18)
יָרֵךְ / יְרֵכַיִם thigh (Num 5:21)
כְּרָע lower leg (below knee) (Exod 12:9 R)
מַרְגְּלוֹת legs (Hobbins); place of feet (DCH) (Ruth 3:4 R)
עָטִין thigh (Hobbins) (Job 21:24 H)
רֶגֶל / רַגְלַיִם leg, foot; penis, genitals (euphemism) (Ezek 25:6)
שׁוֹק leg, calf (Lev 7:33)

Foot

אָפְסַיִם ankles (Hobbins) (Ezek 47:3 H)
אֶצְבַּע finger, toe (1 Chr 20:6)
בֹּהֶן big toe, thumb (Lev 8:23)
יָחֵף barefoot (2 Sam 15:30 R)
כַּף / כַּפַּיִם palm (of hand); sole (of foot) (Deut 2:5)
עָקֵב heel (Gen 3:15)
פַּעַם foot (Hobbins) (Ps 17:5)
קַרְסֹל ankle (2 Sam 22:37 R)
רֶגֶל / רַגְלַיִם foot, feet (Hobbins) (Ezek 25:6)

Body/Muscle

בָּשָׂר flesh, body; person; skin (Wilkinson) (Isa 10:18)
גְּוִיָּה body (Gen 47:18)
גּוּפָה body (Hobbins) (1Chr 10:12)
גִּיד tendon; sinew (Hobbins) (Job 40:17 R)
גֶּלֶד skin (Hobbins) (Job 16:15 H)
גֵּו body; self; back (Exod 21:3 R)
לְחוּם flesh, body (Zeph 1:17 R)
עוֹר skin (Hobbins) (Exod 22:26)
עֹצֶם frame of body (Hobbins) (Ps 139:15 H)
צַד side (Hobbins) (Num 33:55)
קַעֲקַע tattoo (Lev 19:28 H)
שְׁאֵר flesh, self (Lev 18:12)
שָׁרִיר muscle, sinew (Job 40:16 H)

Body Fat

חֵלֶב fat (Hobbins) (Judg 3:22)
מִשְׁמָן fat (Hobbins) (Ps 78:31 R)
פִּימָה fat (Hobbins) (Job 15:27 H)

Corpse

גּוּפָה corpse (1 Chr 10:12 R)
נְבֵלָה corpse, carcass (Ps 79:2)
פֶּגֶר corpse, carcass (1 Sam 17:46)

DISEASE, MORTALITY, AND DISABILITY

Disease

חֳלָאָה disease; rust (Ezek 24:6 R)

חֳלִי disease, malady, sickness (Jer 10:19)

מָזֶה sickness; emaciated, thin (DCH) (Deut 32:24 H)

מַחֲלָה sickness, infirmity (1 Kgs 8:37 R)

מַחֲלֶה disease, sickness, suffering (pl.) (Prov 18:14 R)

נֶגֶף affliction, plague (Exod 12:13 R)

צָרֶבֶת scab, scar, burning; inflammation (DCH) (Lev 13:23 R)

קֶטֶב pestilence; plague; deadly disease; destruction (SDBH) (Deut 32:24 R)

Specific Diseases

גָּרָב eczema (DCH) (Lev 21:20 R)

יַבֶּלֶת wen, seeping sore (Stewart); running sore, perhaps wart (DCH) (Lev 22:22 H)

יַלֶּפֶת tetter, eczema, impetigo (Stewart); scab (DCH) (Lev 21:20 R)

עֹפֶל "plague with swellings" (Kottek); hemorrhoid (DCH) (1 Sam 5:6 R)

צָרַעַת collective term for skin diseases (Grzybowski and Nita); possibilities include eczema or psoriasis, ringworm, scabies, boils, burns (Williams) (Lev 13:2)

קַדַּחַת inflammation, fever (Lev 26:16 R)

שַׁחֶפֶת consumption (SDBH); illness (DCH) (Lev 26:16 R)

Medical Tools, Herbs

General

אָבְנַיִם birthstool (Pritz); pair of stones (used as birthstool) (DCH) (Exod 1:16)

אֵפֶר bandage (Pritz) (1 Kgs 20:38 R)

חִתּוּל bandage (Pritz) (Ezek 30:21 H)

מָזוֹר wound, bandage (Hos 5:13 R)

מְכֵרָה circumcision blade (DCH) (Gen 49:5 H)

תְּעָלָה bandage, plaster; water channel (Jer 30:13 R)

Herbs

אֲהָלוֹת/אֲהָלִים aloes, agarwood; used as purgative (Harrison); used to treat burns and abrasions on skin (Koops) (Num 24:6 R)

אֵזוֹב hyssop; marjoram (Koops); used for digestion and healing animal bites and scratches (Harrison) (Exod 12:22)

בָּצָל onion; used to treat wounds (Williams) (Num 11:5 H)

בָּשֶׂם/בֹּשֶׂם/בֹּשֶׂם balsam, spices; general term for aromatic spices, balms (Nielsen) (Song 5:13)

גַּד coriander; used to aid digestion (Harrison) (Exod 16:31 R)

דְּבֶלֶת תְּאֵנִים fig cake, used to heal skin wounds (Pritz) (2 Kgs 20:7)

דּוּדָאִים mandrake, love apple (SDBH); narcotic, used to aid infertility (Harrison, Williams) (Gen 30:14–16 R)

הֲדַס myrtle; crushed leaves used for skin health (Harrison); also used to treat gum disease and internal ulcers (Williams) (Neh 8:15 R)

זַיִת olive; olive tree, olive grove; olive oil used to treat cuts and wounds (Harrison, Williams) (Exod 23:11)

חֶלְבְּנָה galbanum (resin gum), fennel; used as deodorant (Harrison); milky or white substance (Nielsen) (Exod 30:34 H)

כַּמּוֹן cummin; used to relieve gas and aid digestion (Harrison); used to treat sore throats and possibly also respiratory problems (Williams) (Isa 28:25 R)

כֻּסֶּמֶת fitches, spelt (Harrison); used to relieve gas and aid digestion (Harrison) (Ezek 4:9 R)

כַּרְכֹּם saffron; deodorant and digestive aid (Harrison) (Song 4:14 H)

לֹט ladanum (SDBH); used for coughs and dysentery (Koops) (Gen 37:25 R)

לַעֲנָה wormwood; used to kill internal parasites and as expectorant (Harrison) (Deut 29:17 R)

שְׁחֵלֶת onycha, used to make incense (DCH) (Exod 30:34 H)

מֹר myrrh; used to relieve flatulence (Harrison) (Exod 30:23)

מָרֹר bitter herbs (Exod 12:8 R)

נָטָף stacte resin; used to relieve coughs and stimulate menstruation (Harrison); storax, balm (Nielsen) (Exod 30:34 H)

נְכֹאת gum tragacanth (Koops); ladanum (CDC) (Gen 37:25 R)

נֵרְדְּ nard, spikenard (amber-colored oil) (Song 1:12 R)

עֲרָבִים poplar; willow (pl. only); used as natural aspirin (Williams) (Ps 137:2 R)

פְּקָעִים gourds (pl.); gourd-shaped ornament (DCH); used to make castor oil, a laxative (Harrison) (1 Kgs 6:18 R)

צָרִי storax; balm (SDBH) (Gen 37:25 R)

קִדָּה cassia bark (aromatic); used as aphrodisiac, to aid digestion, and to stimulate blood flow to a part of the body (Harrison) (Exod 30:24 R)

קִיקָיוֹן castor-oil tree; gourd (Harrison); used to make castor oil, a laxative (Harrison, Koops) (Jonah 4:6 R)

קָנֶה calamus reed (Harrison); sweet cane, ginger grass (Koops); unclear use (Harrison) (Ezek 27:19)

קֶצַח nutmeg (black cummin); fitches, spelt, used to relieve gas and aid digestion (Harrison); nigella (Koops); black cumin (DCH) (Isa 28:25 R)

רִמּוֹן pomegranate; pomegranate fruit, pomegranate tree (DCH); used to eradicate intestinal worms (Williams) (Exod 28:33)

שׁוּם garlic; used to expel parasites and heal abcesses (Williams) (Num 11:5 H)

שֶׁמֶן oil, ointment (Pritz) (Isa 1:6)

תְּאֵנָה fig; fig tree (SDBH); used to treat boils (Williams) (2 Kgs 20:7)

תֹּמֶר/תִּמֹּרָה/תָּמָר date-palm; possibly used to treat epilepsy, ear infections, coughs (Williams) (Exod 15:27)

Wound

חַבּוּרָה wound, bruise (Isa 1:6 R)

מַדְקָרָה piercing, stab (Prov 12:18 H)

מָזוֹר wound, bandage (Hos 5:13 R)

מַכָּה wound, blow, slaughter; stroke, blow stripe (DCH) (Prov 20:30)

נָכֵא stricken, wounded (Prov 17:22 R)

פֶּצַע wound, bruise (Isa 1:6 R)

תְּעָלָה bandage, plaster; water channel (Jer 30:13 R)

Pain

חַלְחָלָה writhing, terror, trembling (Ezek 30:4 R)

חַרְצֹב pangs, grief; bands (Ps 73:4)

כְּאֵב pain, anguish (Job 2:13 R)

כָּפָן hunger (Job 5:22 R)

עִצָּבוֹן pain, labor, toil (Gen 3:16 R)

עַצֶּבֶת pain, injury (Ps 16:4 R)

Disabilities

Physical

אִלֵּם unable to speak, "mute" (Olyan) (Isa 35:6 R)

גִּבֵּן curvature of back (Lev 21:20 H)

חָרֵם mutilated, disfigured; flat nose (?) (Lev 21:18)

חֵרֵשׁ hearing impaired, deaf (Isa 42:18 R)

מוּם blemish, defect (Olyan) (Deut 15:21)

מָעוֹג unable to walk, lame person (DCH) (Ps 35:16 H)

עִוֵּר visually impaired, blind (Isa 42:18)

פִּסֵּחַ physically impaired, limp, limping (2 Sam 9:13)

צֹלֵעָה someone with a limp, limper (Olyan) (Zeph 3:19 R)

קָלוּט stunted limb, short stature (Lev 22:23 H)
שָׂרוּעַ stretched, extended; big ear (?) (Lev 21:18 R)
תְּבַלֻּל eye-cataract (Lev 21:20 H)
תָּמִים unblemished, faultless, perfect (Stewart) (Song 5:2)

Mental Illness

מְשֻׁגָּע usually translated "crazy person," but possibly mentally ill (Olyan) (2 Kgs 9:11 R)
שִׁגָּעוֹן madness, mental illness (Olyan) (Deut 28:28 R)

Sexual/Reproductive Dysfunction

זָב genital flow (Olyan), genital discharges (Stewart) (Num 5:2)
כְּרוּת שָׁפְכָה castrated penis (Stewart) (Deut 23:2)
מְרוֹחַ אָשֶׁךְ crushed testicles (Stewart) (Lev 21:20)
עָקָר / עֲקָרָה infertile, barren person (Stewart) (Deut 7:14)
פְּצוּעַ־דַּכָּא crushed testicles (Stewart) (Deut 23:2)
רֶחֶם מַשְׁכִּיל miscarrying womb (Stewart) (Hos 9:14)

Death, Burial, Mourning

Death

אֹבֵד destruction (SDBH) (Num 24:20 R)
אַבְדָן / אָבְדָן destruction; extermination (SDBH) (Esth 9:5 R)
חָלָל slain (Num 19:18)
טֶבַח / טִבְחָה slaughter (of animal) (SDBH) (Ps 44:23)
טֶרֶף / טְרֵפָה prey; victim (SDBH) (Gen 31:39)
מָוֶת death (Gen 25:11)
מַחֲנָק strangling (SDBH) (Job 7:15 H)
מַפָּח breathing one's last (SDBH) (Job 11:20 H)
רְפָאִים dead spirits, ghosts (Prov 21:16 R)
שַׁחַת pit, destruction (Ps 55:24)

Burial

אָרוֹן coffin (Pritz) (Gen 50:26 H)
גָּדִישׁ burial heap; pile of sheaves (Job 21:32 R)
מִטָּה bier, coffin (Pritz) (2 Sam 3:31 H)
מְסֻפָּד embalmer, anointer (Amos 6:10 H)
צַלְמָוֶת grave, death; shadow (Amos 5:8)
צְרִיחַ tomb, grave (Pritz) (1 Sam 13:6 H)
קְבוּרָה sepulcher, grave (Gen 35:20)
קֶבֶר grave, tomb, burial (Gen 23:4)
בֵּית קְבָרוֹת burial site (Hurvitz) (Neh 2:3)
שְׁאוֹל underworld, sheol, grave (Gen 37:35)

Mourning

אָבֵל lamentation; mourning, lamenting; mourner, lamenter (DCH) (Gen 37:35 R)

אֲנָחָה sighing, groaning (Ps 38:10)

אֲנִיָּה groaning (Lam 2:5 R)

בִּגְדֵי־אֵבֶל mourning clothes (Pritz) (2 Sam 14:2)

בְּכִית weeping (Gen 50:4)

מִסְפֵּד wailing, lamentation, mourning (Gen 50:10)

שַׂק sackcloth, mourning clothes (Pritz) (Gen 37:34 R)

FOOD AND SPICES

Food/Drink: General Terms

General

אֲכִילָה food, meal, meat (1 Kgs 19:8 H)
אֹכֶל food (Ps 104:21)
אָכְלָה food (Ezek 15:4)
אֲרֻחָה food, ration (2 Kgs 25:30 R)
בָּרוּת food, meat (Ps 69:22 H)
בְּרִיָּה food, meat, meal (2 Sam 13:10 R)
טֶרֶף food (SDBH); prey of beasts, food for humans (DCH) (Num 23:24)
יְבוּל yield of soil, produce; crops, produce (SDBH) (Hab 3:17)
לֶחֶם food, bread, grain (Lev 23:17)
מַאֲכָל food (Gen 2:9)
מָזוֹן food, meat (2 Chr 11:23 R)
מַכֹּלֶת food (1 Kgs 5:25 H)
מָן manna, connected with Tamarix mannifera (UBS) (Exod 16:15)
מָנָה portion (Esth 2:9)
מַטְעָם morsel, food, delicacy (Prov 23:3 R)
מַרְזֵחַ banquet (Walsh); feasting, funeral meal (DCH) (Jer 16:5 R)
מִשְׁתֶּה banquet (Walsh); feast, drink (DCH) (Esth 1:3)
נָזִיד stew (FAJ) (Gen 25:29 R)
פַּנַּג unknown baked food (Borowski *Agriculture*); millet (Koops); early figs, pastry, millet, or pancakes or opopanax (DCH) (Ezek 27:17 H)
צֵידָה food, game; provision of food (DCH) (Gen 27:3)
תָּפֵל tasteless, insipid food (SDBH) (Job 6:6 R)

Animal Fodder

בְּלִיל fodder, food for animals (SDBH) (Isa 30:24 R)
מִסְפּוֹא fodder, food for animals (SDBH, Koops) (Gen 24:25 R)

Drink

מַיִם water (Gen 21:14)
מִשְׁתֶּה banquet (Walsh); feast, drink (DCH) (Esth 1:3)
עָסִיס juice (Brenner "The Food of Love"); sweet wine, juice (DCH); must, fresh wine (SDBH) (Joel 1:5 R)
שִׁקּוּי beverage, possibly wine (Jordan) (Hos 2:7 R)

Taste

טוֹב sweet, tasty (Brenner "The Food of Love") (Song 1:2)

מָתוֹק sweet (Brenner "The Food of Love"); sweet, sweet thing, sweetness (DCH) (Prov 24:13)

Grains

אָבִיב ripe ears of corn; newly formed ears of grain (Koops); ear of cereal (DCH) (Lev 2:14 R)

אֵיפָה grain measure (40 liters) (Exod 16:36)

בִּכּוּרִים firstfruits (of fruits and grain) (Ezek 44:30)

בְּלִיל fodder, food for animals (SDBH) (Isa 30:24 R)

בַּר grain (Prov 14:4)

גָּדִישׁ sheaves (Koops); shock of grain (DCH) (Job 5:26 R)

גֶּרֶשׁ crushed grains, grits (Lev 2:14 R)

דָּגָן grain; cereal (Borowski *Agriculture*); corn, grain of cereals (DCH) (Ps 4:8)

דֹּחַן millet, sorghum (Ezek 4:9 H)

זֶרַע sowing, seed, grain (Koops) (Gen 47:19)

חִטָּה wheat (1 Kgs 5:25)

יֵרָקוֹן mildew (Koops); rust or mildew (DCH) (1 Kgs 8:37 R)

כֻּסֶּמֶת spelt; spelt, emmer (SDBH); wheat (Koops); emmer wheat (MacDonald); spelt (DCH) (Ezek 4:9 R)

כַּרְמֶל new grain; fruit, growth; raw grain (Borowski *Agriculture*); fresh ears of grain (Koops); fresh ears (of cereal) (DCH) (2 Kgs 4:42 R)

מְלִילוֹת ear of grain (Borowski *Agriculture*); ear of corn (DCH) (Deut 23:26 H)

נִסְמָן sesame (?), millet (?) (Borowski *Agriculture*); "the thing planted" (DCH) (Isa 28:25 H)

סֹלֶת fine flour; semolina, choice wheat or flour (DCH) (Gen 18:6)

עֲבוּר produce, grain (Koops) (Josh 5:11–12 R)

עָמִיר cut grain, sheaves (SDBH) (Jer 9:21 R)

פִּשְׁתָּה flax (Borowski *Agriculture*) (Exod 9:31 R)

קָלִי roasted grain, parched grain; roasted, dried, or baked kernels of grain (Koops); roasted grain, parched grain, or perhaps roasted lentils (DCH) (Lev 23:14 R)

קָמָה ripe, uncut grain plants (Koops); standing grain (DCH); standing grain (SDBH) (Isa 17:5)

קֶמַח flour, meal (Num 5:15)

קַשׁ chaff, straw; stubble, chaff (DCH) (Exod 15:7)

רִיפוֹת crushed grains (pl.); barley groats (DCH) (2 Sam 17:19 R)

שִׁבֹּלֶת ear of grain (Isa 17:5)

שְׂעֹרָה barley (Lev 27:16)
תֶּבֶן straw, grain stalks (Gen 24:25)

Threshing/Winnowing

גֹּרֶן threshing floor (Hos 9:2)
דִּישׁ threshing time; threshing (DCH) (Lev 26:5 H)
חָרוּץ threshing sledge, incised, sharpened (Job 41:22 R)
חָרִיץ sharpened; pickaxe (DCH) (2 Sam 12:31 R)
מוֹרַג threshing sledge (2 Sam 24:22 R)
מִזְרֶה winnowing shovel (fan, fork); pitchfork (DCH) (Jer 15:7 R)
רַחַת winnowing fork; winnowing shovel (DCH) (Isa 30:24 H)

Grain: Baked Goods/Dough/Leaven

בָּצֵק dough, flour (Exod 12:34 R)
לָשָׁד cake; cake, delicacy (DCH) (Num 11:8 R)
חַלָּה ring bread; cake (DCH) (Lev 24:5)
חָמֵץ leavened bread (Lev 7:13)
חֹרִי white bread (Gen 40:16 H)
כַּוָּן cake (for idols), wafer (Jer 7:18 R)
לְבִבוֹת/לְבִיבֹת cakes (pl.); hearty dumplings (FAJ) (2 Sam 13:6 R)
לֶחֶם bread, food; bread, bread grain, grain (Koops) (Lev 23:17)
מָעוֹג cake, bread; loaf or slice of bread or cake (DCH); round silo (DCH) (1 Kgs 17:12 H)
מַצָּה unleavened bread (Exod 12:39)
עֻגָּה cake (on hot stones) (Hos 7:8)
עֲרִיסָה coarse meal, dough; wheat (Brenner "The Food of Love") (Ezek 44:30 R)
צְלִיל/צָלוּל round loaf/cake (Judg 7:13 H)
רָקִיק flat cakes; wafer (SDBH) (Lev 2:4 R)
שְׂאֹר leaven (Exod 12:15 R)

Vine, Wine, Grapes (includes Strong Drink)

Plant Parts

גֶּפֶן vine (2 Kgs 4:39)
זְמוֹרָה twig; branch of vine (Isa 17:10 R)
נָזִיר untrimmed vine (Lev 25:5 R)
שָׂרִיג tendril; branch of vine (DCH) (Gen 40:10 R)
שֹׂרֵק/שְׂרֵקָה vinestock; choice vine (Walsh); variety of grape, choicest grape (Borowski *Agriculture*) (Isa 5:2 R)

Wine/Strong Drink

דַּם־עֲנָבִים / דַּם־עֵנָב poetic phrase for wine, lit "blood of grape(s)" (Borowski *Agriculture*) (Gen 49:11)

חֹמֶץ vinegar (fermented grape plus barley); sour wine, vinegar (SDBH) (Ruth 2:14 R)

חֶמֶר/חֲמֶר wine (root = boil); (fermenting) wine (SDBH); red (?) wine (Borowski *Agriculture*) (Deut 32:14)

יַיִן wine, wine-induced stupor (DCH) (Gen 9:24)

יַיִן הָרֶקַח spiced wine (Borowski *Agriculture*) (Song 8:2)

מֶזֶג mixed wine = spiced; mixed wine (DCH) (Song 7:3 H)

מִמְסָךְ mixed drink, spiced wine (Walsh); ritual wine, libation wine (Jordan) (Prov 23:30 R)

מַמְתַּקִּים sweet wine (SDBH); sweetness, sweet things, perhaps sweet drink (DCH); sweets (Brenner "The Food of Love") (Song 5:16 R)

מֶסֶךְ mixed drink, spiced wine (SDBH) (Ps 75:9 H)

מַשְׁקֶה drink (Lev 11:34 R)

מִשְׁרָה juice; syrup, a grape product forbidden to Nazirites, perhaps equivalent to modern Arabic dibs (Borowski *Agriculture*); juice (DCH) (Num 6:3 H)

סֹבֶא drink, wine, liquor; alcoholic drink (Walsh); strong drink (DCH); wine, possibly beer (Jordan) (Hos 4:18 R)

עָסִיס new wine (Walsh); must, new wine (de Blois); pomegranate wine (Borowski *Agriculture*); sweet wine, juice (DCH) (Joel 1:5 R)

צוּף honeycomb (SDBH); mead (Borowski *Daily Life*) (Ps 19:11 R)

שֵׁכָר liquor, strong drink; date-wine (SDBH); beer (Borowski *Agriculture*); generic term for alcoholic drinks (MacDonald); fermented drink (DCH) (Prov 20:1)

שְׁמָר dregs; lees, dregs of wine, wine matured on the lees (DCH) (Ps 75:9 R)

שִׁקּוּי beverage, possibly wine (Jordan) (Hos 2:7 R)

תִּירוֹשׁ new wine (Isa 65:8)

Cluster/Grape

אֲשִׁישָׁה raisins (Brenner "The Food of Love"), raisin cake (DCH, SDBH, Koops, MacDonald) (2 Sam 6:19 R)

אֶשְׁכּוֹל cluster, bunch (Song 1:14 R)

בֹּסֶר unripe grape (SDBH, Koops) (Isa 18:5 R)

בָּצִיר grape harvest, vintage, clipped (Isa 24:13 R)

זָג grapeskin, pit; skin or seed of grape (DCH) (Num 6:4 H)

חַרְצָן unripe grape, pit, seeds; sour grape (DCH) (Num 6:4 H)

סְמָדַר type of grape, usually translated "grape blossom" (Borowski *Agriculture*); buds or blossoms of vine, perhaps blossom-flavored wine (DCH) (Song 7:13 R)

עֹלְלוֹת grape gleanings (pl.) (Judg 8:2 R)

עֵנָב grape (Hos 9:10)

פֶּרֶט fallen grapes (Lev 19:10 H)

צִמּוּק raisin cake; dried grapes, raisin cake (DCH); raisin (Borowski *Agriculture*) (1 Sam 25:18 R)

Vineyard

גָּדֵר vineyard walls (Walsh) (Isa 5:5)

גַּת winepress, threshing floor (DCH); treading floor (Jordan) (Isa 63:2 R)

כֶּרֶם vineyard (1 Kgs 21:1)

מִשְׁעוֹל narrow (walled) passage (in vineyard); narrow pathway (DCH) (Num 22:24 H)

Winepress

יֶקֶב wine vat; winepress (Walsh); winery, fermentation vat, press (Jordan) (Prov 3:10)

פּוּרָה winepress (Walsh); portable winepress (FAJ); winepress, liquid from winepress (DCH) (Isa 63:3 R)

Dairy

גְּבִינָה cheese (SDBH) (Job 10:10 H)

חָלָב milk; fresh milk or processed dairy products (MacDonald); milk, cheese (DCH) (Gen 49:12)

חַלָּמוּת egg yolk (SDBH, DCH); possibly mallow plant (Koops) (Job 6:6 H)

חֶמְאָה curds (SDBH); curds, butter (DCH) (2 Sam 17:29)

חָרִיץ cheese (SDBH); full idiom חֲרִצֵי הַחָלָב = literally "slices of dairy" (MacDonald) (1 Sam 17:18 R)

שְׂפוֹת cheese (SDBH) (2 Sam 17:29 H)

Nuts

אֱגוֹז walnut; nut (Brenner "The Food of Love") (Song 6:11 H)

בָּטְנִים pistachios; terebinth nuts (Koops) (Gen 43:11 H)

לוּז hazelnut; almond (Koops) (Gen 30:37 H)

מְשֻׁקָּד almond (Koops) (Exod 25:33 H)

שָׁקֵד almond (Gen 43:11 R)

Fruits

אֲבַטִּיחַ melon; watermelon (Koops) (Num 11:5 H)

אֲבִיּוֹנָה caper plant; caper bush, caper berry (Koops, DCH) (Eccl 12:5 H)

אֶשְׁפָּר date cake (SDBH) (2 Sam 6:19 R)

בְּאֻשִׁים fetid fruit (Walsh) (Isa 5:2 H)

בָּכָא unidentified fruit (MacDonald); balsam, or perhaps aspen tree (DCH) (Ps 84:6 R)

בִּכּוּרִים first fruits (of fruits and grain) (Ezek 44:30)

בִּכּוּרָה/בִּכֹּרָה early fig; first fig crop (Borowski *Agriculture*) (Isa 28:4 R)

גַּרְגְּרִים olives (Borowski *Agriculture*); berry, olive, or grape (DCH) (Isa 17:6 H)

דְּבֵלָה pressed fig cake (2 Kgs 20:7 R)

זַיִת olive; olive tree, olive grove (Exod 27:20)

יִצְהָר olive oil; fresh oil (DCH) (Deut 7:13)

מְסֻכָּן mulberry (Koops); mulberry tree or wood, also possibly sisu tree or wood (DCH) (Isa 40:20 H)

נֹקֶף shaking off (olives) (Isa 17:6 R)

עֵץ הָדָר citron (Koops) (Lev 23:40)

פַּג early fig, unripe fig (DCH) (Song 2:13 H)

פְּרֶדֹת dried figs (Joel 1:17 H)

פְּרִי fruit (Lev 25:19)

קַיִץ late fig, second crop (Borowski *Agriculture*); summer fruits, summer produce (DCH); summer fruit (SDBH) (Jer 8:20)

רִמּוֹן pomegranate (Exod 28:33)

שֶׁמֶן oil tree; wild olive; oleaster (SDBH) (1 Kgs 6:23)

שִׁקְמָה sycamore fig; sycamore tree (DCH) (Isa 9:9 R)

תְּאֵנָה fig; fig tree (DCH) (Gen 3:7)

תֹּמֶר/תִּמֹּרָה/תָּמָר date-palm (Exod 15:27 R)

תַּפּוּחַ apple, apricot; peach (Brenner "The Food of Love", Borowski *Agriculture*); quince or apricot (MacDonald); apple tree (DCH) (Prov 25:11 R)

Vegetables

בָּצָל onion (Num 11:5 H)

זֵרוּעַ vegetable (Borowski *Agriculture*); sowing, thing sown (DCH) (Lev 11:37 R)

חָמִיץ chick-pea (?) (Borowski *Agriculture*, Koops); sorrel (DCH) (Isa 30:24 H)

חָצִיר leek; grass; reed (Isa 34:13)

יָרָק vegetable (Borowski *Agriculture*); collective noun meaning herbage, vegetables (DCH) (Deut 11:10 R)

מִקְשָׁה cucumber field; muskmellon, cantalope (Koops) (Isa 1:8 R)

עֲדָשִׁים lentils (2 Sam 17:28 R)

פּוֹל bean; broad bean (MacDonald) (2 Sam 17:28 R)

פְּקָעִים gourds (pl.); gourd-shaped ornament (DCH) (1 Kgs 6:18 R)

קִשֻּׁאָה cucumber; muskmellon, cantalope (SDBH, Koops) (Num 11:5 H)

שׁוּם garlic; used to expel parasites and heal abcesses (Williams) (Num 11:5 H)

Honey

דְּבַשׁ honey; date honey (Borowski *Agriculture*); bee honey or fruit honey (MacDonald) (1 Sam 14:25)

יַעַר/יַעֲרָה honeycomb (Brenner "The Food of Love," DCH) (Song 5:1 R)

נֹפֶת honeycomb (Brenner "The Food of Love"); flowing honey (DCH) (Prov 24:13 R)

צוּף honeycomb (SDBH); mead (Borowski *Daily Life*) (Ps 19:11 R)

Herbs and Spices, Ointments/Resins/Balms, Incense

Herbs and Spices

אֹרֶת herbs; mallow (DCH) (2 Kgs 4:39 H)

גֶּד coriander (Exod 16:31)

דּוּדָאִים mandrake; mandrake, love apple (SDBH) (Gen 30:14–16 R)

חָמִיץ seasoned, salted; chick-pea (?) (Borowski *Agriculture*, Koops); sorrel (DCH) (Isa 30:24 H)

כַּמֹּן cummin (Isa 28:25 R)

כֻּסֶּמֶת fitches, spelt (Harrison) (Ezek 4:9 R)

מֶלַח salt (Job 6:6)

מֶרְקָחָה spices, seasonings; perfume boiler (כלי); pot of ointment, spice (DCH) (Job 41:23 R)

מָרֹר bitter herbs (Deut 32:32 R)

נְכֹאת gum tragacanth (Koops) (Gen 37:25 R)

סַם spice; herb (Exod 25:6)

קִנָּמוֹן cinnamon (Exod 30:23 R)

קֶצַח nutmeg (black cummin); fitches, spelt (Harrison); nigella (Koops); black cumin (DCH) (Isa 28:27 R)

רֶקַח spice (general term) (Song 8:2 H)

Ointments/Resins/Balms

אֲהָלוֹת/אֲהָלִים aloes, agarwood (Num 24:6 R)

בֹּשֶׂם/בֶּשֶׂם/בֹּשֶׂם balsam, spices; general term for aromatic spieces, balms (Nielsen) (Song 5:13)

חֶלְבְּנָה galbanum (resin gum), fennel (Exod 30:34 H)

כֹּפֶר henna (Koops) (Song 1:14 R)

כַּרְכֹּם saffron (Song 4:14 H)

לֹט laudanum (oil), "Rock Rose" (Exod 37:25 R)
מֹר myrrh (Exod 30:23)
נָטָף stacte resin (Exod 30:34 H)
נְכֹאת trangacanth gum; aromatic gum; ladanum (DCH) (Gen 43:11 R)
נֵרְדְּ nard, spikenard (amber-colored oil) (Song 1:12 R)
צָרִי liquid amber (storax), balm; mastic tree (Harrison); balm, balsam (DCH) (Gen 37:25 R)
קִיקָיוֹן castor-oil tree; gourd (Harrison) (Jonah 4:6 R)

Incense

אֲהָלוֹת/אֲהָלִים aloes, agarwood (Num 24:6 R)
בֹּר hammada plant, used for making soap (Job 9:30 R)
בָּשֶׂם/בֹּשֶׂם/בֹּשֶׂם balsam, spices; general term for aromatic spieces (Nielsen) (Song 5:13)
לְבוֹנָה/לְבֹנָה frankincense (Jer 6:20)
מֹר myrrh (either dry or wet) (Exod 30:23)
נָטָף stacte resin; used to relieve coughs and stimulate menstruation (Harrison); storax, balm (Nielsen) (Exod 30:34 H)
נְכֹאת gum tragacanth (Koops) (Gen 37:25 R)
סַם spice; herb; general term for aromatic substances (Nielsen) (Exod 25:6)
צָרִי storax; balm (SDBH) (Gen 37:25 R)
קְטֹרֶת incense; perfume (DCH) (Exod 30:35)

CLOTHING

General Terms

בֶּגֶד clothing, covering (Gen 24:53)
בִּגְדֵי אַלְמְנוּת widow's clothing (Gen 38:14) (Pritz)
גְּלוֹם mantle, clothes, wrapping, wrap; thin garment (Platt) (Ezek 27:24 H)
חֹב fold (of garment) (SDBH) (Job 31:33 H)
לְבוּשׁ attire, clothing, garment (Gen 49:11)
מַד garments; clothing (Pritz) (Lev 6:10 R)
מַחֲלָצוֹת loin cloth (Platt); outer garment, mantle, cloak (Pritz); festive robe (DCH) (Isa 3:22 R)
מַלְבּוּשׁ vestments, apparel (Ezek 16:13 R)
מֶלְתָּחָה royal wardrobe, vestry; clothes store, wardrobe, cloakroom (DCH) (2 Kgs 10:22 H)
מַעֲטֶה vestment (Isa 61:3 H)
סָדִין linen wrapper (undergarment) (Judg 14:12–13 R)
סוּת garment (Gen 49:11 H)
בֶּגֶד עִדִּים menstrual cloth (SDBH) (Isa 64:5 H)
עוֹר animal skin (Pritz) (Gen 3:21)
פְּתִיגִיל some kind of fine garment wrapped around the wearer (Pritz) (Isa 3:24 H)
שֹׁבֶל garment, clothing (Pritz); skirt (DCH) (Isa 47:2 H)
שִׁית attire, dress, clothing, garb; mantle (DCH) (Prov 7:10 R)
שַׂלְמָה / שִׂמְלָה garment, clothing (Pritz) (Exod 22:9)
תִּלְבֹּשֶׁת a garment (Isa 59:17 H)

Old Clothes

בְּלוֹי rag (SDBH) (Jer 38:11 R)
מֶלַח old clothes, rags (SDBH) (Jer 38:11)
קְרָעִים torn pieces of cloth, rags, tattered clothes (SDBH) (Prov 23:21 R)

Outer Garment

כְּסוּת covering, garment (Pritz) (Exod 21:10 R)
מִכְנָסַיִם breeches, drawers (SDBH) (Exod 28:42 R)
מִכְסֶה covering, garment (Exod 26:14)
שַׂלְמָה / שִׂמְלָה / סַלְמָה outer garment; cloak, mantle (DCH) (Deut 29:4)

Robe

מַכְלֻל ornate robe; perfect (Ezek 27:24 H)
מַעֲטָפָה enveloping cape (Platt); cape, mantle, cloak (SDBH) (Isa 3:22 H)
מְעִיל robe (SDBH) (Exod 28:4)
תַּכְרִיךְ long royal robe, mantle (Esther); cloth wrapping, garment (Hurvitz) (Esth 8:15 H)

Band

אֵפֵר band, bandage, cloth (SDBH) (1 Kgs 20:38 R)
אַבְנֵט sash (SDBH) (Exod 28:4 R)
אֵזוֹר belt, band; loincloth, waistcloth (SDBH) (Job 12:18 H)
חֲגוֹר girdle, belt (SDBH) (Gen 3:7 R)
חֲגוֹרָה loincloth (Pritz); belt (DCH) (Gen 3:7 R)
חֵשֶׁב girdle, band (Exod 28:8 R)
חֲתֻלָּה swaddling band (SDBH) (Job 38:9 H)
כֶּסֶת band for wrist or arm (SDBH); wristband, magic charm (Pritz) (Ezek 13:18 R)
מֵזַח waistband, sash, belt (Pritz); girdle (DCH) (Ps 109:19 H)
סָדִין warriors' belts (Platt); linen garment (DCH) (Isa 3:23 R)
קִשֻּׁרִים sashes, bridal bands; sashes, girdles, ribbons (SDBH) (Isa 3:20 R)

Tunic

כְּתֹנֶת tunic, shirt, undergarment (Gen 3:21)
מַעֲטָפָה overtunic, mantle, cloak (Isa 3:22 H)
סָדִין shirt, tunic (Pritz) (Prov 31:24 R)
פַּס long-sleeved tunic; variously colored material (DCH) (Gen 37:3 R)

Hem/Fringes

גְּדִלִים fringes, tassels of garment (Pritz) (Deut 22:12 R)
כָּנָף hem, corner of garment (Pritz) (Num 15:38)
צִיצִת fringes, tassels of garment (Pritz) (Num 15:38 R)
שׁוּל hem, skirt (of robe), bottom edge; train of garment (Pritz) (Exod 28:33)

Cloak

אַדֶּרֶת cloak, mantle, robe (SDBH) (Gen 25:25)
מִטְפַּחַת cloak, spreading garment, wide cloak (Ruth 3:15 R)
תַּכְרִיךְ mantle, cape, cloak (Pritz) (Esth 8:15 H)

Head Covering

טְבוּל turban (Ezek 23:15 H)
טוֹטָפוֹת frontlet, phylactery, headband, sign, mark, reminder (SDBH) (Exod 13:16 R)
כֶּתֶר circlet, diadem, crown (Persian) (Esth 1:11 R)
לִוְיָה wreath, garland (SDBH) (Prov 1:9 R)
מִגְבָּעָה mitre (priest), headband (Exod 28:40 R)
מִצְנֶפֶת turban, diadem, tiara (Ezek 21:26)
נֵזֶר crown, headband (king, high priest) (Exod 29:6)
עֲטָרָה crown, royal diadem (2 Sam 12:30)
פְּאֵר headwrap, turban (Isa 3:20 R)
צִיץ (golden) plate, disk, frontlet, medallion on high priest's turban (SDBH) (Exod 28:36)
צָנִיף headdress (men, priest, women) (Isa 3:23 R)
צְפִירָה crown, wreath (Isa 28:5 H)

Veils

מַסְוֶה face covering (Exod 34:33–35 R)
מִסְפָּחָה / מִטְפַּחַת long veil, scarf (Ezek 13:18 R)
צַמָּה woman's veil (Song 4:1 R)
צָעִיף shawl, wrapper, veil (Gen 24:65 R)
רְדִיד cloak, large veil (Isa 3:23 R)
רְעָלוֹת veils ("tremulous"); beads (Platt) (Isa 3:19 H)

Footwear

מִצְחָת greaves (1 Sam 17:6 H)
נַעַל sandal (Gen 14:23)
סְאוֹן military boot (Isa 9:4 H)
שְׂרוֹךְ thong (sandal); strap of sandal (Pritz) (Gen 14:23 R)

Jewelry

General

חֲלִי / חֲלִיָּה ornament, jewel (SDBH) (Prov 25:12 R)
לְחָשִׁים snake charms (Platt); amulets (DCH) (Isa 3:20 R)
עֲדִי jewelry, ornaments (2 Sam 1:24)
רְעָלוֹת veils ('tremulous'); beads (Platt) (Isa 3:19 H)
תִּפְאָרֶת jewelry, beauty; insignia of office (Platt) (Isa 3:18 R)

Head

פְּאֵר garland crown (Platt); headdress, turban (DCH) (Isa 3:20 R)
שְׁבִיסִים sun- or star-disks (Platt); women's jewelry in the shape of the sun (DCH) (Isa 3:18 H)

שַׁהֲרוֹן crescent (Platt); crescent, little moon (DCH) (Isa 3:18 R)
תּוֹר ornament (SDBH); plait, earring, pendant (DCH) (Song 1:10 R)

Ear

נְטִיפָה pendant (ear) (Isa 3:19 R)
עָגִיל earring (Num 31:50 R)

Nose

חָח nose ring, hook; fibula, brooch (DCH) (Exod 35:22 R)
נֶזֶם nose ring (Prov 11:22)

Neck

בַּיִת house; sachet of perfume worn around neck by women (כלי); container (of perfume) (DCH) (Isa 3:20)
חָח brooch, pin (SDBH) (Exod 35:22)
חֲרוּזִים string of jewels, string of shells (SDBH) (Song 1:10 H)
כּוּמָז neck ornament (golden) (Num 31:50 R)
עָנָק necklace, collar (Prov 1:9 R)
צָוָרוֹן necklace (SDBH) (Song 4:9 H)
רָבִיד necklace, neck-chain (Gen 41:42 R)
שַׁהֲרוֹן crescent, neck pendant (Judg 8:26 R)

Arm

צָמִיד arm-clasp, bracelet (Gen 24:22 R)
צְעָדוֹת armlets (Platt); armband (DCH) (Isa 3:20 H)

Wrist

שֵׁירוֹת wrist-bands; necklace cords (Platt); bracelets, bangles (DCH) (Isa 3:19 H)

Ring/Seal

גָּלִיל rod, ring (DCH) (Esth 1:6 R)
חוֹתָם signature-ring, seal (Gen 38:18)
חֹתֶמֶת signet-ring, seal (Gen 38:25 H)
טַבַּעַת seal, signet, ring (Isa 3:21)

Ankle

אֶצְעָדָה ankle chain, step chain; bracelet (Num 31:50 R)
עֶכֶס anklet, bangle (Isa 3:18 R)
צְעָדָה ankle chain (Isa 3:20 R)

Fabric

אֵטוּן thread, yarn; linen (Prov 7:16 H)
בַּד linen (Exod 28:42)

בּוּץ cotton, byssus; fine undyed linen (CT) (1 Chr 4:21 R)
בְּרֹמִים two-colored fabric, variegated cloth (Ezek 27:24 H)
דְּמֶשֶׁק damask (Amos 3:12 H)
חוּר white linen (Esth 1:6 R)
חֲטֻבוֹת multi-colored embroidered cloth, dark-hued stuff; also considered beautiful (SDBH) (Prov 7:16 H)
חֹפֶשׁ material; saddle-clothes; woven material (DCH) (Ezek 27:20 H)
כַּרְפַּס white linen, cotton cloth (Esth 1:6 H)
מַטְוֶה yarn (SDBH) (Exod 35:25 H)
מַכְבֵּר netted cloth (thick) (2 Kgs 8:15 H)
מֶשִׁי fine fabric (Ezek 16:10 R)
עוֹר leather, skin; hide of animals, skin of humans (DCH) (Gen 27:16)
עֵרֶב woof, web; woven or knitted material (SDBH) (Lev 13:58 R)
פְּלֶדָה cloth (SDBH); covering, blanket, caparison (Nah 2:4 H)
פִּשְׁתָּה linen, flax (Exod 9:31 R)
צֶבַע dyed cloth (SDBH) (Judg 5:30 R)
צֶמֶר wool (Lev 13:47)
קְרָעִים torn pieces of cloth, rags, tattered clothes (SDBH) (1 Kgs 11:30 R)
רִקְמָה / רֹקֵם colorful weaving; embroidered cloth, needlework (SDBH) (Judg 5:30)
שַׁעַטְנֵז mixed linen and wool (Lev 19:19 R)
שֵׁשׁ fine undyed linen (CT); byssus, linen (DCH) (Gen 41:42)
שְׁתִי warp (weaving); woven or knitted material (SDBH) (Lev 13:48 R)

Cosmetics

Eyes

כחל paint eyes with stibium (Ezek 23:40 H)
פּוּךְ black eyeshadow (stibium), dye; antimony, malachite, eye makeup (DCH) (2 Kgs 9:30 R)
מְשַׁקְּרוֹת applying makeup to eyes (CT) (Isa 3:16 H)

Application

מְרוּקִים cosmetics, scraping, rubbing; cosmetic treatment (DCH) (Esth 2:12 H)

Ointment/Perfume

אֲבָקָה fragrant powders (SDBH) (Song 3:6 H)
בָּשֶׂם / בֹּשֶׂם / בֹּשֶׁם spices, perfume, balsam oil (SDBH) (Exod 25:6)
בָּתֵּי הַנֶּפֶשׁ tubular "soul" cases (Platt) (Isa 3:20)

כֹּפֶר henna (CT) (Song 1:14 R)
כַּרְכֹּם saffron fragrance (CT) (Song 4:14 H)
לֹט ladanum (used in perfume) (SDBH) (Gen 37:25 R)
מֻקְטָר perfume, incense (SDBH) (Mal 1:11 H)
מִרְקַחַת ointment, perfumery (Exod 30:25)
נֵרְדְּ nard, spikenard (SDBH) (Song 1:12 R)
נֶשֶׁק pleasant scents (SDBH) (1 Kgs 10:25 R)
צָרִי storax, balm (SDBH) (Gen 37:25 R)
קְטֹרֶת perfume, incense (SDBH) (Exod 25:6)
קִנָּמוֹן cinnamon (SDBH) (Exod 30:23 R)
קְצִיעוֹת / קְצִיעָה cassia (SDBH) (Ps 45:9 H)
רַקָּח ointment maker, perfume (Neh 3:8 H)
רַקָּחָה / רַקָּח perfumer (1 Sam 8:13 H)
שֶׁמֶן oil, fat (Deut 33:24)

Mirror

גִּלָּיוֹן mirror; tablet; papyrus garment (DCH) (Isa 3:23 H)
רְאִי mirror (Job 37:18 H)
מַרְאָה mirror; vision (Exod 38:8)

PART III

THE SOCIAL ORDER

FAMILY AND KINSHIP

Immediate Family

Father/Husband

אָב father (Gen 2:24)
אִישׁ man, husband (Gen 2:24)
בַּעַל husband (Deut 24:4)

Wife/Mother

אֵם mother (Gen 2:24)
אֵשֶׁת/אִשָּׁה wife, woman (Gen 16:3)

Son

בֵּן son (Gen 3:16)
בַּר son (SDBH) (Prov 31:2)
יָלִיד son, born (Gen 17:12)

Daughter

בְּכִירָה eldest daughter (Gen 19:33 R)
בַּת daughter (Gen 20:12)

Brother/Sister

אָח brother (Gen 4:2); nephew (Gen 14:14) (Rattray)
אָחוֹת sister; sister, half-sister (SDBH) (Gen 4:22)
בֶּן־אָח son of brother, nephew (Rattray) (Gen 12:5)

Uncle/Aunt

בֶּן־דּוֹד son of uncle, male cousin (Lev 25:49)
דּוֹד uncle, father's brother (Lev 10:4)
דּוֹדָה aunt, father's brother's wife; father's sister (Rattray) (Exod 6:20 R)

Firstborn

בְּכוֹר firstborn (SDBH) (Gen 4:4)
בְּכִירָה eldest daughter (Gen 19:33 R)
בְּכֹרָה right of firstborn (SDBH) (Gen 25:31)

Relatives/Kin/Offspring

מֹדָע/מֹדַעַת relative, kinsman, kinswoman (DCH) (Ruth 2:1 R)
נֶכֶד (with נִין) offspring; descendents, posterity (SDBH); progeny (DCH) (Gen 21:23)
עֵקֶר family member; offshoot (SDBH) (Lev 25:47 H)
שְׁאֵר בָּשָׂר "near in flesh," close kin (Rattray) (Lev 18:6)
תּוֹאֲמִים/תְּאוֹמִים twins (DCH) (Gen 25:24 R)

In-Laws

חָם father-in-law; father-in-law (of women) (Rattray) (Gen 38:13 R)

חָמוֹת mother-in-law; mother-in-law (of woman) (Rattray) (Ruth 1:14)

חֹתֵן father-in-law (SDBH); father-in-law (of men) (Rattray) (Exod 3:1)

חָתָן groom, son-in-law, daughter's husband; bridegroom (DCH) (Exod 4:25)

חֹתֶנֶת mother-in-law (SDBH); mother-in-law (of men) (Rattray) (Deut 27:23 H)

יָבָם brother-in-law; husband's brother (DCH) (Deut 25:5 R)

יְבָמָה sister-in-law (Ruth 1:15 R)

כַּלָּה bride, daughter-in-law, son's wife (Gen 11:31)

Marriage/Divorce

גֹּאֵל kinsman, redeemer (Ruth 3:13)

חתן to give away in marriage (Gen 34:9)

כְּלוּלֹת betrothal (as bride) (Jer 2:2 H)

מֹהַר bride-price (Gen 34:12 R)

פִּילֶגֶשׁ concubine (SDBH) (Gen 22:24)

צָרָה rival-wife (SDBH) (1 Sam 1:6 H)

שִׁלּוּחִים divorce, bill of divorce (Exod 18:2 R)

שָׂרָה princess, noble woman; mistress (SDBH) (Judg 5:29 R)

Widowhood

אַלְמָנָה widow (Lev 22:13)

אַלְמָנוּת widowhood (2 Sam 20:3 R)

יבם to marry a brother's widow (Gen 38:8 R)

Family/Clan

בֵּית־אָב family, "house of the father" (2 Chr 35:5)

יַחַשׂ genealogy, family list, pedigree (Neh 7:5 H)

מוֹלֶדֶת lineage, offspring, family, relations (Ezek 16:3)

מִשְׁפָּחָה family, clan (Gen 8:19)

תּוֹלְדוֹת descent, family, history (Gen 5:1)

WORSHIP/CULTIC

Structures

אֹהֶל הָעֵדוּת tent of witness (Num 9:15)
אֹהֶל־מוֹעֵד Tent of Meeting (Exod 27:21)
דְּבִיר innermost sanctuary, shrine (1 Kgs 6:19)
הֵיכָל temple (Hos 8:14)
מִשְׁכָּן tabernacle, sanctuary; dwelling-place (2 Sam 7:6)

Ark of the Covenant

אָרוֹן ark of covenant, chest, box (Exod 30:6)
בַּד pole (for side of ark) (Pritz); carrying-pole (כלי) (Exod 25:13)
בֵּית הַכַּפֹּרֶת Holy of Holies (Hurvitz) (1 Chr 28:11)
זֵר rim, molding (of ark) (Pritz) (Exod 25:11)
טַבְּעֹת rings (of gold, for ark) (Pritz) (Exod 25:12)
בֵּית־קֹדֶשׁ הַקֳּדָשִׁים Holy of Holies (Hurvitz) (2 Chr 3:8)
כַּף incense dish (Pritz); handbowl, incense-ladle (כלי) (Exod 25:29)
כַּפֹּרֶת Mercy seat, cover/lid of ark (Pritz) (Exod 25:17)
כְּרוּב / כְּרֻבִים cherubim on lid of ark (Pritz) (Exod 25:18)
מוֹט pole, frame; pole (for side of ark) (Pritz); yoke (כלי) (Num 4:10 R)
מְנַקִּית jars (for wine offerings) (Pritz) (Exod 25:29 R)
פַּעַם leg of table (Pritz) (Exod 25:12)
צֵלָע side (of ark) (Pritz) (Exod 25:12)
קַשְׁוָה jug, jar (libations); jug, jar, flagon, pitcher (SDBH) (Exod 25:29 R)

Altars

אָרִיאֵל / הַרְאֵל altar, hearth (Ezek 43:15 R)
בַּד pole (for side of Tabernacle altar) (Pritz) (Exod 27:6–7)
טַבַּעַת ring (of Tabernacle altar) (Pritz) (Exod 27:4)
כַּרְכֹּב rim, ledge of altar (Pritz) (Exod 27:5 R)
לְבֹנִים incense altars (Pritz) (Isa 65:3)
מוֹקְדָה altar top, altar-plate (for burnt offering) (Lev 6:2 H)
מִזְבֵּחַ sacrificial altar (Gen 8:20)
מִכְבָּר grating of Tabernacle altar (Pritz) (Exod 27:4 R)
מִקְטָר hearth, incense stand (Exod 30:1 H)
קַרְנֹת horns of the altar (Pritz) (Exod 27:2)
שֻׁלְחָן altar, table, incense altar, table for consecrated bread, table for preparing sacrificial victims (Pritz) (Mal 1:7)

Menorah/Lampstand

גָּבִיעַ cup at the top of each stem, for holding candles (Pritz) (Exod 25:31)
יָרֵךְ base of lampstand (Pritz) (Exod 25:31)
מְנֹרָה / מְנוֹרָה menorah, lampstand (Pritz) (Exod 25:31–35)
פֶּרַח flower-shaped decoration on each cup (Pritz) (Exod 25:31)
קָנֶה arm, stem of lampstand (Pritz) (Exod 25:31)

Personnel

חֹזֶה seer; dreamer (DCH) (Isa 56:10 H)
כֹּהֵן priest (Lev 6:15)
כְּהֻנָּה priesthood (Exod 29:9)
מֶכֶר business accessor, temple official valuing sacrifices (DCH) (2 Kgs 12:6 R)
מָשְׁחָה anointing, being anointed (Exod 40:15 R)
מִשְׁמֶרֶת ceremonial office, duty, service (Gen 26:5)
נְבִיאָה / נָבִיא prophet (Deut 18:15)
נָזִיר devoted one; Nazirite (Gen 49:26)
נְתוּנִים those assigned (Ezra 8:17)
עָתָר worshipper, suppliant; odor, incense (Zeph 3:10 H)
פְּקֻדָּה office, appointment, commission (Num 3:36)
רֹאֶה seer; vision (1 Sam 9:9)

Garb (Priestly)

אַבְנֵט sash, girdle (undergarment) (Exod 28:4 R)
אֵפֹד / אֵפוֹד ephod, shoulder-piece, high-priest's shoulder-cape (Exod 25:7)
חֵשֶׁב band (on ephod); girdle of ephod (DCH) (Exod 28:8 R)
חֹשֶׁן breastplate, pocket (Exod 25:7)
כְּתֹנֶת tunic, shirt (Pritz) (Exod 28:4)
מִגְבָּעָה headband, mitre (Exod 28:40 R)
מַד priestly robe (Ps 133:2 R)
מִכְנָסַיִם leggings, breeches (Exod 28:42 R)
מְעִיל priestly robe (Pritz) (Exod 28:4)
מִצְנֶפֶת mitre, turban (Exod 28:4)
פְּאֵר turban, headdress (Pritz) (Exod 39:28 R)
פַּעֲמֹן / פַּעֲמוֹן bells (sewn in hem of priestly robe) (Exod 28:33–34 R)
צִיץ forehead plate (Pritz) (Exod 28:36)
צָנִיף turban, headdress (Pritz) (Zech 3:5 R)

Accoutrements

(For Bowls, etc., see Containers and Implements)

בֶּגֶד tablecloth, covering (Num 4:6)
יָם water tank in Temple (Pritz) (1 Kgs 7:23–25)
יָעֵ shovel; fire-shovel (DCH) (Exod 27:3 R)
כִּיּוֹר / כִּיר washstand, basin, bowl (Pritz) (1 Kgs 7:30)
מַזְלֵג fork (three-pronged) (Pritz) (1 Sam 2:13–14 R)
מְזַמְּרוֹת snuffers, wick trimmers (Pritz) (1 Kgs 7:50 R)
מַחְתָּה fire-pan, censer; small shovel, firepan (Pritz) (Exod 25:38)
מְכוֹנָה moveable stand (Pritz); base, stand (DCH) (1 Kgs 7:27)
מֶלְקָחַיִם snuffers, tongs; forceps, tongs (כלי) (Exod 25:38 R)
מַעֲצָד tongs (Pritz) (Isa 44:12 R)
מִקְטֶרֶת censer, coal-pan (2 Chr 26:19 R)
קְעָרָה plate (as implement in Tabernacle) (Pritz) (Exod 25:29)

Vow

אִסָּר vow of abstinence, binding obligation (Num 30:5)
נֶדֶר vow (Num 30:5)

Sacrifices and Offerings

אַזְכָּרָה memorial offering; token offering (DCH) (Lev 5:12 R)
אִשֶּׁה burnt offering, sacrifice (Exod 29:25)
אָשָׁם guilt-offering (1 Sam 6:4)
הַבְהָב gift, offering (Hos 8:13 H)
זֶבַח sacrifice (Exod 34:15)
חַטָּאָה sacrifice, offense; sin (DCH) (Gen 20:9 R)
חַטָּאָה sin-offering; offense (Exod 34:7 R)
מִנְחָה donation, tribute, offering (Gen 32:21)
מָשְׁחָה consecrated portion (Num 18:8 H)
מַתָּנָה present, sacrificial offering (Num 18:7)
נְדָבָה voluntary offering (Exod 35:29)
נִיחוֹחַ aroma (of sacrifice) (Ezek 6:13)
נֶסֶךְ libation, drink offering (Num 28:14)
עֹלָה whole burnt offering (Exod 29:42)
קָרְבָּן offering, sacrificial present, gift (Lev 1:2)
רֵיחַ aroma, odor, fragrance (Gen 8:21)
שֶׁלֶם peace offering (Num 7:17)
שָׁרֵת ritual service (Num 4:12 R)
תּוֹדָה sacrifice of thanksgiving; adoration, praise (Josh 7:19)
תְּנוּפָה wave-offering, brandishing (Num 8:11)

תְּרוּמָה present, sacrifice, tribute, heave offering (Num 15:19)
תְּרוּמִיָּה sacrificial offering, contribution (Ezek 48:12 H)

Idolatry

אֶבֶן מַשְׂכִּית carved stone, idol (Pritz) (Lev 26:1)
אֱלִיל worthless, vain, idol (Lev 19:4)
אֲשֵׁרָה Asherah, goddess images (Pritz) (Exod 34:13)
בָּמָה high place (shrine, altar) (Lev 26:30)
בַּעַל Baal, lord, husband (Judg 6:31)
גִּלּוּל idol (Lev 26:30)
זְנוּת/זָנוּנִים/תְּזְנוּת idolatry, harlotry (Num 14:33 R)
חַמָּן sun-pillar, altar; incense altar (DCH) (Lev 26:30 R)
כַּוָּנִים sacred cakes for false gods (Pritz) (Jer 7:18 R)
כִּיּוּן statue for deity (Saturn/Kivvun) (Amos 5:26 H)
כֹּמֶר idolatrous priest; priests of foreign cults (DCH) (Hos 10:5 R)
מְלֶכֶת Queen (of Heaven) (Jer 7:18 R)
מַסֵּכָה molten image (Judg 17:4)
מַצֵּבָה stone pillar (Lev 26:1)
מַשְׂכִּית carved image (Lev 26:1)
נֶסֶךְ cast idol; libation; molten image (Pritz) (Isa 41:29)
סֵמֶל idol, image (Pritz) (Ezek 8:3 R)
פֶּסִיל graven image (Deut 7:5)
פֶּסֶל idol; graven image (Pritz) (Lev 26:1)
צִירִים idols (Pritz) (Isa 45:16 R)
צֶלֶם idol, image (Num 33:52)
שִׁקּוּץ idol, detestable thing (Deut 29:16)
תַּבְנִית idol, image (Pritz) (Ps 106:20)
תְּרָפִים Teraphim, household idols (Pritz) (Gen 31:19)

Divination

אוֹב medium, necromancer; ghost (DCH) (1 Sam 28:3)
אִטִּים ghosts (Isa 19:3 H)
אוּרִים lots, dice, stones ("lights"); Urim (DCH) (Exod 28:30 R)
אַשָּׁף enchanter, conjurer; exorcist (DCH) (Dan 1:20 R)
גּוֹרָל lot, stone (Josh 15:1)
חֶבֶר spell, enchantment; noise, spell, incantation (DCH) (Deut 18:11 R)
חוֹבֵר spellcaster (Ps 58:6 R)
חֲכַם חֲרָשִׁים sorcerer, lit. "wise one of sorceries" (DCH) (Isa 3:3 H)
חַרְטֹם magician, astrologer (Exod 9:11)
יִדְּעֹנִי soothsayer, spirit; familiar spirit, medium, necromancer (DCH) (1 Sam 28:3)

כַּשָּׁף sorcerer (Jer 27:9 H)
מְכַשֵּׁף sorcerer, magician (Deut 18:10 R)
מְנַחֵשׁ omen interpreter; diviner (DCH) (Deut 18:10)
מְעוֹנֵן enchanter; diviner of thunder (Mic 5:12 R)
מִקְסָם augury, divination (Ezek 12:24 R)
נַחַשׁ omen; divination (Num 24:1 R)
קֶסֶם prediction, divination, oracle (Ezek 21:27)
רְפָאִים deceased, ghost, shade, spirit (Isa 26:14 R)
תֻּמִּים lots, dice, stones ("perfections"); Thummin (DCH) (Exod 28:30 R)

Dream/Vision/Oracle

חָזוֹן sight, vision, oracle (1 Sam 3:1)
חָזוּת oracle, vision (Isa 21:2 R)
חִזָּיוֹן dream, revelation, vision (Job 20:8 R)
חָלוֹם dream, vision (Isa 29:7)
מַחֲזֶה vision (Num 24:4 R)
מַרְאָה/מַרְאֶה vision, revelation (Ezek 43:3)
מַשָּׂא oracle; burden, load (Isa 13:1)
נְבוּאָה prophecy, prophetic utterance/writing (Hurvitz) (Neh 6:12 R)
נְאֻם utterance, oracle (Amos 2:11)
פִּתְרוֹן interpretation (Gen 40:12 R)

Purity/Impurity

Pure

טָהוֹר pure (Num 19:9)
טָהֲרָה ritual purity, purification, cleansing (1 Chr 23:28)
כִּפֻּרִים atonement (Lev 23:27 R)
נָקִי innocent, clean (Deut 24:5)
קָדוֹשׁ holy, sacred (1 Sam 6:20)
קֹדֶשׁ sacredness, holiness (Joel 4:17)

Impure

זָר profane, strange, foreign (Lev 22:12)
חֹל profane; profaneness (DCH) (Ezek 48:15 R)
חָלִילָה God forbid! Far be it! (Gen 18:25)
חֲנֻפָּה impiety, pollution (Jer 23:15 H)
טָמֵא impure (Num 18:15)
טֻמְאָה religious impurity (Lev 15:25)
נִדָּה menstrual impurity, uncleanness (Ezek 36:17)
פִּגּוּל foul, ritually impure; meat unfit for use (DCH) (Lev 7:18 R)

Circumcision

מול to circumcise (Deut 30:6)
מוּלָה circumcision (DCH) (Exod 4:26 H)
מְכֵרָה circumcision blade (DCH) (Gen 49:5 H)
מלל to circumcise, cut off (DCH) (Josh 5:2 R)
נָמוּל circumcised (Exod 4:26)
עָרֵל uncircumcised (Judg 14:3)
עָרְלָה foreskin (Deut 10:16)

Assembly

מַקְהֵל assembly, choir (Ps 26:12 R)
מִקְרָא assembly, convocation (Lev 23:21)
עֵדָה congregation, gathering (Num 16:5)
עֲצָרָה solemn assembly (Lev 23:36)
קָהָל assembly, congregation (Num 22:4)
קְהִלָּה assembly, congregation (Deut 33:4 R)

Holidays/Festivals

חַג feast, festival (SDBH) (Exod 10:9)
חַג הָאָסִף Feast of the Harvest (Borowski *Agriculture*) (Exod 23:16)
חַג הַמַּצּוֹת Feast of Unleaved Bread, Passover (Borowski *Agriculture*) (Exod 23:15)
חַג סֻכּוֹת Festival of Sukkoth; Feast of Booths (Borowski *Agriculture*) (Lev 23:34)
חַג שָׁבֻעֹת Feast of Weeks (Borowski *Agriculture*) (Exod 34:22)
חֹדֶשׁ New Moon (1 Sam 20:5)
יוֹם הַכִּפֻּרִים Day of Atonement (Lev 23:27–28)
עֲצָרָה festival, holiday (Joel 1:14)
פּוּרִים lots, small pebbles used to decide questions, Purim (SDBH) (Esth 9:28 R)
פֶּסַח Passover (Exod 12:11)
שַׁבָּת Sabbath (Exod 16:23)

LAW AND COVENANT

Laws/Decrees

בְּרִית covenant, treaty, agreement (Gen 17:7)
דָּבָר word, matter, speech; dispute, controversy case, case decided in court, legal decision (Bovati) (Exod 22:8)
דָּת royal edict, decree (Esth 2:8)
חֹק rule, statute (Exod 18:16)
חֻקָּה statute, ordinance (Deut 6:2)
חֵרֶם ban, devoted to destruction (Deut 13:17)
מַאֲמַר word, commandment, decree (Esth 1:15 R)
מִצְוָה commandment, law (Isa 29:13)
מִשְׁפָּט legal decision, sentence, law (Deut 16:18)
פִּקּוּדִים precepts, commandments (Ps 19:9)
פָּרִיץ duty, law (DCH) (Ps 17:4 H)
פִּתְגָם edict, sentence; decree, word (Hurvitz) (Eccl 8:11 R)
צַו precept (Hos 5:11 R)
עֵדוּת treaty stipulations (Van der Toorn) (Deut 4:45 R)
קַו law, precept, statute (DCH) (Ps 19:5)
שֶׁפֶט law, penalty; verdict of court (Bovati) (Exod 12:12)
תּוֹרָה instruction, precept, Torah (Isa 1:10)

Oath/Blessing/Curse

אָלָה oath; curse; covenant or treaty, curses from breaking covenant or treaty (Aitken) (Deut 29:19 R)
אלה to swear an oath, to curse (Aitken) (1 Kgs 8:31)
ארר to curse (Aitken) (Gen 4:11 R)
ברך to bless, (euphemistically) to curse (Aitken) (1 Sam 25:33)
בְּרָכָה blessing, praise, something beneficial (Aitken) (Prov 24:25)
זעם to utter a curse, denounce (Aitken) (Isa 66:14)
נקב to curse, to utter (Aitken "נָקַב II") (Lev 24:11 R)
קבב to curse (Aitken) (Num 22:11)
קלל to curse, call down evil on someone (Aitken) (1 Sam 17:43)
קְלָלָה curse (Gen 27:12)
שְׁבוּעָה oath (Neh 10:30)
תַּאֲלָה curse (Lam 3:65 H)

Justice

אִישׁ רִיב defendant, accused (Bovati) (Judg 12:2)
אִישׁ רִיבִי plaintiff, accuser (Bovati) (Job 31:35)
גֹּאֵל הַדָּם avenger of blood (Bovati) (Num 35:19)

דַּיָּן judge (Bovati) (1 Sam 24:15 R)
דִּין judgment, cause, lawsuit; lawsuits concerning property or other civil matters (Bovati) (Jer 5:28)
שׁפט to enter into a controversy with someone, be at odds legally (Bovati) (Deut 16:18)
יָפֵחַ witness (Bovati) (Prov 12:17 R)
יָרִיב plaintiff, accuser (Bovati) (Isa 49:25 H)
כֹּפֶר monetary compensation in legal case (Bovati); ransom (DCH) (Exod 21:30)
מַזְכִּיר misdeed (legal) (Bovati); recorder (DCH) (Gen 41:9)
מִישׁוֹר equity, justice (Isa 11:4)
מְרִיב plaintiff, accuser (Bovati); contention (DCH) (1 Sam 2:10 R)
נטה to pervert justice (Bovati) (Deut 16:19)
עֵד witness in court, usually for prosecution (Bovati) (Lev 5:1)
פְּלִיל magistrate, judge (Bovati) (Deut 32:31 R)
פְּלִילָה justice, right; judgment, responsibility, decision, intervention (DCH) (Isa 16:3 H)
צַדִּיק just one; innocent (Bovati) (Jer 12:1)
צְדָקָה justice, righteousness (Ps 112:3)
רִיב legal controversy that takes place between two persons (Bovati); argument, case, strife, dispute (DCH); to strive, contend, bring a lawsuit (Gen 13:7)
שֹׁפֵט/שֹׁפְטָה judge (Bovati) (Judg 4:4)

Crime/Evil/Wrong

חֵטְא crime, penalty (Hos 12:9)
חַטָּא criminal, wrongdoer (Ps 51:15)
חֲטָאָה wrong, offense (Gen 20:9 R)
חָמָס violence, wrong (Jer 6:7)
סָרָה crime, apostasy, offense (Deut 13:6 R)
עַוְתָה oppression, wrong (Lam 3:59 H)
רַע bad, evil (Prov 9:16)
רָשָׁע evildoer; rich (DCH) (Prov 11:7 H)
רִשְׁעָה/רֶשַׁע wrong, wickedness, injustice (Mic 6:11)
שְׁגָגָה error, inadvertent sin (Lev 5:15)
שֶׁקֶר lie, falsehood (Exod 5:9)

Freedom

גאל to redeem oneself, free oneself (SDBH) (Lev 25:49)
גְּאֻלָּה redemption (SDBH) (Lev 25:24)
דְּרוֹר freedom (Lev 25:10 R)
חֻפְשָׁה freedom, liberty (Lev 19:20 H)

Poor/Oppressed

אֶבְיוֹן beggar, poor, needy (Exod 23:6)
דַּל/דַּלָּה poor, thin (Exod 23:3)
חֲלוֹף helpless people, destitute people (SDBH); passing away, opposition, foolishness (DCH) (Prov 31:8 H)
מוּך to be, become poor (SDBH); to be low (DCH) (Lev 25:25 R)
מַחְסוֹר impoverishment; lack (DCH) (Prov 6:11)
מִסְכֵּן poor, indigent (Eccl 4:13 H)
מִסְכֵּנֻת poverty (Deut 8:9 H)
עָנָו/עָנִי oppressed, poor, humiliated (Prov 22:22)
עַרְעָר naked, poor, helpless; destitute (DCH) (Ps 102:18 H)
פְּרָזוֹן peasantry (SDBH) (Judg 5:7 R)
רָאשִׁים/רָשׁ/רוּשׁ poor, destitute, needy (1 Sam 8:23)

Wealthy/Rich

חַשְׁמַן nobles (SDBH); envoy, bronze, red cloth (DCH) (Ps 68:32 H)
נָדִיב noble person (SDBH) (Num 21:18)
עֹשֶׁר wealth, riches (Esth 1:4)
פַּרְתְּמִים nobles (SDBH) (Esth 1:3 R)
שׁוֹעַ rich, noble (SDBH) (Job 34:19 R)

PROFESSIONS AND OCCUPATIONS

(For Religious Professions, see Worship/Cultic ➡ Personnel)

Government: Leaders

(See also Military)

Royal Family

גְּבִירָה queen, queen-mother; woman who is in a position of authority over another person as a legal owner, employer, or sovereign (SDBH) (Gen 16:4)
מֶלֶךְ king (Gen 14:1)
מַלְכָּה queen (1 Kgs 10:1)
שֵׁגַל queen (SDBH) (Ps 45:10 R)
שַׁלִּיט prince, warrior; ruler, governor (DCH) (Eccl 7:19 R)
שָׂרָה princess, female noble (Esth 1:18 R)

Nobility

חֹר noble, nobility (SDBH) (1 Kgs 21:8)
נָדִיב noble person (SDBH) (Num 21:18)

General

אַבִּיר chief (SDBH); mighty one, hero (DCH) (1 Sam 21:8)
אָדוֹן lord; master; owner (SDBH) (Gen 18:12)
אַלּוּף chieftain (Gen 36:15)
גְּבִיר lord; master (SDBH) (Gen 27:29 R)
מִמְשָׁל ruler; dominion, rule (DCH) (Dan 11:3 R)
מִנְּזָר courtier, prince (Nah 3:17 H)
נָגִיד leader, commander, prince (2 Chr 6:5)
נְצִיב governor (SDBH) (1 Kgs 4:19)
נָשִׂיא ruler, king, leader; prince (DCH) (Gen 34:2)
סֶגֶן prefect; ruler (DCH) (Ezek 23:12)
סֶרֶן lord; ruler; chief (SDBH) (Josh 13:3)
עַתּוּד leader (SDBH); leader, male goat (DCH) (Isa 14:9)
פֶּחָה prefect, governor (Neh 5:14)
פָּלִיל magistrate, judge (Deut 32:31 R)
פַּרְז chief; leader; commander (SDBH); warrior, ruler (DCH) (Hab 3:14 H)
קָצִין ruler, leader (Josh 10:24)
רֹאשׁ head, leader, ruler (Josh 11:10)
רוֹזֵן ruler (Ps 2:2 R)
שַׂר head person, chieftain, general, prince (Num 31:14)

Foreign Rulers and Leaders

אֲחַשְׁדַּרְפַּן satrap, governor (Persian) (Esth 3:12 R)
מֶלְצַר royal guardian (Persian) (Dan 1:16 R)
פַּרְעֹה Pharaoh (SDBH) (Gen 12:15)
שַׁרְבִיט scepter (Persian) (Esth 4:11 R)
תִּרְשָׁתָא governor (Persian) (SDBH) (Neh 7:65 R)

Royal Ornament: Scepters/Staffs/Crowns/Throne/Footstool

אֶצְעָדָה royal armlet (Salvesen "The Trappings") (2 Sam 1:10 R)
הֲדֹם footstool (Salvesen "The Trappings") (Isa 66:1 R)
כִּסֵּא throne (Salvesen "The Trappings") (1 Kgs 10:9)
כֶּתֶר royal crown (Salvesen "The Trappings") (Esth 1:11 R)
מְחֹקֵק ruler's staff; commander, sceptre (DCH) (Gen 49:10 R)
מַטֶּה rod; tribe; branch (Ps 110:2)
מַקֵּל staff, rod; branch (Jer 48:17)
מִשְׁעֶנֶת staff, support, symbol of authority (כלי) (Num 21:18)
נֵזֶר crown, royal and priestly headgear (Salvesen "The Trappings"); consecration, crown, diadem (DCH) (Ps 89:40)
פַּךְ שֶׁמֶן anointing horn, anointing flask (to anoint kings) (Pritz) (1 Sam 10:1)
עֲטָרָה crown (Salvesen "The Trappings"); garland wreath (Salvesen "עֲטָרָה") (Ezek 21:31)
קֶרֶן anointing horn, anointing flask (to anoint kings) (Pritz) (1 Sam 16:1)
שֵׁבֶט rod, staff; clan, tribe (כלי, Salvesen, "שֵׁבֶט") (Ps 45:7)
שַׁרְבִיט scepter, stick (Esth 4:11)

Government: Administration

אָצִיל leader (SDBH) (Exod 24:11 H)
אַשָּׁף conjurer; enchanter; exorcist; sorcerer (SDBH) (Dan 1:20 R)
גִּזְבָּר treasurer (Hurvitz) (Ezra 1:8 H)
דַּיָּן judge, advocate (1 Sam 24:16)
חָכָם wise, teacher, sage; learned man, scholar (Van der Toorn) (Prov 1:6)
חַרְטֹם magician, diviner (at royal court) (SDBH) (Gen 41:8)
טַבָּחָה/טַבָּח guard; butcher; cook (SDBH) (1 Sam 8:13)
טִפְסָר commander; officer; official; overseer; scribe (SDBH) (Jer 51:27 R)
מַזְכִּיר recorder; chronicler (SDBH); scribe (DCH) (2 Sam 8:16)
מַסְגֵּר women of the harem (DCH) (Jer 24:1 H)
מַשְׁקֶה cup-bearer, royal butler (Gen 40:13)

סֹפֵר scribe (Jer 8:8)
סָרִיס government official, eunuch (foreign) (Esth 1:10)
עֶבֶד slave; servant; officer; official; subject; vassal (SDBH) (Gen 9:25)
פָּקִיד superintendent, overseer (Jer 20:1)
שֹׁטֵר scribe, official, magistrate; military officer (Deut 1:15)
שֹׁפֵט judge; tribal military leader (Ps 94:2)
שָׂרֵי הָרְכוּשׁ royal overseers (of estates) (Borowski *Agriculture*) (1 Chr 27:31)

Artisans

אָמָן/אָמוֹן skilled worker; artisan (SDBH) (Song 7:2 H)
אֹרֵג weaver (Isa 19:9)
בָּחוֹן tester; assayer (SDBH) (Jer 6:27 H)
גַּלָּב barber (SDBH) (Ezek 5:1 H)
חֹקֵק engraver, carver; commander (DCH) (Judg 5:9)
חָרָשׁ/חֶרֶשׁ artisan, craftsman, blacksmith (Exod 28:11)
חֹשֵׁב inventor; designer (SDBH) (Exod 26:1)
יוֹצֵר potter, artisan, sculptor (Isa 41:25)
מְכַבֵּס launderer, cleaner, fuller (Mal 3:2)
מַסְגֵּר locksmith; smith, metalworker (DCH) (Jer 29:2 R)
מַצְרֵף refiner, crucible (for silver); crucible (Guillame, DCH) (Prov 17:3 R)
צוֹרֵף smelter, smith (gold, silver); metal smelter, refiner (DCH) (Isa 40:19)
צָרוּף metal smelter, refiner (DCH) (Jer 6:29 H)
רַקָּחָה/רַקָּח perfumer (1 Sam 8:13 H)
רֹקֵם embroiderer (SDBH) (Exod 26:36 R)

Merchants/Business/Banking

כֶּסֶף silver, money (1 Chr 29:2)
לֹוֶה borrower (Prov 19:17)
מוֹכֵר seller (Neh 13:20)
מַכָּר business accessor, temple official valuing sacrifices (DCH) (2 Kgs 12:6 R)
מִקְנָה price; acquisition (Gen 17:12)
נֹשֶׁה lender, userer (2 Kgs 4:1)
נֶשֶׁךְ interest, usury (Exod 22:24)
סֹחֵר trader, merchant (Isa 23:8)
סַחַר profit, merchandise, mart, trade (Isa 23:18 R)
קֹנֶה/קוֹנֶה buyer (Ezek 7:12)
קִנְיָן purchase (Gen 36:6)

קְשִׂיטָה money, weight; kesitah, weight of silver or gold (DCH) (Job 42:11 R)
רוֹכֵל trader, merchant (Ezek 27:3)
רְכֻלָּה merchandise, stock; trade (DCH) (Ezek 28:5 R)
שָׂכָר wages, payment (Jonah 1:3)

Food Production

אִכָּר farmer, plowman (Joel 1:11)
אֹפֶה baker (Gen 40:1)
בּוֹקֵר herdsman; cattle breeder (SDBH) (Amos 7:14 H)
בּוֹלֵס person who tends sycamore trees for a living (SDBH); fig tender (DCH) (Amos 7:14 H)
בעה to boil (Peters) (Isa 64:1 R)
בשל to boil (Peters) (Joel 4:13)
דָּוָג / דַּיָּג fisherman (Isa 19:8 R)
זיד to boil, to stew (Peters) (Gen 25:29)
זֹרֵעַ sower (Borowski *Agriculture*) (Isa 55:10)
לבב to create (Peters), to bake (DCH) (2 Sam 13:6 R)
מֹשֵׁךְ הַזָּרַע sower (poetic) (Borowski *Agriculture*) (Amos 9:13)
נֹקֵד herdsmen (Steiner); sheep breeder (DCH) (Amos 1:1 R)
עוג to create (Peters), to bake (DCH) (Ezek 4:12 H)
צַיָּד hunter (Jer 16:16 H)
צלה to boil (DCH), to apply dry heat (Peters) (Isa 44:19 R)
קלה to roast (DCH), to apply dry heat (Peters) (Josh 5:11 R)
רֹעֶה shepherd (Ps 23:1)
רֹעֵה shepherd (Isa 38:12 R)
רתח to boil (DCH), to create turbulence with heat (Peters) (Ezek 24:5 R)

Prostitute/Sex Worker

זֹנָה prostitute, sex worker (Gen 34:31)
כֶּלֶב male shrine prostitute, "dog" (epithet) (SDBH) (Deut 23:19 R)
מַסְגֵּר women of the harem (DCH) (Jer 24:1 H)
קָדֵשׁ male temple prostitute (SDBH) (Deut 23:18 R)
קְדֵשָׁה sacred prostitute, female devotee (Gen 38:21 R)

MILITARY

War: General Terms

חֵרֶם ban, total destruction (1 Kgs 20:42)
הֵידָד shout, war-cry (Jer 51:14 R)
לָחָם battle, war; warrior (DCH) (Judg 5:8 H)
מִלְחָמָה war (Num 31:27)
מָצוֹר siege; siege wall (Pritz) (Deut 20:20 R)
קְרָב battle, war, hostile encounter (Ps 55:22 R)
שׁוֹפָר ram's horn (blown to summon forces) (ELT) (Judg 3:27)
תְּרוּעָה war-cry, alarm (of trumpets) (Num 23:21)

Enemy/Victory/Defeat

אֹיֵב adversary, enemy (Num 10:9)
בַּז plunder (Ezek 34:28)
גְּבוּרָה force, victory, valor; might (DCH) (Isa 30:15)
יָרִיב adversary, enemy (SDBH) (Ps 35:1 R)
יְשׁוּעָה deliverance, victory, salvation (Isa 33:2)
מַגֵּפָה slaughter, defeat, plague (Ezek 24:16)
עָר foe, enemy (1 Sam 28:16 R)
צַר enemy (Num 24:8)
קִים enemy, adversary, opponent (SDBH); rebellion (DCH) (Job 22:20 H)
שׁוּר foe, oppressor; watcher (DCH) (Ps 92:12 H)
שׁוֹרֵר enemy (SDBH) (Ps 5:9 R)
שָׂטָן opponent; adversary, Satan (DCH) (Num 22:22)

Army

אַלְקוּם levy, band of soldiers (Prov 30:31 H)
חֵיל army, force; outer wall, outer fortification (SDBH); rampart (DCH) (2 Sam 20:15)
עִזּוּז an army; forcible; mighty (DCH) (Ps 24:8 R)
עַם army; people, nation (Gen 11:6)
צָבָא army; assembly, group, division (DCH) (Exod 6:26)

Officers/Leaders

טִפְסָר military governor; commander, officer, official, overseer, scribe, recruiting officer (SDBH) (Jer 51:27 R)
נָגִיד commander (Ps 76:13)
נְצִיב governor (SDBH) (1 Kgs 4:19)
סָגָן official, prefect (Jer 51:57)

סֶרֶן lord, ruler, tyrant (Judg 16:5)
פֶּחָה governor (1 Kgs 10:15)
שֹׁטֵר / שׁוֹטֵר officer, foreman, supervisor (SDBH) (Exod 5:6)
שַׂלִּיט prince, warrior; subordinate officer (DCH) (Gen 42:6)
שָׁלִישׁ adjutant, general of the third rank; third man, officer (DCH) (1 Kgs 9:22)
שַׂר head, leader; commanders of various ranks within the army (Seevers) (1 Sam 22:7)
תַּרְתָּן commander-in-chief, person with an extremely high position in the Assyrian kingdom (SDBH); Tartan (title) (DCH) (2 Kgs 18:17 R)

Soldiers

אִישׁ הַבֵּנַיִם "man of the interval," champion (in reference to Goliath) (SDBH, DCH) (1 Sam 17:4)
אֶלֶף thousand, clan, division in army (Seevers) (1 Sam 23:23)
אֶרְאֵל / אֲרִיאֵל mighty warrior (SDBH) (Isa 33:7 R)
גִּבּוֹר hero, warrior (Gen 10:8)
גֶּבֶר warrior, valiant man; man (DCH) (Job 38:3)
גְּדוּד band of raiders; troops (SDBH) (Gen 49:19)
גַּמָּדִים brave man, brave soldier (Ezek 27:11 H)
טַבָּח guard; butcher; guard, bodyguard (SDBH) (Gen 37:36)
יוֹרֶה archer (SDBH) (1 Chr 10:3)
מוֹרֶה archer (SDBH) (1 Sam 31:3)
מִשְׁמָר a guard; watch, lookout (Ezek 38:7)
נְצִיב garrison (SDBH) (1 Sam 10:5)
נֹשֵׂא כֵלִים equipment bearer (for an important soldier) (Seevers) (Judg 9:54)
סֹאֵן soldier, warrior (shod) (Isa 9:4 H)
עֹזֵר warrior, hero; helper (DCH) (Ps 30:11)
פְּקוּדִים mustered soldiers, troops; precepts (DCH) (Num 14:29)
פָּרָשׁ horseman, (plural) cavalry (SDBH) (Gen 50:9)
צָבָא soldier fit for war (SDBH); host (DCH) (Num 1:3)
קַלָּע slinger (DCH) (2 Kgs 3:25 H)
רַגְלִי footman, infantry; on foot (DCH) (1 Kgs 20:29)

Weapons/Armor

General Arms

חֹצֶן weapons, arms; war-horses (DCH) (Ezek 23:24 H)
כְּלִי weapon (Gen 49:5)
מְכֵרָה weapon, staff (DCH) (Gen 49:5 H)

מֶשֶׁק arms, military equipment, arsenal; acquisition, possession (DCH) (Gen 15:2 H)
נֵשֶׁק/נָשֶׁק armor, weapons (2 Kgs 10:2)
שׁוֹט whip (SDBH) (1 Kgs 12:11)
שֶׁלַח weapon; missile, shoot (DCH) (Neh 4:17 R)
תְּלִי weapon; quiver ("hang") (Gen 27:3 H)

Armor

דֶּבֶק joint, appendage of armor (Hobbs, DCH) (1 Kgs 22:34 R)
מָעוֹז רֹאשׁ helmet (Pritz) (Ps 60:9)
מִצְחָה greaves (1 Sam 17:6 H)
סָאוֹן military boot (Isa 9:4 H)
קוֹבַע/כּוֹבַע helmet (Ezek 23:24 R)
קַשְׂקֶשֶׂת scale, coat of mail (1 Sam 17:5 R)
שִׁרְיָה coat of mail; arrow; javelin (SDBH) (Job 41:18 H)
שִׁרְיוֹן/סִרְיוֹן coat of mail; breastplate, scale armor (Pritz); chest protector (SDBH) (1 Sam 17:5)
תַּחֲרָא coat of mail (Exod 28:32 R)

Shields

מָגֵן shield; small shield (Pritz) (2 Sam 22:3)
סֹכֵךְ moveable shield, mantelet (Pritz) (Nah 2:6 H)
עֲגֻלּוֹת small shields (Ps 46:10 H)
צִנָּה large shield; buckler; hook; thorn (1 Sam 17:7)
שֶׁלֶט shield; quiver (?); small shield, buckler (Pritz) (2 Sam 8:7 R)

Swords and Sheaths

אִבְחָה brandishing (sword) (Ezek 21:20 H)
בָּרָק lightning; flashing sword (Ps 18:15)
חֶרֶב sword, knife, dagger; butchers' knives, swords, razors; curved sword (Koller) (Gen 34:26)
מְכֵרֹת swords (Pritz); weapons (DCH) (Gen 49:5 H)
נָדָן sheath (1 Chr 21:27 H)
פִּתִּחָה drawn sword (Ps 55:22)
תַּעַר scabbard, sheath; razor (Koller) (1 Sam 17:51 R)

Club/Axe

מַפֵּץ smiter, war club; hammer, club (Hobbs) (Jer 51:20)
מַקֵּל יָד club, war club, mace (Pritz) (Ezek 39:9)
סְגֹר battle-axe (Pritz) (Ps 35:3 H)
תּוֹתָח club, war club, mace (Pritz) (Job 41:21 H)

Sling

אֶבֶן stone (1 Sam 17:40)

מַרְגֵּמָה sling (Pritz) (Prov 26:8 H)
קָלַע sling (Judg 20:16 R)

Bow and Arrow

אַשְׁפָּה arrow-case, quiver (Job 39:23 R)
בֶּן־קָשֶׁת arrow (Pritz) (Job 41:20)
בְּנֵי אַשְׁפָּה arrow (Pritz) (Lam 3:13)
זִק flaming arrow; spark, brand; fiery missile (כלי) (Prov 26:18 R)
חֵץ / חֵצִי arrow, shaft of spear (Gen 49:23 R)
יֶתֶר bowstring (Pritz); cord, bow string, tent ropes, sinews (DCH) (Judg 16:7 R)
מַטֶּה arrow (Pritz); staff, scepter, shaft of arrow, stem of vine (DCH) (Hab 3:9)
מֵיתָר bowstring (Pritz); cord (DCH) (Ps 21:12 R)
רֶשֶׁף arrow (Pritz) (Ps 76:3 R)
קֶשֶׁת / קֹשֶׁט bow (Gen 21:16)
רַב / רַבִּ archer (Pritz) (Job 16:13 R)
רבב shoot an arrow (Gen 49:23 R)
רִבְבוֹת shafts of arrows (Ps 3:7 H)
שֶׁלֶט quiver (?); small shield, buckler (Pritz) (Jer 51:11 R)
תְּלִי quiver (Pritz) (Gen 27:3 H)

Lance/Spear/Missile

חֲנִית javelin, lance (1 Sam 13:19)
כִּידוֹן knife, dart, javelin, scimitar; long straight sword, carried only by foreigners (Koller) (Josh 8:18 R)
לְהָבָה spearhead (Pritz) (1 Sam 17:7)
מַסָּע missile, dart, quarry (1 Kgs 6:7 R)
קַיִן spearhead (Pritz); spear, lance (DCH) (2 Sam 21:16 H)
רֹמַח lance, iron point, spear ("throw"); spear (SDBH) (Num 25:7)
שֵׁבֶט spear, lance (Pritz); rod, staff, lance (DCH) (2 Sam 18:14)
שֶׁלַח spear, missile; branch; weapon (SDBH) (Joel 2:8 R)
שִׁרְיָה javelin (Pritz) (Job 41:18 H)

Battering Ram

חַרְבוֹת battering rams (Pritz); swords (DCH) (Ezek 26:9)
חִשְׁבֹּנוֹת catapult, ballista (Pritz); war engine (DCH) (2 Chr 26:15 R)
כַּר battering ram; camel's saddle; elaborate ladies' saddle (כלי) (Ezek 4:2)
קֹבֶל siege-engine; battering ram (SDBH) (Ezek 26:9 H)

Vehicles, Horses, and Travel

Chariots

גַּלְגַּל/גִּלְגַּל wheel (Isa 5:28); wheel, cart, wagon, chariot (SDBH, Pritz) (Ezek 23:24)
אוֹפָן wheel (Exod 14:25)
אַפִּרְיוֹן palanquin, litter (SDBH) (Song 3:9 H)
אֹרַח caravan, path, way (DCH) (Judg 5:6)
גַּב wheel rim (Pritz) (1 Kgs 7:33)
חִשֻּׁק wheel-spoke, rod (1 Kgs 7:33 H)
חִשֻּׁר hub of wheel (1 Kgs 7:33 H)
יָד axle of wheel (Pritz) (1 Kgs 7:32)
מֶרְכָּבָה chariot (Gen 41:43)
סֶרֶן axle of wheel (Pritz) (1 Kgs 7:30 H)
עֲגָלָה cart, wagon (Gen 45:19)
פָּרָשׁ cavalry, horse (Jer 4:29)
צַב covered wagon, litter (Num 7:3 R)
רַכָּב charioteer (1 Kgs 22:34 R)
רֶכֶב chariotry; chariot, charioteers (DCH) (Gen 50:9)
רִכְבָּה riding, driving (Ezek 27:20 H)
רְכוּב vehicle (Ps 104:3)

Road

אֹרַח way, path; caravan, traveller (Gen 49:17)
דֶּרֶךְ road, way (Gen 24:27)
הֵלֶךְ journey; traveller (1 Sam 14:26 R)
חוּץ street, road (Pritz) (Josh 2:19)
מְסִלָּה highway, path (Num 20:19)
מַסְלוּל highway (Pritz); gatehouse, gateway (DCH) (Isa 35:8 R)
מַסַּע setting out, station, stage, journey (Num 33:2)
מַעְגָּל wagon track, path; moral path (poetic) (Aitken "מַעְגָּל") (Ps 17:5)
מִשְׁעוֹל road, street (Pritz); pathway within vineyard (Aitken "מִשְׁעוֹל") (Num 22:24 H)
נֵס sign, banner, pole; standard, ensign (DCH) (Isa 5:26)
נָתִיב path; traveller (Judg 5:6 R)
פֶּגֶר monument, memorial (SDBH); memorial stele (DCH) (Ezek 43:7 R)
צִיּוּן guidepost, marker, sign, monument, road pillar (2 Kgs 23:17 R)
שְׁבִיל way (Jer 18:15 R)
שׁוּק street, road (Pritz) (Prov 7:8 R)

תַּמְרוּר pillar, road marker (Jer 31:21 H)

Formations/Groups

אֲגַף/אַגַּפִּים forces, wings of an army; band, crowd of troops (Ezek 38:6 R)
גְּדוּד troop (1 Chr 7:4)
חָמֵשׁ battle array (five) (Num 31:32)
מַעֲרָכָה military array (1 Sam 17:21)
מַצָּבָה military guard (1 Sam 14:12 H)

Flags/Standards

אוֹת sign; standards, ensigns (Num 2:2)
דֶּגֶל banners, standards; division (Num 1:52)
נֵס standard, ensign, banner (Pritz) (Isa 5:26)
תֹּרֶן standard, ensign, banner (Pritz); mast, flag, pole (DCH) (Isa 30:17 R)

Fortifications

Fortress

אָגַם fortress (SDBH); pool, swamp (DCH) (Jer 51:32 R)
אַרְמוֹן citadel (1 Kgs 16:18)
בִּירָה fortress, castle, palace (2 Chr 17:12)
בִּצָּרוֹן fortress, castle (Zech 9:12 H)
טִירָה fortress, hamlet, encampment, wall (Song 8:9 R)
מִבְצָר fortification, castle, fortified city (2 Sam 24:7)
מַחֲנֶה encampment (Judg 7:9)
מִלּוֹא citadel, rampart (1 Kgs 9:15 R)
מִסְגֶּרֶת fortress, stronghold (Pritz) (2 Sam 22:46)
מָעוֹז fortified place, defense (Isa 23:11)
מְצָד/מְצוּדָה fort, mountain, fortress, stronghold (2 Sam 5:7)
מָצוֹר/מְצוּרָה mound, rampart, fortification (2 Chr 11:10 R); watchtower, tower (Hab 2:1 R) (Pritz)
מִשְׂגָּב high fort, defense, tower (2 Sam 22:3)
עֹפֶל mound, fortress (Mic 4:8 R)

Wall

חוֹמָה wall (Deut 28:52)
חִיצוֹן exterior (of wall) (2 Kgs 16:18)
חָרוּץ moat (Pritz) (Dan 9:25 H)
כֹּתֶל wall (of house) (Song 2:9 H)
מַעֲקֶה parapet (top of wall) (Deut 22:8 H)
קִיר city wall; side (2 Kgs 4:10)

שׁוּר wall (of rich house) (Gen 49:22 R)
שָׂרָה fortification wall (Jer 5:10 H)
תָּא guardroom (Pritz) (1 Kgs 14:28)

Armory, Arsenal

אוֹצָר armory, arsenal (Pritz) (Jer 50:25)
בֵּית כְּלִי armory, arsenal (Pritz) (2 Kgs 20:13)
נֵשֶׁק/נָשֶׁק armory, arsenal (Pritz) (Neh 3:19)

Tower

אַלְמָנוֹת watchtowers (Pritz); widows (DCH) (Isa 13:22 R)
אָשִׁיָּה bulwark, tower, bastion (SDBH) (Jer 50:15 H)
פִּנָּה watchtower, tower (Pritz) (Zeph 1:16)
מִגְדָּל tower (Judg 8:9)
מָצוֹר tower, fortress, refuge (2 Chr 11:10)
מִצְפֶּה watchtower, tower (Pritz) (Isa 21:8 R)
שֶׁמֶשׁ watchtower, tower (Pritz) (Isa 54:12 H)

Siege

אֹרַח embarkment, earthwork for siege (DCH) (Job 30:12 H)
בַּחַן/בַּחוּן siege tower, watchtower (Isa 32:14 R)
דֵּיק siege wall (2 Kgs 25:1 R)
מֶצָב firing platform, siege tower (Pritz) (Isa 29:3 H)
מָצוֹד siege wall (Pritz) (Eccl 9:14 R)
מְצוּרָה firing platforms, siege towers (Pritz); fortification, fortress (DCH) (Isa 29:3)
סֹלְלָה siege-ramp, siege-mound (2 Sam 20:15)

Bunker

חֵיל entrenchment, rampart, tower (?), fortress (2 Sam 20:15)
צְרִיַּח bunker, underground room; watchtower (?) (Judg 9:46 R)

Post/Outpost

מִצְפֶּה observatory, post; watchtower (DCH) (Isa 21:8 R)
נְצִיב military post, garrison; sentry (1 Sam 10:5)

Spoils, Plunder, Booty

בַּז spoils, plunder (captives, cattle); prey (Ezek 34:28)
בִּזָּה prey, spoils (Dan 11:24)
גָּזֵל robbery; plundered goods (Ezek 22:29 R)
גְּזֵלָה seized goods, stolen goods (Isa 3:14 R)
חֲלִיצָה stripped off (spoils, armour) (Judg 14:19 R)
מֶכֶס tribute, tax (Num 31:37 R)

מַלְקוֹחַ booty (cattle, captives); prey; plunder (DCH) (Num 31:12 R)
מְשִׁסָּה spoils, prey, booty (Isa 42:22 R)
עַד booty (Zeph 3:8 R)
שָׁלָל plunder, booty (Josh 22:8)

Captive/Exile

אַסִּיר/אָסִיר captive, bound; prisoner (DCH) (Job 3:18)
גּוֹלָה exile, exiles (Isa 49:21)
גָּלוּת captivity, exile; diaspora (DCH) (Isa 20:4)
שְׁבוּת exile; prosperity (Deut 30:3)
שְׁבִי captives, captivity (Ezra 2:1)
שִׁבְיָה captivity, captives (2 Chr 28:5 R)
שׁוֹלָל prisoner, captive; nude; barefoot, led in fetters (DCH) (Job 12:19 R)

Chains/Bonds/Fetters

אֲזִקִּים chains, bonds, manacles (Jer 40:1 R)
אֵסוּר bond, manacle (Judg 15:14)
חַרְצֻבָּה bands; grief (Isa 58:6 R)
כֶּבֶל fetter (Ps 105:18 R)
מוֹסֵר fetter, bond (Job 39:5 R)

MARITIME

Ships

אֳנִי fleet, ships, navy (1 Kgs 9:26 R)
אֳנִי־שִׂיט galley, lit. "rowing ship" (Patai) (Isa 33:21)
אֳנִיָּה ship (Gen 49:13)
אֳנִיּוֹת אֵבֶה reed ships (Patai); papyrus ship (DCH) (Job 9:26)
אֳנִיּוֹת תַּרְשִׁישׁ Tarshish ships, large seagoing vessels (Patai) (1 Kgs 22:49)
דֹּבְרוֹת rafts; floats (SDBH) (1 Kgs 5:23 H)
כְּלֵי־גֹמֶא "vessels of papyrus" (Patai) (Isa 18:2)
סְפִינָה ship (SDBH) (Jonah 1:5 H)
עֲבָרָה ferry boat (Patai) (2 Sam 19:19 H)
צִי ship (Dan 11:30 R)
צִי אַדִּיר large ship (Patai) (Isa 33:21)
רַפְסֹדֹת rafts (2 Chr 2:15 H)
שְׂכִיָּה ship (Isa 2:16 H)
תֵּבָה basket; ark (SDBH); e.g., Noah's ark; chest, ark (Patai) (Gen 6:14)

Crew

אַנְשֵׁי אֳנִיּוֹת crew, literally "men of the ship" (Patai) (1 Kgs 9:27)
חֹבֵל sailor ("handles rope") (Jonah 1:6 R)
יֹדְעֵי הַיָּם crew, literally "knowers of the sea" (Patai) (1 Kgs 9:27)
מַלָּח seaman, sailor, mariner (Ezek 27:27 R)
רַב הַחֹבֵל captain of the ship, literally "master roper" (Patai) (Jonah 1:6)
שָׁטִים rowers, oarsmen (Patai) (Ezek 27:26)
תֹּפְשֵׂי מָשׁוֹט oar holders, oarsmen (Patai) (Ezek 27:29)

Structures

חִבֵּל cable, rope; mast (Pritz); perhaps tackle rigging (DCH) (Prov 23:34 H)
חֶבֶל rope, cord holding sail in place (Patai) (Isa 33:23)
חוֹמוֹת sides of a hull (Patai) (Ezek 27:11)
כֵּן socket for mast (Patai) (Isa 33:23)
כֹּפֶר pitch, bitumen (for sealing ship hull) (Patai) (Gen 6:14 H)
לוּחַ plank, board (Ezek 27:5)
מִפְרָשׂ sail (spread out) (Ezek 27:7 R)
מָשׁוֹט / מִשׁוֹט rudder, oar (Ezek 27:6 R)
נֵס ensign, standard; sail; yard, ensign (Patai); sail (Pritz) (Isa 33:23)
קֶרֶשׁ deck, room, mast (Ezek 27:6)

רֹאשׁ חִבֵּל	top of the mast (Patai) (Prov 23:34)
שׁוט	to row (Ezek 27:8)
שַׁיִט	oar (Pritz) (Isa 33:21 H)
תַּחְתִּיִּם	lower decks (DCH) (Gen 6:16)
תֹּרֶן	mast; flagstaff (SDBH) (Isa 30:17 R)

Trade/Cargo

מַעֲרָב	merchandise, goods (Ezek 27:27 R)
עִזְבוֹן	wares, merchandise (Ezek 27:12 R)
ערב	to conduct trade (Ezek 27:9 R)

MUSIC

General Terms and Types

גִּתִּית musical term, meaning unknown; possibly associated with the winepress or with the town of Gath (SBDH); in psalm titles, "perhaps an instrument or melody associated with (musician from) Gath or with winepress" (DCH) (Ps 8:1 R)

זָמִיר song (Isa 25:5 R)

זִמְרָה music, melody, song (Exod 15:2 R)

מִזְמוֹר music, poem, psalm (Ps 30:1)

מַנְגִּינָה mocking song (Lam 3:63 H)

מְנַצֵּחַ musician (2 Kgs 3:15)

נְגִנִים / נְגִינוֹת musicians; possibly a string instrument (Kolyada) (Ps 68:26)

סֶלָה pause (Ps 3:3)

עֲלָמוֹת / עַלְמוּת ambiguous technical notation: high key/register, falsetto (1 Chr 15:20) (Burgh); perhaps sotto voce as musical term (DCH) (Ps 9:1 H)

קוֹל sound, music, melody, rhythm (DCH) (Ps 19:5)

עֹז poetic and musical performance (DCH) (2 Sam 6:14 R)

ענה to sing; utter a shout (DCH) (Isa 13:22)

קִינָה dirge, funeral song; lamentation (2 Chr 35:25)

שִׁיר song, singing (Ps 65:1)

שְׁמִינִית "according to the Sheminith" in Psalm titles, perhaps for psalms played on instrument with eight strings or in the eighth key (DCH); low key/register (Burgh); the eighth (Smith) (Ps 6:1)

שָׁרִים singers (Ps 68:26)

תְּהִלָּה laudation, hymn; psalm, praise, adoration (DCH) (Isa 42:8)

תְּפִלָּה hymn, intersession, supplication (2 Sam 7:27)

Instruments

Flute

חלל play the pipe (1 Kgs 1:40)

חָלִיל flute, pipe; double-reed woodwind instrument (Kolyada); clarinet, oboe (Braun); pipe (Montagu); double pipe (Mitchell); double pipe (Burgh); double reed pipe (Smith) (Isa 5:12 R)

נְחִילוֹת lamentation pipes (Borowski *Daily Life*); flutes (DCH) (Ps 5:1 H)

עוּגָב flute, reed instrument; lute (Borowski *Daily Life*), generic woodwind term (Montagu); pipe, flute (DCH) (Ps 150:4 R)

String

כִּנּוֹר harp, lyre; generic term for all stringed instruments or a specific stringed instrument (Kolyada) (Isa 5:12)

מֵן string (of instrument) (Ps 45:9)

מִנִּים stringed instruments (Braun) (Ps 150:4 H)

נֵבֶל / נֵבֶל harp, lyre; skin-bag; possibly a bass lyre (Kolyada); a large כִּנּוֹר (Borowski *Daily Life*) (Isa 5:12)

נְגִינָה stringed instrument; poem; string music, mocking song (DCH) (Ps 69:13)

נגן to play (a stringed instrument); to accompany song with a stringed instrument (DCH) (1 Sam 16:16)

עָשׂוֹר ten-stringed harp (Ps 92:4)

שְׁמִנִּית eight-stringed harp; "according to the Sheminith" in Psalm titles, perhaps for psalms played on instrument with eight strings or in the eighth key (DCH); low key/register (Burgh); the eighth (Smith) (Ps 6:1)

Horn

חֲצוֹצְרָה / חֲצֹצְרָה trumpet, straight trumpet made of metal (Kolyada); trumpet made of silver (Braun) (Ps 98:6)

יוֹבֵל horn, ram's horn, trumpet; jubilee horn (Kolyada) (Exod 19:13)

קֶרֶן bull horn, ox horn (Kolyada); symbol of strength, might, pride (DCH); ram's horn (Braun) (Josh 6:5)

שׁוֹפָר curved horn, ram's horn; trumpet (DCH) (Josh 6:16)

תְּקוֹעַ trumpet; horn (sounded for battle) (DCH) (Ezek 7:14 H)

תֵּקַע blast (of ram's horn) (DCH) (Ps 150:3 H)

תְּרוּעָה trumpet blast, battle cry, loud noise (Num 23:21)

Cymbals, Shakers, Bells

מִלְחָמָה adaptation, harmony, sistrum (DCH) (Isa 30:32 H)

מְנַעֲנְעִים sistrum (Mitchell); clay rattle (Braun); rattles (Burgh) (2 Sam 6:5 H)

מְצִלָּה bell, tinkler; small bell on horses (HALOT) (Zech 14:20 H)

מְצִלְתַּיִם / מְצִלּוֹת pair of cymbals (Kolyada) (Zech 14:20)

עֲצֵי בְרוֹשִׁים cypress wood clappers (Smith) (2 Sam 6:5)

פַּעֲמֹן / פַּעֲמוֹן bell; bell on high priest's robe (DCH) (Exod 28:34 R)

צֶלְצַל cymbal; whirring; insect; sistrums (Borowski *Daily Life*) (Ps 150:5 R)

שְׁלִשִׁים sistrum (Kolyada); rattle (Montagu); sistrum (Smith) (1 Sam 18:6 H)

תֹּף tambourine; timbrel (DCH); frame drum (Burgh); small, round, hand-held frame drum (Smith) (Ps 81:3)

Dance

חֹלְלִים dancers (root חול) (Ps 87:7) (Smith); flautists (root חלל) (1 Kgs 1:40) (DCH)

מָחוֹל dance, dancing, circle dance (Lam 5:15 R)

מְכַרְכֵּר leaping and whirling about (of David) (Montagu) (2 Sam 6:14 R)

שׂחק to dance, play (an instrument) (Smith); play (games), entertain (DCH) (2 Sam 6:5)

EDUCATION

Teachers and Students

בֵּית מִדְרָשׁ school (Van der Toorn) (not used in Hebrew Bible; see Sir 51:23)

דַּעַת knowledge (Widder) (Isa 40:14)

חָכָם wise, teacher, sage; learned man, scholar (Van der Toorn) (Prov 1:6)

חָכְמָה wisdom, prudence (including in religious matters) (Van der Toorn) (Deut 4:6)

לֶמֶד pupil, apprentice, student; thing taught, teaching (DCH); instruction (Widder) (Isa 8:16 R)

לֶקַח learning, teaching (Deut 32:2 R)

מַדָּע knowledge, thought (Hurvitz) (Eccl 10:20 R)

מִדְרָשׁ written composition, study/exegesis of a written (sacred) text (Hurvitz) (2 Chr 13:22 H)

מוֹדִיעִים religious officials (Widder); astrologers (DCH) (Isa 47:13 R)

מוּסָר instruction in behavior, discipline, punishment (Widder) (Prov 1:8)

מְלַמֵּד teacher (Widder) (Ps 119:99 R)

מוֹרֶה teacher, priestly teacher (Widder) (Isa 30:20 R)

סֹפֵר scribe, scholar of texts (Van der Toorn) (2 Chr 34:13)

תּוֹרָה Torah, parental instruction, priestly instruction (Widder) (Jer 18:18)

תַּלְמִיד student, apprentice (Hurvitz); scholar (DCH) (1 Chr 25:8 H)

Writing Tools and Implements

(For Writing on Paper/Stone, see Tools ➡ Artisanal Tools ➡ Carving/Writing)

אִגֶּרֶת letter, missive, epistle, royal letter, edict (Hurvitz) (Neh 2:7)

גִּלָּיוֹן blank scroll (Zhakevich); tablet for writing on (DCH) (Isa 8:1 H)

דְּיוֹ ink (Zhakevich) (Jer 36:18 H)

דֶּלֶת door, column, writing board (Zhakevich); column of writing in a scroll (כלי) (Jer 36:23 H)

חֶרֶשׂ potsherd (Zhakevich) (Isa 30:14)

כְּתָב document, letter, edict, writing (DCH) (Esth 1:22)

לוּחַ tablet (Notebaart); tablet, board, plank (Zhakevich) (Isa 30:8)

מְגִלָּה scroll made of papyrus or leather (Zhakevich) (Jer 36:23)

מְגִלַּת־סֵפֶר scroll document (Zhakevich) (Ezek 2:9)

מִכְתָּב writing, script, document, inscription (DCH) (Exod 39:30 R)

נִשְׁתְּוָן official letter (Persian) (כלי) (Ezra 4:7 R)

סֵפֶר scroll (Notebaart); document, record, book, register, epistle, literature (DCH) (Isa 30:8)

סִפְרָה document, scroll, learning (DCH) (Ps 56:9 H)

סִפֹּרָה literacy, art of writing (DCH) (Ps 71:15 H)

עוֹר skin of human or animal, perhaps used for vellum (Zhakevich) (Lev 8:17)

קֶסֶת cup, ink well; scribal palette (Zhakevich); writing case (DCH) (Ezek 9:2 R)

תַּעַר הַסֹּפֵר scribal knife, scribal razor (Zhakevich, Koller) (Jer 36:23)

PART IV

THE CONSTRUCTED ORDER

BUILDINGS AND STRUCTURES

Town and Village

חַוָּה settlement (SDBH); tent village (DCH) (Num 32:41 R)
חֵיל town (SDBH) (1 Kgs 21:23 R)
חָצֵר village, settlement (SDBH) (Gen 25:16)
טִירָה camp, encampment, village (SDBH) (Gen 25:16 R)
מְדִינָה province, district (Esth 1:1)
עִיר city; town (SDBH) (Gen 4:17)
פְּרָזוֹת unwalled towns, villages (SDBH) (Ezek 38:11)
קֶרֶת city, town (SDBH) (Job 29:7 R)
רְחוֹב town square, marketplace (Pritz) (Gen 19:2)

Buildings

(For Roads, see Military ➡ Vehicles, Horses, and Travel ➡ Road)
(For Fortifications, see Military ➡ Fortifications)

General

בַּיִת house (1 Sam 25:1)
בִּנְיָה a structure, building (Ezek 41:13 H)
בִּנְיָן edifice; structure, building (Hurvitz) (Ezek 40:5 R)
מִבְנֶה building (Ezek 40:2 H)
מִגְדָּל tower for military or agricultural purposes (Walsh); watchtower, platform (Pritz) (Isa 5:2)
מְלוֹן אֹרְחִים inn (Pritz) (Jer 9:2)
מִסְכְּנוֹת pillared or tripartite building (Borowski *Daily Life*); supply store, garrison (DCH) (1 Kgs 9:19 R)
פַּרְוָר summer house, treasury (DCH) (2 Kgs 23:11 R)
קִרְיָה building; town (Deut 2:36)

Royal/Palace

אַרְמוֹן citadel (1 Kgs 16:18)
בִּירָה palace; fortress, royal citadel, the temple (Hurvitz) (Esth 1:2)
בַּיִת palace (Pritz) (Gen 12:15)
בֵּית־הַמֶּלֶךְ palace (Pritz) (2 Sam 11:2)
בִּיתַן palace (Esth 1:5 R)
הֵיכָל palace (Pritz); temple; hall (1 Kgs 21:1)
הַרְמוֹן castle; high place (DCH) (Amos 4:3 H)
מִבְצָר fortification, fortress (DCH); fortress, stronghold, castle, citadel, fort (Pritz) (Hos 10:14)
מִסְגֶּרֶת panel, rim, stronghold (DCH) fortress, stronghold, castle, citadel, fort (Pritz) (2 Sam 22:46)

מְצָד stronghold, mountain fastness (DCH); fortress, stronghold, castle, citadel, fort (Pritz) (Jer 51:30)

מָצוֹר fortification, fortress (DCH) fortress, stronghold, castle, citadel, fort (Pritz) (Zech 9:3 R)

מִשְׂגָּב stronghold (DCH); fortress, stronghold, castle, citadel, fort (Pritz) (2 Sam 22:3)

צְרִיחַ citadel, crypt, underground chamber, vault (DCH); fortress, stronghold, castle, citadel, fort (Pritz) (Judg 9:46 R)

Temple

בִּירָה palace; fortress, royal citadel, the temple (Hurvitz) (Esth 1:2)

דְּבִיר inner sanctuary of temple (1 Kgs 6:19)

הֵיכָל temple, palace, large public building; hall (2 Kgs 18:16)

מִקְדָּשׁ sanctuary (Exod 15:17)

עֲזָרָה court, enclosure of temple (Hurvitz); ledge, court (DCH) (2 Chr 4:9 R)

Prison

בּוֹר prison; cistern (Gen 40:15)

בֵּית הָאֵסוּר prison (SDBH) (Jer 37:15)

בֵּית הָאֲסִירִים prison, dungeon (Pritz) (Judg 16:21 R)

בֵּית הַפְּקֻדֹּת prison, dungeon (Pritz) (Jer 52:11 H)

בֵּית מִשְׁמָר prison (Gen 42:19)

חָגוּת prison, cell, vault (Jer 37:16 H)

כֶּלֶא prison (1 Kgs 22:27)

כְּלִיא prison; confinement (DCH) (Jer 37:4 H)

מַטָּרָה jail, prison; target (Neh 3:25)

מַסְגֵּר dungeon (Ps 142:8 R)

מִשְׁמָר watch, imprisonment (Gen 40:3)

סֹהַר dungeon; enclosure (DCH) (Gen 40:3 R)

עֹצֶר prison, dungeon (Pritz) (Isa 53:8 R)

Storehouse

אוֹצָר treasury, storehouse (Josh 6:19)

אָסָם storehouse; grain store, silo (Pritz); grain pit (Borowski *Agriculture*); barn, granary (SDBH) (Deut 28:8 R)

אָסֹף storehouse (Neh 12:25 R)

בֵּית הָאוֹצָר storehouse, treasury (Hurvitz); storehouse; treasury; armory; granary; (wine) cellar (SDBH) (Mal 3:10)

גֶּנֶז treasury (Hurvitz) (Esth 3:9 R)

גִּנְזָךְ storeroom, treasury (Hurvitz) (1 Chr 28:11 H)

מַטְמוֹן secret storehouse; treasure (DCH) (Gen 43:23 R)

מִסְכְּנוֹת storagehouse, magazine (1 Kgs 9:19)

גְּנֹאת treasure house, treasury (SDBH) (2 Kgs 20:13)
פִּרְוָר summer house, treasury (DCH) (2 Kgs 23:11 R)

Granary/Barn

אָסָם storehouse; grain store, silo (Pritz); grain pit (Borowski *Agriculture*); barn, granary (SDBH) (Deut 28:8 R)
מַאֲבֵס grain-store, silo (Jer 50:26 H)
מְגוּרָה barn, granary; a fright; grain-store, silo; storehouse (Hag 2:19 H)
מְזָוִים barns, storehouses, cells; barns, granaries (SDBH) (Ps 144:13 H)
מַמְגֵרוֹת granaries (DCH) (Joel 1:17 H)
מָעוֹג round silo (DCH); cake, bread; loaf or slice of bread or cake (DCH) (1 Kgs 17:12 H)
קַרְקַע barn; floor (DCH) (Num 5:17 R)

Tent

אֹהֶל tent (Gen 4:20)
אַפְּדָן pavilion, palace tent (Dan 11:45 H)
דּוֹר dwelling (SDBH) (Isa 38:12 H)
חַוָּה tent camp; tent village (DCH) (Num 32:41)
חֻפָּה tent; canopy; pavilion (SDBH) (Ps 19:6 R)
יָתֵד tent-peg, stake, nail, pin; peg on wall of house, for hanging objects (Pritz) (Exod 27:19)
סֻכָּה vineyard booth (Walsh) (Isa 4:6)
מֵיתָר tent rope; cord (Ps 21:13 R)
מִשְׁכָּן tent (Pritz); tabernacle (DCH) (Num 24:5)
קֻבָּה pavilion, tent, bedchamber (Num 25:8 H)

Structural Features

Entryway

אַיִל gate, gateway (Pritz); pillar (DCH) (1 Kgs 6:31)
אַמּוֹת doorposts (Pritz) (Isa 6:4 H)
דֶּלֶת door, gate, lid (Gen 19:6)
מְזוּזָה doorpost (Exod 12:7)
מִפְתָּן threshold (1 Sam 5:4–5)
מַשְׁקוֹף lintel, top beam of doorframe (Pritz) (Exod 12:7 R)
סַף foundation, door, threshold, doorsill (Pritz) (Amos 9:1)
עֹב architrave (?), threshold (?); canopy (DCH) (1 Kgs 7:6 R)
פֶּתַח opening door, entrance (Gen 4:7)
פֶּתַח הַשַּׁעַר gate, gateway (Judg 18:16–17)
שַׁעַר gate (Esth 2:19)

Door Locks/Bars/Hinges

בְּרִיחַ bar (Exod 26:28)
גְּלִילִים hinges (Pritz); hinged (DCH) (1 Kgs 6:34 R)
כַּפּוֹת הַמַּנְעוּל locks (Pritz) (Song 5:5)
מַפְתֵּחַ key (Pritz); connotation of authority (כלי) (Judg 3:25 R)
נעל lock (Pritz) (Judg 3:23 R)
סגר to lock (Pritz) (Judg 9:51)
פֹּתוֹת hinges (Pritz); socket, secret parts (DCH) (1 Kgs 7:50 R)
צִיר hinge (Pritz) (Prov 26:14 H)

Stairs

לוּלִים stairs, steps (Pritz) (1 Kgs 6:8 H)
מַעֲלָה stair, step (Pritz) (Exod 20:26)
סֻלָּם stairway, steps (Pritz); ladder (DCH) (Gen 28:12 H)

Windows

אֲרֻבָּה lattice, window; chimney (Gen 7:11 R)
אֶשְׁנָב latticed window; window (DCH) (Judg 5:28 R)
חַלּוֹן window (Gen 8:6)
מָחֲזֶה window; light (1 Kgs 7:5 R)
צֹהַר window (Pritz); roof (DCH) (Gen 6:16 H)
שְׁקֻפִים windows (Pritz); window frame (1 Kgs 6:4 R)

Location

חוּץ outdoors (Lev 18:9)
פְּנִימָה indoors (2 Kgs 7:11)

Walls

גְּבוּל boundary wall, fence, boundary-marking stone (Pritz) (Ezek 40:12)
גדר to build a wall or fence up (Pritz) (Job 19:8)
חוֹמָה boundary wall, fence (Pritz) (Lam 2:7)
חַיִץ boundary wall, fence (Pritz); interior wall; shaky wall (SDBH) (Ezek 13:10 H)
יָתֵד tent peg, stake, nail, pin; peg on wall of house, for hanging objects (Pritz) (Exod 27:19)
כֹּתֶל wall (of house) (Song 2:9 H)
מְגֻרָעוֹת recesses, ledges (in wall) (1 Kgs 6:6 H)
מְשֻׂכָה boundary wall, fence (Pritz); hedge (DCH) (Prov 15:19 H)
קִיר boundary wall, fence (Pritz); wall, side, barrier (SDBH) (Ps 62:3)
שׂוּך to build a wall or fence up (Pritz) (Job 1:10 R)
שׂוּר wall (rich houses); boundary wall, fence (Pritz) (Gen 49:22 R)

Cornerstone/Capstone

אֶבֶן הָרֹאשָׁה cornerstone, keystone, capstone (Pritz) (Zech 4:7)
אֶבֶן פִּנָּתָה cornerstone, keystone, capstone (Pritz) (Job 38:6)
פִּנָּה cornerstone, keystone, capstone (Pritz) (Zech 10:4)
רֹאשׁ פִּנָּה cornerstone, keystone, capstone (Pritz) (Ps 118:22)

Rooms

בַּיִת room (Pritz) (1 Chr 28:11)
גֵּב room (Pritz); back, brow, mound, platform for worship (DCH) (Ezek 16:24)
חֶדֶר apartment, chamber (Gen 43:30)
חֶדֶר בְּחָדֶר inner room with no outside windows (Pritz) (1 Kgs 20:30)
חֶדֶר הַמִּטּוֹת bedroom (Pritz) (2 Kgs 11:2)
חֶדֶר הַפְּנִימִים inner rooms with no outside windows (Pritz) (1 Chr 28:11)
חֶדֶר מִשְׁכָּב bedroom (Pritz) (Exod 8:3)
חֻפָּה bridal chamber, marriage bed (Pritz) (Joel 2:16 R)
יָצִיעַ room; wing (of building) (HALOT); terrace (DCH) (1 Kgs 6:5 R)
לִשְׁכָּה room; chamber (DCH) (1 Sam 9:22)
מַעֲלֶה upper room, roof chamber (Pritz) (Amos 9:6)
נִשְׁכָּה chamber, temple cell (Neh 3:30 R)
סַף vestibule; threshold (DCH) (Exod 12:22)
עֲלִיָּה stairway; upper room (Ps 104:13)
צֵלָע side chamber, cell (1 Kgs 6:5); plank, board (1 Kgs 6:16)
תָּא chamber, guardroom (1 Kgs 14:28)

Cooking Area

מְבַשְּׁלוֹת cooking hearths (Ezek 46:23 H)
מִקְטָר hearth place; place of burning, incense altar (DCH) (Exod 30:1 H)

Floor/Foundation

מוֹסָד foundations (Pritz); foundation, ruins, remains (DCH) (Deut 32:22)
מָכוֹן foundation (Pritz) (Ps 104:5)
סַף foundation, door (Pritz); threshold (DCH) (Amos 9:1)
קַרְקַע floor (Num 5:17 R)
רִצְפָּה pavement, floor (Esth 1:6)

Roof

גֵּב crossbeam, rafter (Pritz); trench; coffer, recess in paneled ceiling (DCH) (1 Kgs 6:9 R)
גָּג roof (Deut 22:8)

דֶּלֶף leaky roof (Prov 27:15 R)
כָּפִיס girder, rafter; crossbeam (Pritz) (Hab 2:11 H)
מַעֲקֶה parapet (Deut 22:8 H)
מִקְרֶה roof, housetop (Pritz); beam-work, rafter (DCH) (Eccl 10:18 H)
זֵר concave molding surrounding top of object or building, i.e., cavetto cornice (Eichler "The Meaning of Zçr"); border (DCH) (Exod 25:11)
סִפֵּן ceiling (1 Kgs 6:15 H)
קוֹרָה rafter; roof; log, beam (DCH) (Gen 19:8 R)
קרה to lay ceiling beams (Hurvitz) (Ps 104:3 R)
שְׁדֵרָה roof; board; aligned beams (HALOT); row, plank (DCH) (1 Kgs 6:9 R)

Curtain/Screen

דֹּק door of tent, dividing curtain (Pritz) (Isa 40:22 H)
יְרִיעָה curtain, hanging (Ps 104:2)
מָסָךְ curtain, screen (Exod 26:36)
פָּרֹכֶת curtain (Exod 26:31)
קֶלַע curtain, hanging (Exod 27:9)

Materials

גָּזִית ashlar, hewn stone (1 Kgs 6:36)
טוּר course, row (of ashlar or wood) (1 Kgs 6:36)
לְבֵנָה brick (Exod 24:10)
מַלְבֵּן brick kiln; brick pavement (SDBH) (Jer 43:9 R)

Boards/Planks

לוּחַ board, plank (Exod 27:8)
קֶרֶשׁ board, plank (Exod 26:15)
שָׁחִיף board (planed) (Ezek 41:16 H)

Mortar

גִּר chalk, lime (CT); plaster (Pritz) (Isa 27:9 H)
זֶפֶת pitch, tar, asphalt (Isa 34:9 R)
חֵמָר bitumen (Gen 14:10 R)
חֹמֶר clay, "clay material used for pottery as well as mud plaster and mortar utilized for construction purposes" (Zhakevich) (Gen 11:3)
טִיחַ mortar, plaster (Ezek 13:12 H)
שִׂיד lime, whitewash (CT); quicklime plaster (Zhakevich); lime, mortar (DCH) (Isa 33:12 R)
תָּפֵל plaster; frivolity; mud-based plaster unmixed with reinforcing elements (Zhakevich) (Ezek 13:10–15 R)

Enclosures

גָּדֵר / גְּדֵרָה / גְּדֵרֹת wall, stone fence (Num 22:24 R)
חָצֵר court, enclosure (Exod 8:9)
רְחוֹב plaza; square, street (DCH) (Neh 8:1)

Portico and Columns

אֶדֶן pedestal, socket (Exod 26:25)
אוּלָם / אֵילָם portico, porch (1 Kgs 6:3)
אַיִל pilaster; pillar (DCH) (1 Kgs 6:31)
אֹמְנוֹת columns; doorposts (Pritz) (2 Kgs 18:16 H)
דְּבִיר column (Pritz); inner sanctuary, room (DCH) (2 Chr 3:16)
זָוִית column (Pritz); corner (Hurvitz) (Psa 144:12 R)
כִּיּוֹר platform (Pritz) (2 Chr 6:13)
כַּפְתּוֹר capital of pillar; capital of column (Pritz); knob, ornament, capital of pillar (DCH) (Amos 9:1)
כֹּתֶרֶת capital of column (Pritz) (Jer 52:22)
מִסְעָד support pillar; balustrade; table, bench, bannister, support (DCH) (1 Kgs 10:12 H)
מָצוּק / מְצֻק column (Pritz); pillar (DCH) (1 Sam 2:8 R)
עַמּוּד column, stand, platform (Judg 16:25–26)
רֹאשׁ capital of column (Pritz) (2 Chr 3:15)

Water Storage

בּאֹר / בְּאֵר / בֵּיר cistern; pit, cistern (DCH); well (Pritz) (Gen 16:14)
בְּרֵכָה pool (Pritz) (2 Sam 2:13)
גֹּב / גֻּבָּא well, cistern, keg; ditch for irrigation (DCH) (Jer 14:3 R)
מִקְוֶה / מִקְוָה pool (Pritz); collection of water, reservoir (DCH); tank (SDBH) (Exod 7:19 R)
צִנּוֹר water shaft, water tunnel, water channel, water supply (Pritz) (2 Sam 5:8 R)

Furniture

Couch/Bed

יָצוּעַ bed, couch (Pritz) (Gen 49:4 R)
מִטָּה bed, sofa; bier (Gen 47:31)
מֶסַב bed, couch (Pritz); couch, surroundings (DCH) (Song 1:12 R)
מַצָּע couch, bed (Isa 28:20 H)
מְרַאֲשׁוֹת headrest; place of head, head support (DCH) (Gen 28:11)
מִשְׁכָּב bed (Gen 49:4)
פַּעֲמֹת feet (of furniture) (Eichler "The Meaning of *Pa'am*") (Exod 25:12)
עֶרֶשׂ couch, divan; bed (SDBH) (Deut 3:11)

Carpet, Rug

גֶּנֶז carpet, rug (Pritz); treasure chest (DCH) (Ezek 27:24 H)

מַד carpet, rug (Pritz); cloth, rug, garment (DCH) (Judg 5:10 H)

צָפִית cloth, rug (SDBH) (Isa 21:5 H)

שְׂמִיכָה carpet, rug (Pritz) (Judg 4:18 H)

Seat

אָבְנָיִם birthstool (Pritz); stones (dual), pair of stones used as birthstool (DCH) (Exod 1:16 R)

כִּסֵּא throne; chair, seat (Pritz) (Judg 3:20)

מוֹשָׁב seat, chair (Pritz) (1 Sam 20:18 R)

מֶרְכָּב seat; chariot (Song 3:10 R)

תְּכוּנָה seat, chair (Pritz); fixed placer (DCH) (Job 23:3 R)

Footstool

הֲדֹם footstool; metaphor for obeisence and submission (Salvesen "הֲדֹם") (Isa 66:1 R)

כֶּבֶשׁ footstool (2 Chr 9:18 H)

Table/Storage

מֶלְתָּחָה closet, cabinet, cupboard (Pritz); clothes, store, wardrobe (DCH) (2 Kgs 10:22 H)

מֵסַב bed, couch (Pritz); table (DCH) (Song 1:12 R)

שֻׁלְחָן table (Judg 1:7)

Lamps

לָפִיד lamp, torch; cresset (כלי) (Judg 7:16)

מָאוֹר luminary, lightbearer (כלי) (Exod 27:20)

מְנוֹרָה/מְנֹרָה menorah; lampstand (DCH) (2 Kgs 4:10)

נִיר/נֵר lamp, light (Num 8:2)

פִּשְׁתָּה flax (for linen, wicks); wick of a lamp, made of flax (כלי) (Exod 9:31 R)

CONTAINERS AND IMPLEMENTS

General Terms

חֶרֶשׂ vessel made of cheap material (Pritz); pot, potsherd, earthenware (DCH) (Prov 26:23)

כְּלִי vessel, implement, utensil, apparatus (Ruth 2:9)

צָמִיד lid or cover (Kelso and Albright) (Num 19:15 H)

קֶרֶן horn of animal used as container (SDBH) (1 Sam 16:1)

Chest/Box

אַרְגַּז chest, box; bag (SDBH) (1 Sam 6:11 R)

אָרוֹן box, chest, coffin (SDBH) (Gen 50:26)

Cup

גָּבִיעַ goblet, calyx; pitcher (Kelso and Albright); special cup made of silver (Pritz) (Gen 44:12)

כּוֹס cup; drinking vessel similar to bowl (Walsh); cup, purse (DCH) (2 Sam 12:3)

כִּיס cup, bag (for money, weights); bag, purse (SDBH) (Deut 25:13 R)

קֻבַּעַת goblet; small bowl (Kelso and Albright); cup, bowl, goblet (SDBH) (Isa 51:17 R)

קֶסֶת cup, ink well; scribal palette (Zhakevich); writing case (DCH) (Ezek 9:2 R)

Crucible

מַצְרֵף crucible (for silver) (Prov 27:21 R)

עֲלִיל crucible, furnace (Ps 12:7 H)

Bowl, Basin

אַגָּן bowl; large banquet bowl (Kelso and Albright) (Song 7:2 R)

אֲגַרְטָל dish, bowl (SDBH); basket (DCH) (Ezra 1:9 R)

גֻּלָּה basin, bowl (Eccl 12:6)

כִּיּוֹר bowl (Kelso and Albright); basin for washing (DCH); cooking pot, kettle (Pritz) (Exod 30:18)

כְּפוֹר bowl, basin; frost (1 Chr 28:17 R)

מִזְרָק bowl, wine bowl, basin; bowl used for alcohol, ritual contexts (Walsh); shallow metal drinking-offering bowls (Greer); large banquet bowl (Kelso and Albright) (Amos 6:6)

מַחֲלָפִים vessels of various kinds (Pritz); knives (DCH) (Ezra 1:9 H)

מְנַקִּית sacrificial bowl (Exod 25:29 R)

סַף basin, goblet, bowl; vestibule; small bowl for sacrifice or wine (Kelso and Albright); cup (Pritz) (Zech 12:2 R)

סֵפֶל basin, bowl; large banquet bowl (Kelso and Albright); cup (Pritz) (Judg 15:25 R)

צְלֹחִית bowl (Kelso and Albright); jar (DCH) (2 Kgs 2:20 H)

קְעָרָה bowl, dish, platter (Exod 25:29)

רַחַץ wash basin (SDBH); washing (DCH) (Ps 60:10 R)

סִיר רַחָץ basin, washbasin (Pritz) (Ps 60:10)

מַשְׂרֵת bowl with perforated base, colander, strainer (FAJ); bread bowl for kneading dough (Kelso and Albright); pan, tray (DCH) (2 Sam 13:9 H)

Jug, Jar

אָסוּךְ oil jar (Kelso and Albright) (2 Kgs 4:2 H)

בַּקְבֻּק decanter (Kelso and Albright); jug (DCH) (1 Kgs 14:3 R)

דְּלִי pail, jar; bucket (SDBH) (Num 24:7 R)

כַּד earthenware jar, pail; jar for water or flour (Kelso and Albright) (Gen 24:14)

כִּירַיִם jar stand (Kelso and Albright); cooking furnace (DCH); double cooking stove (כלי) (Lev 11:35 H)

צְנִצֶנֶת vase, jar, pot (Exod 16:33 H)

קַשְׁוָה jug, jar (libations); flagon, pitcher (SDBH) (Exod 25:29 R)

Pot, Kettle

אָח firepot; brazier (כלי) (Jer 36:22 R)

דּוּד kettle, pot, basket; deep cooking pot (Kelso and Albright) (2 Kgs 10:7 R)

כּוּר smelting pot (for gold) (Prov 27:21 R)

כִּיּוֹר cauldron, chafing dish, fire pot; pedestal or palanquin (DCH) (1 Sam 2:14 H)

סִיר pot; thorn; hook; wide-mouth cooking pot, wash basin (Kelso and Albright) (Exod 16:3 R)

פָּרוּר cooking pot (Num 11:8 R)

קַלַּחַת kettle, cauldron, pot; stewpot (כלי) (1 Sam 2:14 R)

Pans

כַּף pan; palm of hand; ladle, spoon, saucer (DCH) (Exod 25:29)

מַחֲבַת pan, griddle, plate (Lev 2:5 R)

מַחְתָּה pan for live coals; firepan (DCH) (1 Kgs 7:50)

מֶרְחֶשֶׁת baking pan, stove pan; cooking pan for deep-fat frying (Kelso and Albright); griddle (Pritz) (Lev 7:9 R)

צַלַּחַת shallow pan; medium sized bowl (Kelso and Albright); cooking pot, kettle (Pritz) (2 Kgs 21:13 R)

Flask

אָסוּךְ oil flask (2 Kgs 4:2 H)
בַּקְבֻּק flask, bottle; jug (SDBH) (1 Kgs 14:3 R)
פַּךְ flask, vial; small perfume juglet (Kelso and Albright) (1 Sam 10:1 R)
צַפַּחַת pilgrim flask, small oil jar (Kelso and Albright); clay jar (Pritz) (1 Sam 26:11 R)
קֶרֶן horn, flask (1 Sam 16:13)

Pottery

Formed Clay

חַרְסוּת potsherd, pottery (Jer 19:2 H)
חֶרֶשׂ pottery; earthenware vessel, clay pot (SDBH) (Lev 11:33)
כְּלֵי יוֹצֵר potter's vessel (Kelso and Albright) (Ps 2:9)
עֶצֶב pottery vessel (?) (Kelso and Albright) (Jer 22:28 H)

Unformed Clay

אֲדָמָה land, soil (Gen 2:5); topsoil, humus (HCW); dry native clay (Kelso and Albright) (Isa 45:9)
אֶרֶץ earth, land; dry native clay (Kelso and Albright) (Ps 12:7)
חֹמֶר clay, "clay material used for pottery as well as mud plaster and mortar utilized for construction purposes" (Zhakevich) (Gen 11:3)
טִיט mud, mire, silt, clay (HCW) (Job 41:22)
עָפָר dust, raw clay (Kelso and Albright) (Job 10:9)

Oven

כִּבְשָׁן kiln, smelting furnace (Gen 19:28 R)
כִּיר stove, furnace (Lev 11:35 H)
תַּנּוּר oven, furnace, fire-pot (Lev 11:35)

Hearth

אֲרִיאֵל hearth (CHB) (Ezek 43:15 R)
יָקוּד hearth (CHB); glowing fire (כלי) (Isa 30:14 H)
מוֹקְדָה hearth (CHB) (Lev 6:2 H)

Sacks, Bags, Skins

אֹבוֹת wineskins, water bags (Pritz) (Job 32:19 H)
אַמְתַּחַת sack, bag; grain-storage bag carried by pack animals (כלי) (Gen 42:27)
חֵמֶת wineskin, water bag (Pritz) (Gen 21:14 R)
חָרִיט purse, bag (SDBH); wallet (Platt); purse (DCH) (2 Kgs 5:23 R)

יְלֻקוּט (shepherd's) pouch, bag (SDBH) (1 Sam 17:40 H)
מֶשֶׁךְ leather bag, pouch (כלי) (Job 28:18 R)
מִשְׁפְּתַיִם saddlebags, donkey packs (כלי) (Gen 49:14 R)
נֹאד skin, bottle; made of animal skin (Walsh) (Josh 9:4 R)
נֵבֶל / נֵבֶל wineskin, jar, pitcher; large storage jar (Kelso and Albright); clay jar (Pritz) (Isa 30:14)
צִקְלוֹן satchel, saddlebag, sack, bag (2 Kgs 4:42 H)
צְרוֹר bundle, parcel, pouch; money pouch, purse (כלי) (Prov 7:20 R)
שַׂק sackcloth, bag (Isa 3:24)

Basket

אֵיפָה basket, specific measure of a basket (Pritz); tub, barrel (SDBH) (Lev 19:36)
דּוּד kettle, pot, basket; deep cooking pot (Kelso and Albright) (2 Kgs 10:7 R)
טֶנֶא basket (Deut 26:2 R)
כְּלוּב wicker basket (fruit); bird trap, cage (Jer 5:27 H)
סַל / סַלְסִלּוֹת bread basket, woven basket (Exod 29:3)
תֵּבָה basket (Pritz); ark (SDBH) (Exod 2:3)

Cutting Instruments

חֶרֶב sword, knife (Josh 5:2–3)
מַאֲכֶלֶת knife (eating); used to cut animal flesh (Koller) (Gen 22:6 R)
מַזְמֵרָה pruning knife (Joel 4:10 R)
מַחֲלָפִים slaughter-knives; specifically for ritual use in temple (Koller) (Ezra 1:9 H)
צֹר / צַר knife, stone (flint) (Isa 5:28 R)
שַׂכִּין knife (Prov 23:2)
תַּעַר knife, razor; scabbard (Num 6:5 R)

Fork

מַזְלֵג fork (three-pronged) (Pritz) (1 Sam 2:13–14 R)
מַעֲצָד tongs (Pritz); axe, billhook (DCH) (Isa 44:12 R)
קִלְשׁוֹן fork, points (Hurvitz) (1 Sam 13:21 H)

TOOLS

(Many other categories contain "Tools" vocabulary as well:
for Animal Husbandry Tools, see Animals ➡ Animal Husbandry Tools;
for Hunting Tools, see Animals ➡ Snares and Traps;
for Medical Tools, see Disease, Mortality, and Disability ➡ Medical Tools, Herbs;
for Harvesting Tools, see Food and Spices ➡ Threshing/Winnowing;
for Military Tools, see Military ➡ Weapons/Armor;
for Literacy, see Education ➡ Writing Tools and Implements)

General Tools

General

כְּלִי vessel, utensil, tool (כלי) (2 Sam 8:10)
מַטְאֲטֵא broom (Pritz) (Isa 14:23 H)

Rope/Cord/Ties

אֲגֻדָּה cord (SDBH); bond tying one to yoke (DCH) (Isa 58:6 R)
אַגְמוֹן rope, cord (Pritz); rush, used as barb (DCH) (Job 41:2 R)
חֶבֶל rope, cord (Pritz) (Job 18:10)
חוּט thread, cord (DCH) (Gen 14:23 R)
יֶתֶר cord; string; cord, sinew, tent rope, bowstring (DCH) (Judg 16:7 R)
לֻלָאָה loop (Exod 26:4)
מֵיתָר rope, cord (Pritz) (Exod 39:40 R)
מִשְׁכוֹת ropes, cords (Pritz); belts (DCH) (Job 38:31 H)
נְקִפָּה rope (Isa 3:24 H)
עֲבֹת rope, cord, gold chains connecting ephod and shoulder straps on priestly garment (Pritz) (Exod 28:14)
פְּתִיל cord; thread (Gen 38:18)

Restraints/Chains

אֲזִקִּים chains, bonds, manacles (Jer 40:1 R)
אֵסוּר thong; strap; bond; fetter; cord; bond, fetter (DCH) (Judg 15:14 R)
זֵק chain; fetter (Job 36:8 R)
כֶּבֶל shackles, fetters, manacles (Pritz) (Ps 105:18 R)
מַהְפֶּכֶת stocks (Jer 20:2 R)
מוֹסֵר thong; strap; bond; fetter; cord; bond, fetter (DCH) (Job 39:5 R)
מַעֲדַנּוֹת chains (Pritz) (Job 38:31 R)
מִשְׁכוֹת chains (Pritz) (Job 38:31 H)
נְחֻשְׁתַּיִם shackles, fetters, manacles (Pritz); bronze fetters (DCH) (Judg 16:21 R)

סַד stocks (Pritz) (Job 13:27 R)
צִינֹק iron collar; neck irons (Jer 29:26 H)
רַתּוּקוֹת chains (Pritz) (1 Kgs 6:21 R)

Barber/Haircutting

מוֹרָה razor (Pritz) (Judg 13:5 R)
תַּעַר razor (Pritz) (Num 6:5 R)

Artisanal Tools

Textile Production

אֶרֶג loom, shuttle of loom (Job 7:6 R)

Pottery

חוֹתָם press mold (Kelso and Albright); seal, signet ring (DCH) (Job 38:14)

Hammer

הַלְמוּת hammer, mallet (Judg 5:26 H)
לטש to hammer out, sharpen; to sharpen, whet, forge (DCH) (Gen 4:22 R)
מַסְמֵר / מַשְׂמְרוֹת nail, peg; nail, perhaps scepter (DCH) (1 Chr 22:3 R)
מַקֶּבֶת hammer (Judg 4:21 R)
מִקְשָׁה hammered work (Exod 25:18 R)
פַּטִּישׁ forge hammer (Isa 41:7 R)
רַקַּע hammer (Pritz) (Num 16:38)
רקע to hammer (DCH) (Ezek 6:11)

Carving/Writing

(For Writing Implements, see Education ➡ Writing Tools and Implements)

חֶרֶט chisel (Zhakevich); stylus (Pritz) (Exod 32:4 R)
מְחוּגָה compass; lathe (DCH); callipers (כלי) (Isa 44:13 H)
מִכְתָּב writing, script, document, inscription (DCH) (Exod 39:30 R)
מִכְתָּם inscription (DCH) (Ps 16:1 R)
מַקְצֻעָה chisel, scraper; carpenter's knife, used for sharpening curved wood (Koller) (Isa 44:13 H)
מַרְצֵעַ awl (Pritz) (Exod 21:6 R)
עֵט iron or reed pen; for writing on hard surfaces, e.g. rock or metal (כלי) (Jer 17:1 R)
צִפֹּרֶן שָׁמִיר emery point (Notebaart); hard stone tip of an עֵט (Zhakevich); stylus point (DCH); nail, tip of angle-tint tool (כלי) (Jer 17:1)
שָׂרָד scribing-awl; chalk; tool used by a carpenter in the preparation of wood to be cut up (Zhakevich); marker, stylus (DCH) (Isa 44:13 H)

Saw

מְגֵרָה saw; used for cutting stones (Koller); axe (DCH) (2 Sam 12:31)

מַשּׂוֹר saw, possibly carpenter's saw (Koller) (Isa 10:15 H)

Agricultural Tools

Axe

גַּרְזֶן axe; axe, pickaxe, adze (DCH) (Deut 19:5 R)

כֵּילַף axe, club, sledge hammer; crowbar (DCH); synonymous with קַרְדֹּם (Koller) (Ps 74:6 H)

כַּשִּׁיל feller, axe, hatchet; smaller version of גַּרְזֶן used to chop wood (Koller) (Ps 74:6 H)

מַגְזֵרָה cutting implement, blade, axe (2 Sam 12:31 H)

מַעֲצָד axe; reaping tool, type of hoe (Borowski *Agriculture*); adze (Notebaart); used to carve and shape wood (Koller) (Isa 44:12 R)

קַרְדֹּם axe; double-bladed, with axe on one side and adze on the other; used for chopping wood, pruning trees, and digging up plants and roots (Koller) (Judg 9:48 R)

Plow/Hoe/Farming/Harvesting/Threshing

אוֹפַן עֲגָלָה wheel-thresher (Borowski *Agriculture*) (Isa 28:27)

אֵת hoe, plowshare; generic digging tool (Borowski *Agriculture*); blade (DCH) (1 Sam 13:20 R)

גֹּרֶן threshing floor (Borowski *Agriculture*) (Num 15:20)

חֶרְמֵשׁ flint sickle (Borowski *Agriculture*) (Deut 16:9 R)

חָרוּץ iron tooth for threshing sledge (Borowski *Agriculture*); threshing sledge (DCH) (Job 41:22 R)

יָתֵד digging tool (Borowski *Agriculture*); peg, nail, digging stick (DCH) (Deut 23:14)

כִּבְרָה sieve (Borowski *Agriculture*) (Amos 9:9 H)

מַגָּל sickle (Pritz) (Joel 3:13 R)

מוֹרַג threshing sledge (Borowski *Agriculture*) (Isa 41:15 R)

מַזְמֵרָה pruning knife; pruning tool (Walsh); smaller than מַגָּל, specialized for pruning, especially grape vines (Koller) (Joel 4:10 R)

מִזְרֶה winnowing fork (Borowski *Agriculture*) (Isa 30:24 R)

מַחֲרֵשָׁה plowshare, pick-axe, mattock; possibly identical to מַעְדֵּר (Koller) (1 Sam 13:20–21 R)

מַטֶּה threshing stick (Isa 28:27) (Borowski *Agriculture*); rod, club, shepherd's staff (Gen 38:18) (Pritz)

מַעְדֵּר hoe (Isa 7:25 H)

נָפָה sieve (Borowski *Agriculture*) (Isa 30:28 H)

רַחַת winnowing shovel (Borowski *Agriculture*) (Isa 30:24 H)
שְׁלֹשׁ קִלְשׁוֹן fork for picking up piles of cuttings (Pritz) (1 Sam 13:21)

Mortar and Pestle

מְדֹכָה mortar (Num 11:8 H)
מַכְתֵּשׁ mortar (beaten out thing); hollow place (Prov 27:22 R)
עֲלִי pestle; crucible, cauldron (DCH) (Prov 27:22 H)

MEASUREMENT

General Terms

חֶבֶל measuring line, rope (2 Sam 8:2)
חוּט measuring tape, string (1 Kgs 7:15 R)
מַד measure (Jer 13:25 R)
מִדָּה tall; measure, size; tax (Lev 19:35)
מִסְפָּר number (Deut 25:2)
מַתְכֹּנֶת proportion, measurement, amount (Ezek 45:11 R)
פְּתִיל measuring rod, measuring line (Pritz) (Ezek 40:3)
קַו measuring line, measuring rod (DCH, Pritz) (Isa 28:17)
קָנֶה measuring rod, measuring line (Pritz) (Ezek 41:8)
שָׁלִישׁ threefold measure (Isa 40:12 R)
שַׁעַר a measure (grain) (Gen 26:12 H)
תֹּכֶן fixed quantity, measure (Ezek 45:11 R)

Liquid

כֹּר *kor*-measure = 10 *baths* = 60 gallons (1 Kgs 5:2 R)
בַּת *bath*-measure = 6 הִין (1 Kgs 7:26)
הִין *hin*-measure = 3 קַב (Exod 29:40)
קַב *qab*-measure = 4 לוֹג (2 Kgs 6:25 H)
לוֹג *log*-measure = smallest unit (Lev 14:10 R)

Dry

כֹּר *kor*-measure = 10 *ephahs* = 6.5 bushels (1 Kgs 4:22 R)
חֹמֶר *homer* = 10 *ephahs*; about 220 liters or 6 bushels (SDBH) (Lev 27:16)
לֶתֶךְ *letek*-measure = 5 *ephahs* (Hos 3:2 H)
אֵיפָה *ephah*-measure = 20 quarts (Exod 16:36)
סְאָה *seah*-measure = 1/3 *ephah*, equivalent to 7.3 liters or 7 quarts (SDBH); about 12 liters (DCH) (Gen 18:6 R)
קַב *qab*-measure = 1/8 *ephah* (2 Kgs 6:25 H)
עֹמֶר *omer*-measure = 2 quarts; heap, sheaf; 1/10 *ephah* (SDBH) (Exod 16:16 R)
עִשָּׂרוֹן tenth-part (of *ephah*) (Lev 23:17)

Width

עֳבִי thickness, width (1 Kgs 7:26 R)
רַחַב width; wide (DCH) (Exod 3:8)
רֹחַב width; breadth (DCH) (Gen 13:17)
רְחוֹב/רְחֹב width; avenue; area (Gen 19:2)

Height

בָּמָה high place, height, *bamah*-altar (Num 21:28)
גָּבֹהַּ elevated, powerful, arrogant; height (SDBH) (Gen 7:19)
מָרוֹם altitude, height (Jer 17:12)
נוֹף elevation; height; loftiness (SDBH) (Ps 48:3 H)
קוֹמָה height; stature (SDBH) (Gen 6:15)
רוּם height; hautiness (Prov 25:3)
רָמָה height, high place (1 Sam 22:6 R)
תְּלוּל high (SDBH) (Ezek 17:22 H)

Length

General

אֹרֶךְ length (Deut 30:20)
אָרֵךְ long (SDBH) (Ezek 17:3)
כְּבָרָה length, measure, distance; stretch of land (DCH) (Gen 48:7 R)

Specific Lengths (Short to Long)

אֶצְבַּע finger ("inch") (Jer 52:21 H)
טֹפַח handwidth (Pritz) (Exod 25:25 R)
זֶרֶת hand-span (1/2 cubit) (Exod 28:16 R)
גֹּמֶד span, cubit (Judg 3:16 H)
אַמָּה cubit (18 inches) (Gen 6:15–16)
קָנֶה measuring rod of six cubits and a palm = 3.5 meters (Pritz) (Ezek 42:18)
שָׂדֶה furrow length, about 20–30 meters (SDBH) (1 Sam 14:14)
צֶמֶד *tsamad*-measure = as much as what a yoke of oxen can plough in a day, roughly an acre (DCH, Walsh) (Isa 5:10)

Weight

General

כֹּבֶד heaviness, weight, mass (Nah 3:3 R)
מִשְׁקוֹל weight (Ezek 4:10 H)
מִשְׁקָל weight, weighing (1 Kgs 10:14)
מִשְׁקֹלֶת / מִשְׁקָלֶת weight, plummet; levelling implement (DCH) (2 Kgs 21:13 R)

Specific Weights (Light to Heavy)

גֵּרָה 1/20 shekel = *gerah*-weight, small weight (Exod 30:13 R)
בֶּקַע 10 gerahs = half-shekel, *beka*-weight (Gen 24:22 R)
פִּים 2/3 shekel = *pim*-weight (1 Sam 13:21 H)
שֶׁקֶל 2 bekas = shekel, weight (Gen 23:15–16)
מָנֶה 50 shekels = *mina*; measured amount (Ezek 45:12 R)

כִּכָּר 10 *minas* (75 lbs) talent (weight); load; circle, valley (Exod 25:39)

Currency

אֲגוֹרָה piece of silver (used as payment) (SDBH) (1 Sam 2:36 H)
אַדַּרְכֹּן / דַּרְכְּמוֹן daric, drachma (SDBH) (1 Chr 29:7 R)
כֶּסֶף silver (Pritz) (Gen 13:2)
קְשִׂיטָה piece of money; coin; *kesitah* (SDBH) (Gen 33:19 R)
שֶׁקֶל shekel, currency (Gen 23:15–16)

Scales

אֶבֶן stone weight for scale (Pritz) (Lev 19:36)
כִּיס bag for money and weights (Deut 25:13 R)
מֹאזְנַיִם scales, balance (Lev 19:36)
פֶּלֶס balance, scale (Prov 16:11 R)
קָנֶה balance, scale (Pritz) (Isa 46:6)

APPENDIX ONE: GUIDE TO FURTHER READING

Throughout our book, we note many specialized studies that cast light on difficult and rare terms. Here we wish to say a few words about the most relevant studies as they apply to the major categories and subcategories. In addition to the specific works discussed in this appendix, we note that probably the best place to start exploring semantic domains in Biblical Hebrew is the *Semantic Dictionary of Biblical Hebrew* (SDBH) project, sponsored by the United Bible Societies under the editorship of Reinier de Blois. The entire database is freely available online at sdbh.org. While some of the sources gathered in our book are written by specialists in lexicography and semantics, including those working on the Semantics of Ancient Hebrew Database project, others are written by archaeologists or literary scholars.

Heavens and Earth

For Hebrew cosmology and topography, the classic study is Stadelmann's *The Hebrew Conception of the World: A Philological and Literary Study*. On weather terms, see Scott, "Meteorological Phenomena and Terminology in the Old Testament," and, more recently, Wiggins's *Weathering the Psalms: A Meteorotheological Survey*.

Metals, Stones, Gems, Minerals, and Pearls

This area of research is in need of new work. SDBH is the best starting point by far. Brenner's *Colour Terms in the Old Testament* discusses some gems, while Notebaart's "Metallurgical Metaphors in the Hebrew Bible" contains the best (though still limited for our purposes) discussions of metallurgical terms.

Colors

The two key sources for this list are Brenner's *Colour Terms in the Old Testament* and Hartley's *The Semantics of Ancient Hebrew Colour Lexemes*. Each work offers unique elements and perspectives. Hartley's book, part of the Semantics of Ancient Hebrew Database project, is more current and covers each of its terms more in-depth. Brenner's book, however, integrates more terms that convey colour figuratively, such as jewels and textiles. She also includes evidence from Mishnaic Hebrew.

Time

A superb, comprehensive overview of time measurement in ancient Israel is Miano's *Shadow on the Steps: Time Measurement in Ancient Israel*. Dated and more theoretical, but still useful, is Barr's *Biblical Words for Time*.

Animals

Hope's *All Creatures Great and Small: Living Things in the Bible*, part of the UBS Technical Helps for Translators series, is the best place to start here. For animals that are kept for animal husbandry, Borowski's *Every Living Thing: Daily Use of Animals in Ancient Israel* and his *Agriculture in Iron Age Israel* are also a great help.

Flora

Our book separates cultivated plants from wild plants, placing the former under Food and Spices and the latter under Flora. On wild plants, Koops and Slager's *Each According to Its Kind: Plants and Trees in the Bible* is the single best resource available. Harrison discusses several plants as well in Healing Herbs of the Bible, though his book has some limits (see comments on this book under "Foods and Spices," below).

Human

Familial terms in the Hebrew Bible seem to be an understudied subject. The most useful works for this section were Eng's *The Days of Our Years: A Lexical Semantic Study of the Life Cycle in Ancient Israel*, which maps out age-related terms, and Parker's *Valuable and Vulnerable: Children in the Hebrew Bible*, which studies several different terms pertaining to children.

Human Anatomy

There is no English-language study of the semantics of human body parts in Biblical Hebrew. The most helpful source is Wilkinson, "The Body in the Old Testament," as well as two 2007 blog posts by Semitic linguist John Hobbins.

Disease, Mortality, and Disability

A useful place to start on diseases is Williams's "A Talmudic Perspective on Old Testament Diseases, Physicians and Remedies," though the subject has much room for further study. Harrison's *Healing Herbs of the Bible* lists many medicinal herbs and speculates on their specific use. On disability, Olyan's *Disability in the Hebrew Bible: Interpreting Mental and Physical Differences* is the best starting point, and Stewart's "Sexual Disabilities in the Hebrew Bible" covers sexual disabilities more specifically.

Foods and Spices

The best starting point for this subject is Koops and Slager's *Each According to Its Kind: Plants and Trees in the Bible*. Like the other books in the UBS Technical Helps for Translators series, this book contains vocabulary from both Testaments. On different types of crops and terms related to animal husbandry, Borowski's *Agriculture in Iron Age Israel* is superb, and it even includes an index of Hebrew terms. On herbs and spices, Harrison's *Healing Herbs of the Bible* is serviceable. Though light on textual analysis, he discusses some plants not mentioned in the Bible but only known from archaeology or comparative Near Eastern sources. For incense, see Nielsen's *Incense in*

Ancient Israel. On viticulture specifically, Walsh's *The Fruit of the Vine: Viticulture in Ancient Israel* is a thorough investigation incorporating both archaeological and textual data, with discussions of Hebrew terms throughout. While Walsh's book focuses on archaeology, Jordan's "An Offering of Wine," a 2002 dissertation, foregrounds semantic analysis of viticulture terminology. Two other books deserve mention. Nathan MacDonald's *What Did the Ancient Israelites Eat?: Diet in Biblical Times* is a highly readable guide to ancient Israelite diet. However, he does not discuss Hebrew terminology, making his book less useful for the Hebrew-language student. Kurtis Peters's *Hebrew Lexical Semantics and Daily Life in Ancient Israel: What's Cooking in Biblical Hebrew?* is a superb study of various terms for cooking activities.

Clothing

Like the metals and gems list, there is a surprising dearth of literature on this subject. SDBH and Pritz's *The Works of Their Hands: Man-Made Things in the Bible* are the best guides.

Family and Kinship

Almost no literature exists on familial terms in Biblical Hebrew. The best place to start, however, is Rattray's "Marriage Rules, Kinship Terms and Family Structure in the Bible."

Worship/Cultic

There are no guides to worship terminology in Biblical Hebrew. The best starting point is chapter 4, "Religion," in Pritz's *The Works of Their Hands: Man-made Things in the Bible.*

Law and Covenant

The main source here for legal terms is Bovati's *Re-Establishing Justice: Legal Terms, Concepts and Procedures in the Hebrew Bible.* On the language of oath, blessing, and cursing, see Aitken's *The Semantics of Blessing and Cursing in Ancient Hebrew,* published as part of the Semantics of Ancient Hebrew Database project.

Professions

There is no lexical study on professions overall in ancient Israel, although SDBH contains a category on "Professions" that is very useful. Apart from that, the terms for this must be gleaned from various studies on particular professions. For example, while Borowski's *Daily Life in Biblical Times* discusses different kinds of professions in the Old Testament, he seldom discusses specific Hebrew terms. His *Agriculture in Iron Age Israel* is useful, but only for terms relating to agricultural professions. There is no study on the terminology of political leadership in particular.

Military

For weapons, fortifications, and those engaged in war, see chapter 2, "Warfare," in Pritz's *The Works of Their Hands: Man-Made Things in the Bible.* On war in ancient

Israel more generally, see first Hobbs's *A Time for War: A Study of Warfare in the Old Testament*, and second, Seevers's *Warfare in the Old Testament: The Organization, Weapons, and Tactics of Ancient Near Eastern Armies*.

Maritime

Little exists on the terminology of seafaring in ancient Israel. Patai's *The Children of Noah: Jewish Seafaring in Ancient Times* is a good resource, which also includes Greek-language Jewish sources and Talmudic terminology. For a more focused examination of terminology in particular, see chapter 8, "Transportation," in Pritz's *The Works of their Hands: Man-Made Things in the Bible*.

Music

There is a large quantity of research into music in ancient Israel. The strongest guides to this subject integrate archaeological, textual (including non-biblical), and comparative ancient Near Eastern evidence on various musical instruments and those who played them. The most helpful resources for this category are Braun's *Music in Ancient Israel/Palestine: Archaeological, Written and Comparative Sources*, Burgh's *Listening to the Artifacts: Music Culture in Ancient Palestine*, and Montagu's *Musical Instruments of the Bible*.

Education

On terms relating to education in particular, see Van der Toorn's superb and readable *Scribal Culture and the Making of the Hebrew Bible*, which speculates on the social context of schools and scribes in ancient Israel. Widder's *"To Teach" in Ancient Israel: A Cognitive Linguistic Study of a Biblical Hebrew Lexical Set* is a more technical, linguistic study, focusing primarily on verbs but including some discussion of nouns related to education. On scribal tools in particular, see Zhakevich's dissertation "The Tools of an Israelite Scribe: A Semantic Study of the Terms Signifying the Tools and Materials of Writing in Biblical Hebrew," as well as Rollston's *Writing and Literacy in the World of Ancient Israel: Epigraphic Evidence from the Iron Age*.

Buildings and Structures

"Buildings and Structures," chapter 3 of Pritz's *The Works of Their Hands: Man-Made Things in the Bible*, is the main starting point for this topic. Borowski's *Agriculture in Iron Age Israel* details some of the buildings used in agriculture. His book has the advantage of including an index of Hebrew terms with glosses.

Containers and Implements

The best place to start here is Pritz's *The Works of Their Hands: Man-Made Things in the Bible*. Part of the UBS Technical Helps for Translators series, this book contains both Hebrew Bible and New Testament terminology. Another excellent starting point is Kelso and Albright's "The Ceramic Vocabulary of the Old Testament." Shafer-Elliot's article in *Biblical Interpretation*, "Food in the Hebrew Bible," is freely available online and contains many terms for implements used in cooking. The כלי *Database: Utensils in the Hebrew Bible*, an initiative of several Dutch biblical scholars, is far from comprehensive but boasts some very focused studies of the terms it does cover. Their results are freely available online.

Tools

Pritz's *The Works of Their Hands: Man-Made Things in the Bible* is the best starting point on biblical tools. The כלי *Database: Utensils in the Hebrew Bible*, an initiative of several Dutch biblical scholars mentioned above, is far from comprehensive but boasts some very focused studies of the terms it does cover. Their results are freely available online. For agricultural tools specifically, see Borowski's *Agriculture in Iron Age Israel* and Walsh's *The Fruit of the Vine: Viticulture in Ancient Israel.* On writing tools and materials, see Philip Zhakevich's recent dissertation, "The Tools of an Israelite Scribe: A Semantic Study of the Terms Signifying the Tools and Materials of Writing in Biblical Hebrew," freely available online in UT Austin Texas ScholarWorks. On cutting tools, see Koller's *The Semantic Field of Cutting Tools in Biblical Hebrew: The Interface of Philological, Semantic, and Archaeological Evidence.*

Measurement

As with the clothing list, there is also a surprising lack of literature on this subject. SDBH and Pritz's *The Works of Their Hands: Man-Made Things in the Bible* are the best places to start. Scott's "Weights and Measures of the Bible" also has some limited usefulness, though it is dated and he does not specifically discuss Hebrew terms. He does discuss some of the pitfalls in trying to "translate" biblical measurements into contemporary systems of measurement.

APPENDIX TWO: CLUSTER VERSES FOR STUDY

Reading biblical vocabulary in contexts that are particularly revealing of a word's meaning can be quite helpful for memorization. We offer here a list of some of the more useful passages for this purpose. Cluster verses are individual verses or passages that contain several words from one category or subcategory. Memorizing these lists is a useful way to increase your Biblical Hebrew vocabulary, but these cluster verses enable you to learn these words in context. Some cluster verses are specific to a subcategory, while others are for a list overall. While the verses listed here are by no means exhaustive, we encourage students and instructors to use them as a model for developing their own examples and to email the authors with any cluster verses they may find.

I. The Created Order

Heavens and Earth: Gen 22:17; Deut 28:12, 32:22; Judg 5:4; 1 Sam 13:6; 2 Kgs 23:5; Ps 18:7–16, 29:7–9, 77:16–19, 83:13–15, 104:3, 135:7; Prov 8:24–29; Job 38:22; Isa 29:6, 51:13–15; Jer 10:13, 17:6, 51:16; Ezek 38:20–22

Stars: Job 9:9; Amos 5:8

Earth: Isa 40:4

Rain/Storm: Deut 32:2; Ps 65:10–11

Water: Exod 15:8; Ezek 31:4

Metals, Stones, Gems, Minerals, and Pearls: Gen 2:12; 1 Kgs 10:22

Metals: Exod 25:3; Num 31:22; Lam 4:1–2; Prov 27:21

Gems: Exod 28:17–20; Ezek 28:13

Specific Colors: Gen 30:32, 49:12; Exod 25:4, 26:31, 28:8, 35:6–7; Lev 13:19; Isa 1:18; Zech 1:8, 6:2; Song 5:10–11; Lam 4:7–8; Esth 8:15

Time: Gen 7:11, 8:22; 1 Kgs 6:1, 6:37–38

Animals: Gen 15:9; Deut 14:4–6; Lev 11:1–8; 1 Sam 17:34; Song 1:8

Birds: Lev 11:13–19; Deut 14:11–18; Isa 34:15

Cattle: Gen 12:16; Job 1:3

Sheep, Goats: Gen 30:32–35

Horses, Mules, Asses: 1 Chr 27:30

Lions: Gen 49:9; Ezek 19:1–6; Nah 2:12

Lizards/Reptiles: Lev 11:29–30

Snakes: Deut 32:33; Isa 14:29

Arthropods: Lev 11:22–23

Locusts: Joel 1:4
Snares and Traps: Job 18:8–10
Flora: Num 24:6; Judg 8:9–15; 2 Kgs 19:26
Trees: Gen 30:37; Lev 23:40; Neh 8:15; Song 1:17; Isa 41:19, 44:14; Hos 4:13; Ps 45:9
Reeds: Exod 2:3
Flowers and Plants: Song 2:1
Parts of Trees and Plants: Gen 1:11; Lev 23:40; Isa 11:1

II. The Human Order

Human: Lev 21:13–14
Human Anatomy: Lev 13; Song 4:1–5
Disease, Mortality, and Disability: Lev 13, 21:18–21, 26:16; Num 5:2; Deut 15:21
Disabilities: Exod 4:11; Lev 19:14; Deut 23:1, 28:28; 2 Sam 5:8
Food and Spices: Deut 8:8; 2 Sam 17:27–29; 2 Kgs 4:39, 18:31–32; Mic 6:15; Song 1:10–14, 6:11
Grains: Exod 9:31; Ezek 4:9
Grain: Baked Goods/Dough/Leaven: Lev 23:17; Isa 28:24–29
Vine, Wine, Grapes (includes Strong Drink): Gen 49:11–12; Prov 23:30–31; Isa 5:1–4, 16:10; Jer 2:21, 48:32–33; Mic 7:1
Dairy: Judg 5:26
Fruits: Num 13:23; Joel 1:12
Vegetables: Num 11:5
Herbs and Spices: Gen 37:25; Exod 30:23–25
Jewelry: Num 31:50; Isa 3:18–23
Fabric: Esth 1:6

III. The Social Order

Immediate Family: Lev 18:6–18
Worship/Cultic: 1 Kgs 7
Ark of the Covenant: Exod 25:10–22
Menorah/Lampstand: Exod 25:31–39
Garb (Priestly): Exod 28:4, 28:39
Accoutrements: 1 Kgs 7:41–45, 7:48–50
Vow: Num 30:5
Idolatry: Lev 26:1
Divination: Exod 28:30; Deut 18:10; 1 Sam 28:3
Law and Covenant: Gen 20:5, 31:36; Exod 23:6–7; Lev 5:1, 19:15; Deut 16:18–20, 19:15–19, 25:1–2; 1 Sam 24:15; 2 Sam 15:4
Professions and Occupations: 1 Sam 8:13
Merchants/Business/Banking: Isa 23:8

Military: Num 31:14; 1 Sam 17:4–7; 1 Chr 14:7–8; Jer 51:20–21
Vehicles, Horses, and Travel: 1 Kgs 7:33; 1 Sam 8:11
Spoils, Plunder, Booty: Num 31:10–12
Maritime: Ezek 27:4–9, 27:25–30; Jonah 1:4–6
Music: Gen 4:21; Exod 15:20; 1 Sam 10:5, 18:6; 2 Sam 6:5; 1 Kgs 1:39–41; 1 Chr 16:5, 25:1; Pss 33:2, 68:24–25, 81:2–3, 150:3–5; Isa 5:12, 24:8; Amos 5:23, 6:5
Writing Tools and Implements: Jer 36:18; 36:23

IV. The Constructed Order

Buildings and Structures: 1 Kgs 6:3–6, 7:1–22; Ezek 13:14
Containers and Implements: Judg 6:19
Pottery: Lev 11:33–35
Artisanal Tools: 1 Kgs 6:7; Isa 44:12–13; Judg 5:26
Agricultural Tools: 1 Sam 13:20–21
Dry Measurement: Ezek 45:11

HEBREW WORD INDEX

אָב 92
אָב/אָבִיב 45
אֹבֵד 74
אֲבַדּוֹן 35
אֹבְדָן/אָבְדָן 74
אֵבֶה 57
אַבּוּס 49
אֵבוֹת 134
אִבְחָה 109
אֲבַטִּיחַ 80
אָבִיב 77
אֶבְיוֹן 102
אֲבִיוֹנָה 80
אַבִּיר 50
אָבַל 48, 103
אֶבֶן 33, 38, 74, 109, 142
אֶבֶן הַבְּדִיל 37
אֶבֶן הָרֹאשָׁה 128
אֶבֶן יְקָרָה 38
מַעֲמָסָה אֶבֶן 31, 38
אֶבֶן מַשְׂכִּית 97
אֶבֶן פִּנָּתָה 128
אַבְנֵט 85, 95
אֲבָנִים 71, 131
אָבַק 29
אֲבָקָה 88
אֶבְרָה 49
אֶבְרָה 46
אַגָּדָה 28, 64, 136
אָגוֹז 80
אֲגוֹרָה 142
אֶגְלֵי־טָל 34
אֲגַם 34, 112
אַגְמוֹן 57, 136
אַגָּן 132
אֲגַף/אַגָּפִים 112
אַגַּרְטָל 132
אֶגֶרֶת 120
אָדוֹם/אֹדֶם 41
אָדוֹן 64, 103
אדם 64
אָדָם 64
אֹדֶם 39
אֲדַמְדַּם 41
אֲדָמָה 29, 134
אֶדֶן 130
אֵדֶר 45
אֲדַרְכּוֹן/דַּרְכְּמוֹן 142
אַדֶּרֶת 85
אֹהֶל 126
אֹהֶל הָעֵדוּת 94
אֹהֶל־מוֹעֵד 94
אֲהָלוֹת/אֲהָלִים 71, 82, 83
אוֹב 97
אוּבָל 35
אוּל 67
אוּלָם/אֵילָם 130
אוֹפֶן 111
אוֹפַן עֲגָלָה 138
אוֹצָר 113, 125
אוֹר 28
אוּר 32, 36
אוּרִים 97
אוֹת 112
אַזּוּב 58, 71
אֵזוֹר 85
אַזְכָּרָה 96
אֹזֶן/אוֹזֶן/אָזְנַיִם 65
אֲזוּקִים 114, 136
אֶזְרָח 64
אֵת 92, 133
אַח 52
אָחוּ 57
אָחוֹר 36, 65
אֲחוֹת 92
אִחְלָמָה 39
אֲחַשְׁדַּרְפְּנִים 103
אֵטֶד 58
אֵטוּן 87
אִטִּים 97
אִי 29, 52
אַיִב 107
אֵיהָ 47
אֵיל 52
אַיִל 126
אֵיל הַמִּלָּאִים 48
אַיֶּלֶת אֵיֶלֶת/ 52
אֵיפָה 77, 135, 140
אִישׁ 62, 92
אִישׁ הַבְּנִים 108
אִישׁ רִיב 100
אִישׁ רִיבִי 100
אִישׁוֹן 65
אֵיתָנִים 45
אֲכִילָה 76
אֹכֶל 76
אָכְלָה 76
אֹכֶר 106
אֶלְגָּבִישׁ 33
אֵלָה 100
אֹלָה 100
אָלָה/אַלָּה 56
אֵלוּל 45
אֵלוֹן/אֵלּוֹן 56
אַלּוּף 63
אֶלוּף/אֶלֶף 48
אַלִּיָּה 48
אֲלִיל 97
אֵלֶם 73
אֲלֻמִּים/אֲלֻגּוּמִים 56
אַלְמָנָה 93
אַלְמָנוֹת 113
אַלְמָנוּת 93
אֶלֶף 64
אַם 92
אַמָּה 64
אַמָּה 141
אָמָה 64
אָמוֹן 64
אֲמוֹת 126
אָמִיר 30, 59
אָמֵן/אָמוֹן 105
אֹמְנוֹת 130
אֹמֶץ 41
אֵמֶר 52
אֶמֶשׁ 43
אִמְתִּחַת 134
אֲנוֹשׁ 62
אַנְחָה 75
אֲנִי 115
אֲנִי־שִׁיט 115
אֲנִיָּה 75
אֳנִיָּה 115
אֳנִיּוֹת אֵבֶה 115
אֳנִיּוֹת תַּרְשִׁישׁ 115
אֶנֶךְ 37
אֲנָפָה 47
אֲנָקָה 53
אַנְשֵׁי אֳנִיּוֹת 115
אָסוּף 133, 134
אֵסוּר 114, 136
אַסִּיר/אָסִיר 114
אֹסֶם 125
אָסָף 125

אֲסִפְסָף 64
אֵסֶר 96
אַף 65
אַפֹּד/אֵפוֹד 95
אַפְדָּן 126
אֹפֶה 106
אֲפוֹא/אֵפוֹ 44
אָפִיק 35
אֹפֶן 44
אֲפָסִים 70
אֶפְעֶה 53
אֲפִקֵי יָם 34
אֵפֶר 32
אֲפַר 71, 85
אָפְרֹחַ 46
אַפְרִיוֹן 111
אֶצְבַּע 66, 70, 141
אַצִּיל 66
אָצִיל 104
אֲצִילוֹת יָד 67
אֲצִילֵי יָד 67
אֶצְעָדָה 87
אֶקְדָּח 38
אַקּוֹ 49
אֲרִאֵל/אֲרִיאֵל 108
אַרְבֶּה 127
אַרְבֶּה 54
אַרְבַּע כַּנְפוֹת הָאָרֶץ 28
אַרְבָּעָה רָאשִׁים 34
אַרְבֹּת הַשָּׁמַיִם 28
אֶרֶג 137
אֹרֶג 105
אַרְגָּוָן/אַרְגָּמָן 42
אַרְגֵּז 132
אַרְוָה 49
אָרוֹן 74, 94, 132
אֶרֶז 56
אֹרַח 111, 113
אָרְחָה 76
אָרִי 52
אֲרִיאֵל 94, 134
אַרְיֵה 52
אֹרֶךְ 141
אָרֵךְ 141
אַרְמוֹן 112, 124
אֹרֶן 56
אַרְנֶבֶת 53
אֶרֶץ 29, 134
אֶרֶץ תַּחְתִּיּוֹת/אֶרֶץ תַּחְתִּית/
אֶרֶץ תַּחְתִּיּוֹת 35
אֹרֶר 100
אֹרֶת 82
אֵשׁ 32, 34
אֶשֶׁד 30
אֲשֵׁדָה 35
אִשְׁדֹּת 30
אִשָּׁה 62
אֶשּׁוּן 43
אִשִּׁיָּה 113
אִשִּׁשָׁה 79
אֶשֶׁף 69
אֶשְׁכּוֹל 79
אֵשֶׁל 56
אֶשֶׁם 96
אַשְׁמוּרָה 43
אַשְׁמֹרֶת הַבֹּקֶר 43
אַשְׁמֹרֶת הַתִּיכוֹנָה 43
אֶשְׁנָב 127
אֹשֶׁף 97, 104
אִשְׁפָּה 110
אֶשְׁפָּר 81
אֲשֻׁרִים/תַּאֲשׁוּר 56
אֲשֵׁרָה 97
אִשָּׁה/אִשֶּׁה 92
אֵת 138
אָתוֹן 51
אֶתְמוֹל/תְּמוֹל 43

בָּאִים בַּיָּמִים 63
בּוֹר/בֹּאר/
בְּאֵר/בֵּיר 33, 34, 40, 130
בָּאְשָׁה 57
בְּאֵשִׁים 81
בָּבָה 65
בֶּגֶד 84, 96
בֶּגֶד עֹדִים 84
בִּגְדֵי אַלְמָנוּת 84
בִּגְדֵי-אֵבֶל 75
בַּד 87, 94
בְּדִיל 37
בְּדַל-אֹזֶן 65
בְּדֹלַח 40, 58
בֶּהָט 39
בְּהֵמָה 46, 48
בְּהֵמוֹת 51
בֹּהֶן 67, 70
בּוּל 45
בּוֹלֵס 106
בּוּץ 88
בּוֹקֵר 106
בּוֹר 33, 35, 125
בּוֹר שָׁאוֹן 35
בּוֹר תַּחְתִּיּוֹת 35
בֹּז 107, 113
בֻּזָּה 113
בָּזָק 32
בָּחוֹן 38, 105
בָּחוּר 63
בְּחוּרוֹת/בְּחוּרִים 63
בַּחֵן/בַּחוּן 113
בֹּחֶן 38
בָּטֶן 67
בֵּיצָה 46, 53
בִּירָה 112, 124, 125
בַּיִת 87, 124, 128
בֵּית הָאוֹצָר 125
בֵּית הָאֲסִירִים 25
בֵּית הַכִּפֻּרֶת 94
בֵּית הַפְּקֻדֹּת 125
בֵּית קְבָרוֹת 74
בֵּית כְּלִי 113
בֵּית מִדְרָשׁ 120
בֵּית־אָב 93
בֵּית־הַמֶּלֶךְ 124
בִּיתָן 124
בֹּכֶא 56
בְּכוֹר 62, 92
בְּכוֹרָה 62
בִּכּוּרָה/בִּכֻּרָה 81
בִּכּוּרִים 77
בְּכִירָה 92
בְּכִית 75
בֹּכֶר 51
בְּכֹרָה 92
בִּכְרָה 51
בְּלוּץ 84
בְּלִיל 76, 77
בָּמָה 97, 141
בָּמוֹת 68
בֵּן 92
בֶּן-אָח 92
בֶּן-דֹּד 92
בֶּן־קֶשֶׁת 110
אַשְׁפַּת בְּנֵי 110
בִּגְיָה 124
בִּגְיָן 124
בֹּסֶר 79
בְּעִיר 48
בַּעַל 92
בַּעֲלָה 62
בֹּץ 29
בְּצָה 34
בָּצִיר 79
בְּצָל 71, 81
בְּצַק 78
בְּצָרָה 49
בְּצָרוֹן 112
בַּצֶּרֶת 33
בַּקְבֻּק 133
בֶּקֶע 141
בִּקְעָה 31
בָּקָר 43
בְּקָר 48
בַּר 77, 92
בֹּר 83

בְּרַבִּרִים 46
בְּרַד 33
בָּרַד 42
בְּרוּת 76
בְּרוֹת/בְּרוֹשׁ 56
בַּרְזֶל 37
בִּרְיָה 76
בְּרִיחַ 27
בְּרִית 100
בְּרִית 40
בֶּרֶךְ 100
בֶּרֶךְ/בִּרְכַּיִם 69
בִּרְכָּה 33, 130
בְּרֹמִים 88
בֹּרֶק 32, 109
בַּרְקָנִים 58
בָּרְקַת 39
בֹּשֶׂם/בֻּשֶׂם/בֹּשֶׂם 72, 82, 83, 88
בָּשָׂר 69, 70
בְּשַׂר עָרְוָה 69
בַּת 92, 140
בַּת־הַיַּעֲנָה 47
בַּתָּה 35
בְּתוּל 63
בְּתוּלָה 63
בְּתֵי הַנֶּפֶשׁ 88
בִּתְרוֹן 43

גֹּאֵל 93
גאל 101
גֹּאֵל הַדָּם 100
גְּאֻלָּה 101
גֵּב 65, 111, 128
גָּב 128
גַּב/גָּבָא 33, 130
גָּבֹהַּ 141
גְּבוּל 127
גִּבּוֹר 108
גְּבוּרָה 107
גִּבֵּחַ/גַּבַּחַת 65
גִּבִּי 54
גְּבִינָה 80
גְּבִיעַ 95, 132
גְּבִיר 103
גְּבִירָה 103
גָּבִישׁ 39
גִּבֵּן 73
גַּבְנֻנִּים 30
גִּבְעָה 30
גֶּבֶר 62
גָּג 128
גַּד 72, 82
גְּדוּד 30, 108, 112
גִּדִּי 49
גְּדִיָּה/גְּדָיָה 35
גְּדִישׁ 74, 77
גְּדֵלִים 85
גדר 127
גֶּדֶר 80
גֶּדֶר/גְּדֵרָה/גְּדֵרֹת 130
גִּדְרַת צֹאן 49
גֹּו/גַּו/גָּוָה 68
גּוֹזָל 46
גּוֹי 64
גְּוִיָּה 70
גּוֹלָה 114
גּוּפָה 70
גּוֹר/גּוּר 52
גּוֹרָל 97
גִּזְבָּר 104
גִּזִּית 38, 129
גֵּזֶל 113
גְּזֵלָה 113
גֵּזֶם 54
גֵּזַע 59
גִּזְרָה 65
גָּחוֹן 67
גַּחֶלֶת 32
גֵּיא 31, 35
גִּיד 70
גַּל 34
גֹּלֶב 105
גַּלְגַּל/גִּלְגָּל 32, 57
גֻּלְגֹּלֶת 65
גָּלֶד 70
גַּלָּה 132
גָּלוּל 97
גָּלוּם 84
גָּלוּת 114
גִּלְיוֹן 89, 120
גְּלִילִים 127
גֹּלֶם 67
גֻּמָּא 57
גֻּמְּדִים 108
גֹּמֶד 141
גָּמוּל 62
גָּמָל 51
גֹּמֶל 62
גַּן 60
גַּנָּה/גִּנָּה 60
גָּנָז 125, 131
גַּנְזַךְ 125
גַּף 70
גֹּפֶן 78
גֹּפֶן סְדֹם 57
גֹּפֶר 56
גְּפֻרִית 38
גֵּר 129
גַּר 64
גָּרֵב 71
גַּרְגְּרוֹת 66
גַּרְגְּרִים 81
גָּרָה 141
גָּרוֹן 66
גַּרְזֶן 138
גֶּרֶם 67
גֹּרֶן 60, 78, 138
גֶּרֶשׁ 77
גֹּשֶׁם/גֶּשֶׁם 33
גַּת 80
גִּתִּית 117

דְּאָה/רְאָה 47
דֹּב 51
דְּבוֹרָה 54
דְּבִיר 94, 125, 130
דְּבֵלָה 81
דְּבֶלֶת תְּאֵנִים 72
דֶּבֶק 109
דֹּבֶר 50
דָּבָר 100
דִּבְרוֹת 115
דֶּבֶשׁ 82
דָּג/דָּגָה 54
דֶּגֶל 112
דָּגָן 77
דֹּד 66
דַּדִּים 66
דַּדָּג/דַּיָּג 106
דּוּד 133, 135
דּוֹד 92
דּוּדָאִים 72, 82
דּוֹדָה 92
דּוּה 69
דּוּכִיפַת 47
דּוֹר 43, 64, 126
דֹּחַן 77
דַּיָּה 47
דָּיוֹ 120
דַּיָּן 101, 104
דִּין 101
דָּיַק 113
דַּיִשׁ 45, 60, 78
דִּישׁוֹן 51
דַּכָּא 29
דַּל/דַּלָּה 102
דַּל שְׂפָתַיִם 65
דֹּלָה 65
דְּלִי 133
דְּלִית 60
דֶּלֶת 120, 126
דַּלְתַּיִם 28
דָּם 66
דַּם־עֲנָבִים/דַּם־עֵנָב 79
דֹּמֶן 68

דִּמְעָה 65
דְּמָשֶׁק 88
דַּעַת 120
דֹּק 129
דִּר 39
דְּרָכָן 50
דַּרְדַּר 58
דָּרוֹם 36
דְּרוֹר 47, 101
דֶּרֶךְ 111
דֶּשֶׁא 57
דָּת 100

הַבְהָב 96
הָבְנִים/הוֹבְנִים/הָבְנִי 56
הָדֹם 104, 131
הָדַס 56, 72
הַוּוֹת 33
הוָה 95
הַיְדֵד 107
הֵיכָל 94, 124, 125
הֵילֵל 28
הִין 140
הֹפֶל 28
הֶלֶךְ 111
הַלְמוּת 137
הַר 30
הַרְמוֹן 124
הָרָר 30

וָלָד 63

זְאֵב 52
זָב 74
זְבוּב 54
זֶבַח 96
זָג 79
זָהָב 37
מִכְלוֹת זָהָב 37
זוּ 45
זוּלַת 130
זִיז 66
זַיִת 72
זָכָר 62
זֵלֶל 59
זְמוֹרָה 78
זָמִיר 59, 117
זָמָן 44
זָמָר 49
זִמְרָה 117
זֹנָה 106
זְנוּת/זָנוּן/תִּזְנוּת 97
זַעַם 66
זִעַם 100
זָפֶת 129

זָק 110, 136
זָקָן 65
זָקֵן 62, 63
זָקָן 63
זָקָן מְאֹד 63
זִקְנָה 63
זְקָנִים 63
זָר 94, 129
זָר 64, 98
זְרוֹעַ 67
זְרוּעַ 81
זַרְזִיף 33
זִרְזִיר 46
זִרְמָה 69
זֹרַע 106
זֶרַע 77
זֶרֶת 141

חֹב 84
חַבּוּרָה 73
חֶבֶל 115
חֶבֶל 55, 115, 140
חֹבֵל 115
חֶבֶל הַיָּם 29
חֲבַצֶּלֶת 57
חָבֵר 63
חָבָר 97
חֹבֵר 97
חַג 44, 99
חַג הָאָסִף 44, 99
חַג הַמַּצּוֹת 44, 99
חַג סֻכּוֹת 44, 99
חַג שָׁבֻעוֹת 44, 99
חָגָב 54
חָגוֹר 85
חֲגוֹרָה 85
חֶדֶל 29
חֵדֶק 58
חָדָר 128
חֶדֶר בְּחֶדֶר 128
חֲדַר הַמִּטּוֹת 128
חֲדַר הַפְּגָרִים 128
חֲדַר מִשְׁכָּב 129
חַדְרֵי־בֶטֶן 67
חֹדֶשׁ 44, 99
חוּג הָאָרֶץ 28
שָׁמַיִם חוּג 28
חָוָה 124, 126
חוֹחַ 29, 58, 87
חוּט 136, 140
חוֹל 29
חוּם 41
חוֹמָה 112, 127
חוֹמוֹת 115
חוֹמֶר 140

חוּץ 111, 127
חוֹר 41
חוּר 88
חוֹתָם 87, 137
חָזֶה 66
חָזוֹן 98
חָזוּת 98
חִזָּיוֹן 98
חֲזִיז 31, 32
חָזִיר 51
חָח 50, 87
חֵטְא 101
חַטָּא 101
חַטָּאָה 96, 101
חֲטָבוֹת 41
חִטָּה 77
חֹטֶר 59
חַי/חַיָּה 46
חַיִל 107, 124
חֵילָה 113
חַיִץ 127
חִיצוֹן 112
חִיק 67
חֵךְ 65
חִכָּה 55
חַכְלִילִי 42
חַכְלִלוּת 42
חָכָם 104, 120
חָכְמָה 120
חֹל 98
חֵלְאָה 38, 71
חֵלֶב 70
חֵלֶב 80
חֲלִבְנָה 72, 82
חֹלֶד 53
חֵלָה 78
חָלוֹם 98
חִלּוֹן 127
חָלוּף 102
חֲלִחְלָה 73
חָלִי 71
חֳלִי/חֳלִיָּה 86
חָלִיל 117
חֲלִילָה 98
חֲלִיצָה 113
חלל 117
חָלָל 74
חֲלָלִים 119
חַלְמוּת 80
חֲלָמִישׁ 31, 39
חֲלָצַיִם 68, 69
חָם 93
חֲמָאָה 80
חֲמָה 29
חָמוּץ 42

חֲמוֹר 51
חֲמוֹת 93
חֹמֶט 53
חָמִיץ 81
חָמֵץ 97
חָמֵשׁ 101
חָמַץ 78
חֹמֶץ 79
חֵמָר 129
חֹמֶר 29, 129, 134
חֶמֶר 79
חָמַשׁ 112
חֹמֶשׁ 67
חֲמֻת 134
חָנוּת 125
חָנִית 110
חֲנֻמָל 32
חֲנֻפָּה 98
חֲסִידָה 47
חָסִיל 54
חַפָּה 128
חֹפֶן 67
חַפַרפָּרָה 53
חֹפֶשׁ 88
חַפְשָׁה 101
חֵץ/חֵצִי 110
חֲצוֹצְרָה/חֲצֹצְרָה 118
חָצִיר 57, 81
חוֹצֵן 108
חָצֵץ 31, 39
חָצַר 124, 130
חֹק 100
חַקָּה 100
חֹקֵק 105
חַקַר תְּהוֹם 34
חֹר 41, 103
חָרְאִים 68
חָרֵב 109, 135
חָרְבָּה 31
חֲרֻבוֹן 29
חֲרֻבוֹת 110
חָרְגֹל 54
חָרוּז 40, 87
חָרוּל 58
חָרוּץ 37, 78, 112, 138
חָרֵט 137
חַרְטֹם 97, 104
חֹרִי 78
חָרִיט 134
חָרִיץ 78, 80
חָרִישׁ 45
חֵרֶם 55, 100, 107
חָרָם 73
חָרְמֵשׁ 138
חָרֵס 29
חַרְסוּת 134
חֹרֶף 45
חִרְצָב 73
חַרְצֻבָּה 114
חַרְצָן 79
חֲרָרִים 31
חֹרֶשׁ 56
חָרַשׁ 73
חָרֶשׁ 120, 134
חָרֹשׁ/חָרֶשׁ 105
חָשַׁב 85
חֹשֵׁב 105
חִשְׁבֹנוֹת 110
חַשְׁמַל 38
חַשְׁמֹן 102
חֹשֶׁן 95
חֹשֶׁק 111
חֹשֶׁר 111
חָשַׁשׁ 57
חִתּוּל 71
חֲתֻלָּה 85
חוֹתֶמֶת 87
חוֹתֵן 93
חָתָן 93
חתן 93
חֹתֶנֶת 93

טְבוּל 86
טַבּוּר 67
טַבּוּר הָאָרֶץ 28
טַבָּח 104
טֶבַח/טִבְחָה 74
טִבְחָה/טַבָּח 104
טַבְּעֹת 94
טַבַּעַת 87, 94
טֶבֶת 45
טָהוֹר 98
טָהוֹר זָהָב 37
טָהֳרָה 98
טוֹב 77
טוֹטָפוֹת 86
טוּר 129
טְחוֹן 39
טַחוֹת 68
טִיחַ 129
טִיט 30, 134
טִירָה 112, 124
טַל 34
טָלָא 42
טָלֶה 48
טָמֵא 98
טָמְאָה 98
טֶנֶא 135
טַף 62
טֹפַח 141
טִפְסָר 104, 107
טֶרֶף 76
טָרָף 60
טֶרֶף/טְרֵפָה 74

יְאֹר 35
יְבוּל 35
יְבוּל/יֶבֶל 34
יַבֶּלֶת 71
יָבֶם 93
יבם 93
יַבֶּשָׁה 29
יָד 111
יָד/יָדַיִם 67, 69
יָדִיד 63
יִדְעֵי הַיָּם 115
יִדְעֹנִי 97
יַהֲלֹם 39
יוֹבֵל 48, 118
יוּבָל/אוּבָל/יֻבָל 35
יוֹם 43
יוֹם הַכִּפֻּרִים 99
יוֹמָם 43
יָזֵן 30
יוֹנָה 46
יוֹנֵק 62
יוֹנֶקֶת 59
יוֹצֵר 105
יוֹרֶה 108
יַחְמוּר 52
יָחֵף 70
יַחַשׁ 93
יַיִן 79
יֵין הָרֶקַח 79
יַלְדָּה 63
יַלְדָה/יֶלֶד 63
יַלְדוּת 63
יָלִיד 64, 92
יַלֶּפֶת 71
יָלַק 54
יַלְקוּט 50, 135
יָם 34, 36, 96
יָמִין 67
בֵּית־קֹדֶשׁ הַקֳּדָשִׁים 94
יִמְתֹנֶם 69
יְנִיקָה 59
יֹנֵק 62
יְנֻשׁוּף 47
יַע 96
יָעֵל 49
יַעֲלָה 49
יָעַן 47
יַעַר 56, 82
יָפַח 101
יִצְהָר 81

יָצוּעַ 130
יָצִיעַ 128
יָקַב 80
יָקוּד 32, 134
יָקוּשׁ 55
יָרוֹק 57
יָרֵחַ 44
יָרֵחַ 29
יָרִיב 101, 107
יְרִיעָה 129
יָרַד 68, 69, 95
יָרַד/יְרָדִים 69
יָרַדְתִּי-אֶרֶץ 28
יָרַכְתֵּי-בוֹר 35
יֶרֶק 57, 81
יָרָק 42
יַרְקוֹן 41, 77
יַרְקְרַק 42
יַרְקְרַק חָרוּץ 37
יְשׁוּעָה 107
יְשִׁימוֹן 29, 31
יָשִׁישׁ 63
יָשָׁן 43
יִשְׁפֵּה 39
יָתֵד 126, 127, 138
יָתוֹם 62
יֶתֶר 44, 110, 136

כְּאֵב 73
כֹּבֶד 141
כָּבֵד 68
כָּבֵל 114, 136
כֶּבֶר 43
כִּבְרָה 141
כִּבְרָה 138
כֶּבֶשׂ 48, 131
כִּבְשָׁה 48
כִּבְשָׁן 38, 134
כַּד 133
כִּדְכֹּד 39
כֵּהָה 41
כֹּהֵן 95
כְּהֻנָּה 95
כּוֹכָב 28
כּוּמָז 87
כּוּן 78
כִּוּנִים 97
כּוֹס 47, 132
כּוּר 38, 133
כּוֹשׁ 53
כָּחֵל 42
כֹּחֵל 88
כִּידוֹד 32
כִּידוֹן 110
כִּיוֹן 133

כִּיּוּן 28, 197
כִּיּוֹר 130, 132
כֵּילַף 138
כִּימָה 28
כִּיס 132, 142
כִּיר 134
כִּיר/כִּיּוֹר 96
כִּירַיִם 133
כִּכָּר 142
כֶּלֶא 125
כֶּלֶב 52, 106
כַּלְבֵי צָאן 52
כַּלָּה 93
כְּלוּב 95, 135
כְּלוּלֹת 93
כְּלִי 132, 136
כְּלֵי הַבָּקָר 50
כְּלֵי הָרֹעִים 50
כְּלִי יוֹצֵר 134
כְּלֵי-גֹמֶא 115
כְּלִיא 125
כִּלְיָה 68
כַּמּוֹן 72, 82
כֵּן 115
כֵּן/כִּנֵּם 54
כִּנּוֹר 118
כָּנָף 85
כְּנֹת 64
כֶּסֶא 29, 44
כִּסֵּא 104, 131
כְּסוּת 84
כְּסִיל 28
כֶּסֶל/כְּסָלִים 68
כִּסְלָו 45
כַּסְמֹת 72, 77, 82
כֶּסֶף 37, 105, 142
כֶּסֶת 85
כַּף 67, 94, 133
כָּף 31, 39
כַּף/כַּפַּיִם 70
כַּף הַיָּרֵךְ 68
כִּפָּה 59
כְּפוֹר 35, 132
כַּפּוֹת הַמַּנְעוּל 127
כְּפִיס 129
כְּפִיר 52
כֶּפֶן 73
כְּפָרִים 98
כֹּפֶר 58, 82, 89, 101, 115
כִּפֹּרֶת 94
כַּפְתּוֹר 130
כְּקָדָה 95
כַּר 49, 110
כֹּר 140
כַּר הַגֶּמֶל 50

כְּרוּב/כְּרֻבִים 94
כְּרוּת שָׁפָכָה 74
כַּרְכֹּב 94
כַּרְכֹּם 72, 82, 89
כִּרְכָּרָה 51
כֶּרֶם 60, 80
כַּרְמִיל 42
כַּרְמֶל 60, 77
כְּרַע 69
כַּרְפַּס 88
כְּרַשׁ 67
כַּשִּׁיל 138
כַּשָּׁף 98
כְּתָב 120
כֹּתֶל 112, 127
כֶּתֶם 37
כֻּתֹּנֶת 85, 95
כְּתַף 66
כֶּתֶף 30
כֶּתֶר 86, 104
כֹּתֶרֶת 130

לְאֹם 64
לֵב/לֵבָב 66
לֶבֶא 52
לְבִאוֹת 52
לְבִבוֹת/לְבִיבֹת 78
לְבוּשׁ 84
לְבִיא 52
לְבִיָּה 52
לְבָן 41
לֶבֶן 41
אֲדַמְדָּם לָבָן 41
לְבוֹנָה/לְבֹנָה 83
לְבֹנָה 129
לְבָנָה 29
לִבְנָה 56
לְבֵנִים 94
לַהַב 32, 42
לֶהָבָה 110
לוּג 140
לוּז 105
לוּז 80
לוּחַ 115, 120, 129
לוּיָה 86
לוּיָתָן 53
לוּלִים 127
לְחוּם 70
לְחִי/לְחָיַיִם 65
לֶחֶם 107
לֶחֶם 76, 78
לְחָשִׁים 86
לֵט 72, 89
לְטָאָה 53
לִטְשׁ 137

מַחְסוֹם 50
מַחְסוֹר 102
מָחוֹקֵק 104
מָחָר 43
מַחֲרֵשָׁה 138
מַחְתָּה 96, 133
מִטְאֲטָא 136
מִטָּה 59, 104, 110
מִטָּה 74, 130
מַטְוֶה 88
בַּרְזֶל מִטִּיל 37
מַטְמוֹן 125
מַטָּע 60
מִטְפַּחַת 85
מֶטֶר/מָטָר 33
מַטָּרָה 125
מִיכָל 35
מַיִם 33, 76
מִישׁוֹל 101
מִישׁוֹר 31
מֵיתָר 110, 126, 136
מְכַבֵּס 105
מִכְבָּר 94
מַכָּה 73
מָכוֹן 128
מְכוֹנָה 96
מִכְלָא 49
מַכְלֹל 85
מַבֹּלֶת 76
מִכְמָר/מִכְמֹר 55
מִכְמֶרֶת 55
מִכְנָסַיִם 84, 95
מֶכֶס 113
מַכָּר 64, 95, 105
מְכַרְכֵּר 119
מְכַרָּה 71, 99, 108
מִכְשׁוֹף 98
מִכְתָּב 120, 137
מִכְתָּם 137
מַכְתֵּשׁ 139
מַלְבּוּשׁ 84
מַלְבֵּן 129
מִלּוּא 112
מִלּוּחַ 57, 58
מְלוֹן אֹרְחִים 124
מְלוּנָה 49
מֶלַח 82, 84
מֶלַח 115
מִלְחָה 31, 40
מִלְחָמָה 107, 118
מְלִילוֹת 77
מֶלֶךְ 103
מְלֻכָּדֶת 55
מַלְכָּה 103
מַלְכֶּת 64
מוֹט 94
מוֹטָה 50
מוּךְ 102
מוֹכֶר 105
מוּל 99
מוֹלֶדֶת 93
מוּלָה 99
מוּם 73
מוֹסָד 128
מוֹסְדֵי הָרִים 30
מוּסָר 120
מוֹסָר 50, 114, 136
מוֹעֵד 44
מוֹצָא 36
מוֹקֵד 32
מוֹקְדָה 94, 134
מוֹקֵשׁ 55
מוֹרָג 78, 138
מוֹרָד 30
מוֹרָה 33, 108, 120
מוֹרָה 137
מוֹשָׁב 131
מָעֻת 74
מִזְבֵּחַ 94
מֶזֶג 79
מָזֶה 71
מְזוּזָה 126
מְזָוִים 126
מָזוֹן 76
מָזוֹר 55, 71, 73
מַזַּח 85
מַזְכִּיר 101, 104
מִזְלָג 96, 135
מַזָּלוֹת 28
מִזְמוֹר 117
מִזְמֶרָה 135, 138
מִזְמֹרוֹת 96
מִזְקָק זָהָב 37
מִזְרָח 36, 37
מִזְרָה 78, 138
מִזְרוֹת 28
מִזְרָק 132
מַח 67
מַחֲבַת 133
מְחוּגָה 137
מָחוֹל 119
מַחֲזֶה 98
מֶחֱזֶה 127
מַחִים 49
מַחֲלָה 71
מַחֲלָיִים 71
מַחֲלָפִים 132, 135
מַחֲלָצוֹת 84
מַחֲנֶה 112
מַחֲנָק 74
לַיְלָה/לֵיל 43
לִילִית 47
לַיִשׁ 52
לַלָּאָה 136
לִמֻּד 120
לַע 66
לְעָנָה 57, 72
לָפִיד 131
לָקַח 120
לָשַׁד 78
לָשׁוֹן 65
לִשְׁכָּה 128
לֶשֶׁם 39
לָתַךְ 140

מַאֲבֵס 126
מְאוֹר 131
מֹאזְנַיִם 142
מַאֲכָל 76
מַאֲכֶלֶת 135
מַאֲמַר 100
מָבוֹא 36, 43
מְבוּל 34
מְבוּעַ 34
מְבוּשִׁים 69
מִבְחֵי נְהָרוֹת 34
מִבְנֶה 124
מִבְצָר 112, 124
מָבֵשׁ 69
מְבַשְּׁלוֹת 128
מִגְבָּעָה 86, 95
מִגְדָּל 113, 124
מְגוּרָה 126
מַגְזֵרָה 138
מִגֵּל 138
מְגִלָּה 120
מְגִלַּת־סֵפֶר 120
מָגֵן 109
מַגֵּפָה 107
מִגְרָה 138
מִגְרָעוֹת 127
מַד 84, 95, 131, 140
מִדְבָּר 31, 50, 65
מִדָּה 140
מִדְלָכָה 139
מַדְמֵנָה 68
מִדָּע 120
מֹדָע/מֹדַעַת 92
מֹדָע/מוֹדָע 64
מַדְקֵרָה 73
מַדְרֵגָה 30
מִדְרָשׁ 120
מַהְפֶּכֶת 136
מֹהַר 93
מוֹדִיעִים 120

מִלֶּכֶת 97
מלל 99
מִלְמֹד 50
מִלְמֹד 120
מֶלֶצַר 104
מִלְקוֹחַ 114
מַלְקוֹחַיִם 65
מַלְקוֹשׁ 33
מָלְקָחַיִם 96
מַלְתָּחָה 84, 131
מַמְגֵרוֹת 126
מִמְסָךְ 79
מִמְשָׁל 103
מִמְתַּקִּים 79
מִן 58, 76
מִן 118
מַנְגִּינָה 117
מִנְגִּנָּה 117
מָנָה 141
מָנָה 76
מִנְחָה 96
מְנֻחָשׁ 98
מִנִּים 118
מְנֹרָה/מְנוֹרָה 95, 131
מֵסֶב 130, 131
מַסְגֵּר 104, 105, 106, 125
מִסְגֶּרֶת 112, 124
מַסֵּוָה 86
מָסָךְ 129
מָסָךְ 79
מַסֵּכָה 97
מִסְכָּן 81
מִסְכֵּן 102
מִסְכְּנוֹת 124
מִסְלָה 111
מַסְלוּל 111
מַסְמָר/מַשְׁמֹרוֹת 137
מַסָּע 31, 55, 110
מַסַּע 111
מִסְעָד 130
מִסְפֵּד 75
מִסְפּוֹא 76
מִסְפָּחָה/ מִסְפֹּחֶת 86
מִסְפָּר 74, 140
מְסֻגָּל 111
מַעֲדַנּוֹת 136
מַעְדֵּר 138
מָעָה 30
מַעֲה/מַעִים 67
מָעוֹג 73, 78, 126
מָעוֹז 112
מְעוֹז רֹאשׁ 109
מְעוֹנֵן 98
מַעֲטֶה 84
מַעֲטָפָת 85
מְעִיל 85, 95
מַעְיָן 34
מַעֲלָה 30
מַעֲלָה 127, 128
מַעֲמַקֵּי־יָם 34
מַעֲנֶה 29
מַעֲצָד 96, 135, 138
מַעֲקֶה 112, 129
מַעַר 69
מַעֲרָב 36, 116
מְעָרָה 31
מַעֲרָכָה 112
מַפַּח 38
מַפָּח 74
מַפָּץ 109
מִפְרָץ 33
מַפְרֶקֶת 66
מִפְרָשׂ 115
מִפְשָׁעָה 68
מַפְתֵּחַ 127
מִפְתָּן 126
מָצָב 113
מַצָּבָה 112
מַצֵּבָה 38
מַצֵּבָה 97
מָצָד 112, 125
מַצָּה 78
מָצוֹד 55, 113
מְצוּדָה 100
מָצוּק/מִצָּק 130
מָצוֹר 107, 125
מָצוֹר/מְצוּרָה 113
מְצוּרָה 113
מַצּוּ 65
מִצְחָת 86
מִצְלָה 118
מְצֻלּוֹת יָם 34
מְצֻלָּתַיִם/מְצִלּוֹת 118
מִצְנֶפֶת 86, 95
מַצָּע 130
מִצְפֶּה 113
מִצְרָף 38, 105, 132
מַקֶּבֶת 31, 137
מִקְדָּשׁ 125
מַקְהֵל 64, 99
מִקְוֶה/מִקְוָה 130
מָקוֹר 34
מִקְטָר 94, 128
מַקְטֵר 83
מִקְטֶרֶת 96
מַקֵּל 50, 69, 104
מִקַּל יָד 109
מִקְנָה 48
מִקְנָה 105
מִקְסָם 98
מִקְצָעָה 137
מִקְרָא 99
מִקְרָה 129
מִקְשָׁה 60, 81, 82, 137
מֹר 72, 82, 83
מַרְאָה 89
מַרְאָה/מַרְאֶה 98
מַרְבֶּה 49
מַרְבִּץ 49
מַרְגְּלוֹת 69
מַרְגֵּמָה 110
מְרוֹחַ אֶשֶׁךְ 74
מָרוֹם 141
מְרוּקִים 42, 88
מַרְזֵחַ 76
מֶרְחֶשֶׁת 133
מְרִיא 48
מְרִיב 101
מֶרְכָּב 131
מֶרְכָּבָה 111
מִרְעֶה 50, 57
מַרְעִית 50
מִרְצַע 137
מֶרְקָחָה 82
מֹר 72, 82
מְרֹרָה 68
מַשָּׂא 98
מִשְׁבְּצָה 38
מַשְׁבֵּר 67
מִשְׁבָּר 34
מִשְׁגָּב 112
מִשְׁגֶּה 74, 125
מְשׁוֹט/מַשּׁוֹט 115
מְשׁוּכָה/מְסוּכָה 58
מַשּׂוֹר 138
מִשְׁחָה 95, 96
מִשְׁחָר 43
מֶשִׁי 88
מֶשֶׁךְ 135
מֹשַׁךְ הַזֶּרַע 106
מִשְׁכָּב 130
מִשְׁכּוֹת 136
מַשְׁכִּים 69
מַשְׁכִּית 97
מִשְׁכָּן 94, 126
מִשְׁמָן 70
מִשְׁמָר 108
מִשְׁמֶרֶת 95
מִשְׁסָה 114
מִשְׁעוֹל 80, 111
מִשְׁעֶנֶת 50, 104
מִשְׁפָּחָה 93
מִשְׁפָּט 100
מִשְׁפְּתַיִם 135
מֶשֶׁק 109

נְשָׁמָה 66
נֶשֶׁף 43
נָשַׁק/נֶשֶׁק 109, 113
נֶשֶׁק 89
נָשַׁר 48
נִשְׁתְּוָן 120
נְתוּגִים 95
נָתִיב 111
נָתָר 40

סְאָה 140
סְאוֹן 86, 109
סַאֵן 108
סֹבֶא 79
סְבַךְ 58
סְגוּר זָהָב 37
סְגוֹר לֵב 66
סָגֵן 107
סָגֵן 103
סְגֹר 109
סגר 127
סַגְרִיר/סַגְרִיד 33
סֵד 137
סָדִין 84, 85
סֹהַר 125
סִיג/סוּג 38
סוּגֵר 55
סוּס 50
סוּס/סִיס 47
סוּף 57
סוּפָה 32
סוּת 84
סֹחַר 105
סֹחֶרֶת 39
סִיוָן 45
סִיר 133
סִיר/סִירָה 58
סִיר דּוּגָה 55
סֻכָּה 126
סֹכֶךְ 109
סֶל/סַלְסִלּוֹת 135
סֶלָה 117
סְלוֹן 58
סְלִלָה 113
סֻלָּם 127
סֶלַע 31
סֶלְעָם 54
סֹלֶת 77
סַם 82, 83
סְמָדַר 80
סֵמֶל 97
סְנֶה 59
סַנְסִנָּה 59
סָס 54
סְעִיף 59

נְחַשְׁתַּיִם 136
נטה 101
נְטִיפָה 87
נְטִישָׁה 59
נָטָף 72, 83
נִיחוֹחַ 96
נִיסָן 45
נִיצוּץ 32
נִיר 30
נִיר/נֵר 131
נָכָא 73
נְכֹאת 72, 82, 83, 126
נָכַד (with נִין) 92
נְכָרִי 64
נְמוּל 99
נְמֻלָה 54
נָמֵר 51
נֵס 111, 112, 115
נֶסֶךְ 97
נִסְמָן 77
נְעוּרִים 63
נעל 127
נַעַל 86
נַעֲצוּץ 58
נַעַר 63
נַעַר 63
נַעַר קָטֹן 63
נַעֲרָה 63
נֶפֶה 138
נֹפֶךְ 39
נֶפֶץ 33
נֶפֶשׁ 62, 66
נֶפֶת 30
נֹפֶת 82
נֵץ 47, 60
נְצָה 60
נְצוּח 44
נֵצַח 66
נְצִיב 103, 107, 108, 113
נִצָּן 40
נֵצֶר 59
נקב 100
נְקֻבָה 62
נֹקֵד 106
נָקֹד 42
נָקִי 98
נֹקֶף 81
נִקְפָּה 136
נֶרֶד 72, 83, 89
נשא כֵלִים 108
נִשֶּׁה 105
נֶשֶׁה 68
נָשִׂיא 32, 103
נֶשֶׁךְ 105
נִשְׁכָּה 128

מִשְׁקָד 80
מִשְׁקָה 79, 104
מִשְׁקוֹל 141
מִשְׁקוֹף 126
מִשְׁקָל 141
מִשְׁקֹלֶת/מִשְׁקָלֶת 37
מִשְׁקָרוֹת 88
מִשְׂרָה 79
מַשְׂרַת 133
מִשְׁתֶּה 76
מַת 62
מֶתֶג 50
מְתוֹק 77
מִתְּכֹנֶת 140
מִתְּנָה 96
מָתְנַיִם 68

נאד 135
נָאָה 50
נְבוּאָה 98
נֶבַח 52
נִבְחַר חָרוּץ 37
נְבִיאָה/נְבִיא 95
נֵבֶךְ 34
נִבְכֵיהֶם 34
נֶבֶל/נֵבֶל 135
נְבֵלָה 46, 70
נַבְלוּת 69
נֶגֶב 36
נָגִיד 103, 107
נְגִינָה 118
נגן 118
נְגִנִים/נְגִינוֹת 117
נֶגַע 71
נְדָבָה 96
נִדָּה 98
נָדִיב 102, 103
נִדָּן 109
נֶדֶר 96
נַהֲלֹל 50
נְהָר 35
נַהֲרָה 43
נָוֶה 50
נָוֶה 31
נֹאַם 98
נוֹף 141
נָזִיד 76, 78, 95
נִזְלִים 34
נֵזֶם 87
נֵזֶר 86, 104
נְחוּשָׁה/נְחֹשֶׁת 37
נְחִילוֹת 117
נַחַל 35, 56
נַחַשׁ 98
נָחָשׁ 53

סְעַפָּה/סַרְעַפָּה 59
סַעַר/שַׂעַר/סְעָרָה 32
סַף 126, 128, 133
סְפִינָה 115
סָפִיר 40
סֶפֶל 133
סִפֵּן 129
סֹפֵר 104
סָפַר 121
סִפְרָה 121
סִפֹּרֶת 121
סָרְבִים 58
סָרָה 101
סָרָן 103, 107, 111
סִרְפַּד 58
סְתָיו 45

עָב 58, 126
עֶבֶד 64, 105
עֲבוּר 77
עֵבִי 140
עֶבְרָה 115
עֵבֶת 60, 136
עֻבֹּת/עֲבוֹת 50
עֹגָה 78
עָגוּר 46
עָגִיל 87
עֵגֶל 48
עֶגְלָה 111
עֶגְלָה 48
עֶגְלוֹת 109
עַד 114
עַד 101
עֵדָה 99
עֵדִי 86
עֵדֶר 49
עֲדָשִׁים 81
עֵדוּת 100
עוּגָב 117
עָוִיל 62
עוּל 62
עוֹלֵל 62
עוֹלָם 28, 44
עוֹף 46
עוֹר 70, 84, 88, 121
עוֹר 73
עַוְּתָה 101
עֹז 117
עֹז 28, 49
עִזְבוֹן 116
עִזּוּז 107
עֲזוּנִיָּה 48
עֹזֶר 108
עֲזָרָה 125
עַט 137
עָטִין 69
עָטַלֵּף 53
עֲטָרָה 86, 104
עִי 62
עִיט 46
עַיִן 34
עַיִן/עֵינַיִם 66
עִיר 51
עִיר 124
עִישׁ/עָשׁ 28
עִכְּבִישׁ 54
עִכְּבָר 53
עֶכֶס 87
עֹל 50
עָלָה 60
עָלָה 96
עֲלוּמִים 63
עֲלוּקָה 54
עֲלָטָה 43
עֲלִי 139
עֲלִיָּה 128
עֲלִיל 38, 132
עֲלֻלוֹת 80
עֹלָם 63
עַלְמָה 63
עֲלָמוֹת/עַלְמוּת 117
עִם 64, 107
עִמּוּד 130
עָמִיר 77
עָמִית 64
עֵמֶק 31
עֹמֶר 140
עֵנֶב 80
עֹנָה 117
עָנִי/עָנִו 102
עָנָן 32
עֲנַן בֹּקֶר 32
עֲנָנָה 32
עָנָף 59
עָנָף 59
עָנָק 87
עָסִיס 76, 79
עֹפֶל 71, 112
עַפְעַפַּיִם 66
עֵפֶר 30, 35, 134
עֹפֶר 52
עֹפֶרֶת 37
עֵץ 56
עֵץ הַדַּר 81
עֵץ שֶׁמֶן 56
עֶצֶב 134
עִצָּבוֹן 73
עַצֶּבֶת 73
עֶצָה 67
עֲצֵי בְרוֹשִׁים 118
עֶצֶם 67
עֹצֶם 70
עֹצֶר 125
עֲצֻרָה 99
עָקֵב 70
עָקֹב 29
עִקְּבֵי־סוּס 50
עֹקֶד 42
עֶקֶר 92
עֶקֶר/עֲקָרָה 73
עַקְרָב 54
עָר 107
עֶרֶב 43
עֵרֶב 47
עֵרֶב 116
עֶרֶב 88
עֶרֶב/עָרֶב 64
עֲרֻבָּה 31
עֲרָבִים 56, 72
עָרוֹב 54
עֲרוּגָה 60
עָרוֹד 51
עֶרְוָה 69
עֵרוּץ 35
עֲרִיסָה 78
עֲרִיפִים 28
עָרִיץ 56
עֵרֶל 99
עַרְלָה 69, 99
עַרְמוֹן 56
עַרְעָר 102
עֲרֹעֵר/עַרְעָר 56, 59
עֹרֶף 66
עֶרְפֶּל 32
עֶרֶשׂ 130
עָשׁ 54
עָשַׁב 57
עָשׁוֹר 118
עִשָּׂרוֹן 140
עֵת 44
עַתָּה 44
עַתּוּד 49, 103
עִתִּי 44
עֶתֶר 95

פֵּאָה 65
פְּאֵר 86, 95
פֹּאֲרָה 60
פָּארוּר 42
פְּאַת זָקָן 65
פְּאַת פָּנִים 66
פְּאַת רֹאשׁ 65
פֵּג 81
פִּגּוּל 98
פֶּגֶר 70

פֶּה 66
פּוּךְ 41, 88
פּוֹל 81
פּוּר 31, 39
פּוּרִים 44, 99
פּוּרָה 80
פָּז 37
פַּח 55
פַּחַד 69
פָּחָה 103
פַּחַת 55
פִּטְדָה 40
פָּטוּר 60
פִּטִּישׁ 137
פִּטְרָה/פֶּטֶר 62
פִּילֶגֶשׁ 64, 93
פִּים 141
פִּימָה 70
פַּךְ 134
שֶׁמֶן פַּךְ 104
פֶּלֶג/פְּלַגּוֹת 35
פִּלְדָה 88
פֶּלַח 39
פָּלִיל 101, 103
פְּלִילָה 101
פֶּלֶס 142
פִּגֵּג 76
פִּגָּה 128
פָּנִים 66
פְּנִינִים 40
פַּס 85
פֶּסַח 44, 99
פִּסֵּחַ 73
פָּסִיל 97
פֶּסֶל 97
פַּעַם 38, 70, 94
פַּעֲמוֹן/פַּעֲמֹנוֹן 95, 118
פַּעֲמֹת 130
פְּצוּעַ-דַּכָּא 74
פָּצַע 73
פְּקוּדִים 108
פִּקּוּדִים 100
פָּקִיד 105
פְּקָעִים 72, 81
פַּקֵּעוֹת 57
פַּר/פָּר 48
פֶּרֶא 51
פֶּרֶד 51
פִּרְדָּה 51
פִּרְדֵּס 60
פְּרֵדוֹת 81
פָּרָה 48
פַּרְוָר 124, 126
פְּרוּר 133
פָּרַז 103
פְּרִזּוֹן 102
פְּרָזוֹת 124
פֶּרַח 60, 95
פֶּרֶט 80
פְּרִי 81
פְּרִיץ 100
פְּרֹכֶת 129
פֶּרֶס 48
פַּרְסָה 46
פֶּרַע 65
פִּרְעֹה 104
פַּרְעֹשׁ 54
פָּרָשׁ 51, 108, 111
פָּרָשׁ 68
פַּרְתֻּמִּים 102
פִּשְׁתָּה 57, 77, 88, 131
פֹּת/פַּאָה/פַּאֲתַיִם 65
פִּתְאֹם/פִּתְאוֹם 44
פִּתְגָּם 100
פִּתּוֹת 127
פֶּתַח 126
פֶּתַח הַשַּׁעַר 126
פִּתְחָה 109
פִּתְיֶגֶל 84
פְּתִיל 136, 140
פֶּתֶן 53
פֶּתַע 44
פִּתְרוֹן 98

צֵאָה / צֹאָה 68
צָאֳלִים 58
צֵאת הַשָּׁנָה 44
צֵב 53, 111
צָבָא 107, 108
צְבוּעַ 42, 52
צְבִי/צְבִיָּה 51
צָבַע 88
צַד 70
צָדִיק 101
צְדָקָה 101
צָהֹב 42
צֹהַב 42
צֹהַל 42
צֹהַר 127
צֹהֳרַיִם 43
צוּ 100
צוּאר 66
צוּף 79, 82
צוּר 31, 39
צִוּרוֹן 87
צוֹרֵף 105
צֵחַ 29, 41
צְחִיחַ 41
צָחֹר 42
צָחֵר 41
צִי 115
צִי אַדִּיר 115
צַיִד 106
צֵידָה 76
צִיָּה 31
צִיּוֹן 31
צִיִּים 52
צִינֹק 137
צִיץ 60, 86, 95
צִיצִת 65, 85
צִיר 127
צִירִים 97
צלח 106
צְלוּחִית 133
צַלַּחַת 133
צְלִיל/צְלוּל 78
צֶלֶם 97
צַלְמָוֶת 74
צֶלַע 30, 67, 94, 128
צֹלָעָה 73
צְלָצַל 118
צִלְצַל דָּגִים 54
צִמְאוֹן 31
צֶמֶד 141
צֶמָה 59
צִמָּה 86
צְמוּק 80
צָמִיד 87, 132
צַמִּים 55
צֶמֶר 88
צַמֶּרֶת 60
צַן 58
צִנָּה 109
צֹנֶה/צֹאן 49
צִנּוֹר 130
צִנּוֹת 55
צִנִּינִים 58
צָנִיף 86, 95
צִנְצֶנֶת 133
צָעְדָה 87
צָעְדוֹת 87
צָעִיף 86
צְעִירָה 63
צָפוֹן 36
צִפּוֹר 47
צִפְחַת 134
צָפִיר/צְפִיר 49
צְפִירָה 86
צָפִית 44
צָפְנָה 36
צָפַע 53
צִפְצָפָה 56
צְפַרְדֵּעַ/צְפַדֵּעַ 53
צִפֹּרֶן 67
צִפֹּרֶן שָׁמִיר 137

צִקְלוֹן 135
צַר 107
צֹר/צַר 31, 39, 135
צַרֶבֶת 71
צָרָה 93
צָרוֹף 38, 105
צָרוֹר 31, 39, 50, 135
צָרִי 72, 83, 89
צְרִיחַ 74, 113, 125
צַרְעָה 54
צָרַעַת 71
צָרַף 38

קָאַת 47
קַב 140
קבב 100
קַבָּה 67, 68
קַבָּה 126
קִבּוּרָה 74
קֹבֶל 110
קַבַּעַת 132
קֶבֶר 36, 74
קֹדֶה 56, 72
קְדוּמִים 44
קָדוֹשׁ 98
קַדַּחַת 71
קְדָרִים 36
קֶדֶם 36
קַדְמֹנִי/קַדְמוֹנִי 36
קַדְמֹנִי 44
קִדְקֹד 65
קֶדֶר 41
קַדְרוּת 41
קָדַשׁ 106
קֹדֶשׁ 98
קְדֵשָׁה 106
קָהָל 99
קְהִלָּה 99
קַו 100, 117, 140
קוֹבַע/כּוֹבַע 109
קוֹמָה 141
קוֹף 51
קוֹץ 58
קְוָצוֹת 65
קוֹרָא/קֹרָא 47
קוֹרָה 129
קָטֹב 71
קֹטֶן 67, 69
קִטֹּרֶת 83, 89
קִיא 67
קִיטוֹר 32
קִים 107
קִין 110
קִינָה 117
קִיץ 45, 81
קִיקָיוֹן 72, 83
קִיר 112, 127
קָלוּט 74
קַלַּחַת 133
קָלִי 77
קלל 100
קְלָלָה 100
קָלַע 129
קָלַע 110
קָלַע 108
קִלְשׁוֹן 58
קָמָה 77
קָמוּשׁ 58
קָמַח 77
קֵן 46
קַנָּא 38
קָנָה 56, 72, 142
קָנָה 57, 67, 95, 140, 141
קֹנֶה/קוֹנֶה 105
קָנָה הַטּוֹב 56, 72
קָנֶה־בֹשֶׂם 56, 72
קִנָּן 105
קַנָּמוֹן 82, 89
קֶסֶם 98
קֶסֶת 121, 132
קַעֲקַע 70
קִעֲרָה 96, 133
קִפּוֹד 46, 53
קִפּוֹז 53
קַצְוֵי־אֶרֶץ 28
קָצָה 72, 82
קָצִין 103
קְצִיעוֹת/קְצִיעָה 56
קָצִיר 45
קָרַב 107
קָרַב 67
קַרְבָּן 96
קַרְדֹּם 138
קָרָה 35
קרה 129
קָרַח 35
קֶרַח/קָרַחַת/קָרְחָה 65
קָרְיָה 124
קֶרֶן 30, 104, 118, 132, 134
קַרְנַת 94
קַרְסֹל 70
קְרָעִים 84, 88
קֶרֶץ 54
קַרְקַע 126, 128
קַרְקַע הַיָּם 34
קֶרֶשׁ 115, 129
קֶרֶת 124
קַשׁ 77
קִשְׁאָה 82
קִשְׁוָה 94, 133
קִשִּׁיטָה 105, 142
קִשְׁקֶשֶׁת 109
קִשָּׁרִים 85
קֶשֶׁת/קֹשֶׁט 33, 110

רֹאֶה 95
רְאִי 89
רְאֵם 48
רָאמוֹת 40
רֹאשׁ 30, 58, 65, 103, 130
רֹאשׁ חִבֵּל 116
רֹאשׁ פִּנָּה 128
רָאשִׁים/רָשׁ/רוּשׁ 102
רֵאשִׁית 44
רַב/רַבּ 110
רַב הַחֹבֵל 115
רבב 110
רִבְבוֹת 110
רְבִיבִים 33
רְבִיד 87
רֶגֶב 30, 69
רֶגֶל/רַגְלַיִם 69, 70
רַגְלִי 108
רֶגַע 44
רְדִיד 86
רֶהָטִים 49
רוּחַ 32, 66
רוּחַ מִדְבָּר 32
רוֹכֵל 106
רוּם 141
רֹחַב 140
רֹחַב 140
רְחוֹב/רֹחוֹב 140
רְחוֹב 124, 130
רַחֲמִים 39
רָחֵל 49
רָחָם 47
רֶחֶם 68
רֶחֶם מַשְׁכִּיל 74
רַחַץ 133
רַחְץ סִיר 133
רַחַת 78, 139
רִיב 101
רֵיחַ 96
רִיפוֹת 77
רַכָּב 111
רֶכֶב 111
רָכֶב 39
רִכְבָּה 111
רְכוּב 111
רְכָלָה 106
רֶכֶס 30
רְכָסִים 30
רֶכֶשׁ 51
רָמָה 141

שׁוֹאָה/שׁוֹא 33
שׁוּחָה 35, 69
שׁוּחָה/שַׁחַת/שִׁיחָה 55
שׁוֹט 34, 109
שׁוּט 116
שׁוּל 85
שׁוֹלָל 114
שׁוּם 73, 82
שׁוֹעַ 102
שׁוּעָל 52
שׁוֹפָר 107, 118
שׁוֹק 69
שׁוּק 111
שׁוּר 107, 113, 127
שׁוֹר 28, 48
שׁוּרָה 60
שׁוֹרֵר 107
שׁוּשָׁן 58
שְׁחוֹר 41
שַׁחַל 52
שְׁחֹלֶת 54, 59, 72
שַׁחַף 47
שַׁחֲפֶת 71
שַׁחַק 32
שַׁחַר 43
שׁחר 41
שְׁחַרְחֹר 41
שַׁחַת 36, 74
שִׁטָּה 57
שִׁטִּים 50
שִׁטִּים 115
שָׁטָף 34
שֹׁטֵר 195
שֹׁטֵר/שׁוֹטֵר 108
שִׁיט 116
שִׁיז 68
שִׁיר 117
ירוֹתֹשׁ 87
שֵׁישׁ/שֵׁשׁ 39
שִׁית 84
שִׁית 39
שִׁכְבָּה 130
שְׁכֶם/שִׁכְמָה 68
שֵׁכָר 79
שֶׁלֶג/שָׁלָג 35
שִׁלּוּחִים 93
שָׁלַח 109, 110
שַׁלְחֶן 94, 131
שָׁלָט 109, 110
שִׁלְיָה 62
שַׁלִּיט 103, 108
שָׁלִישׁ 108, 140
שָׁלֵךְ 46
שָׁלָל 114
שָׁלָם 96
שִׁכְיָה 115
שַׁכִּין 135
שָׁכִיר 64
שָׁכָר 106
שָׁלַו 47
שַׁלְמָה/שִׁלְמָה 84
שְׁמוּאֵל 36, 67
שִׁמִּיכָה 131
שְׁמָמִית 54
שְׂעִיר 33, 49
שְׂעִירָה 49
שַׁעַר 65
שַׁעֲרָה 78
שְׂפָה/שְׂפָתַיִם 66
שֶׁפֶם 65
שָׁקַל 75, 135
שַׁר 103, 108
שׁר/שָׁרַר 68
שָׁרַד 137
שָׁרָה 62, 93, 103
שְׁרוֹדְ 86
שָׁרוּעַ 74
שָׂרֵי הָרְכוּשׁ 105
שָׁרִיג 59, 78
שָׁרַף 53
שָׁרַק 42
שֹׂרֵק/שָׂרֵקָה 78

שְׁאוֹל 36, 74
שְׁאַר 70
שְׁאַר 62
שְׁאַר בָּשָׂר 92
שַׁאֲרָה 62
שָׁבוֹ 39
שְׁבוּעַ 43
שְׁבוּעָה 100
שְׁבוּת 114
שַׁבָּט 50, 110
שֵׁבֶט 45, 104
שְׁבִי 114
שִׁבְיָה 114
שְׁבִיל 111
שְׁבִיסִים 86
שֵׂכֶל 84
שַׁבְלוּל 54
שִׁבֹּלֶת 35, 77
שֶׁבַע 43
שְׁבָרִים 31
שַׁבָּת 99
שִׁגְיוֹנָה 101
שְׁגַל 103
שִׁגָּעוֹן 74
שֵׁד/שֵׁדִים 66
שֹׁהַם 40
שַׁהֲרוֹן 87
רִמָּה 54
רִמּוֹן 73, 81
רֹמַח 110
רֶמֶשׂ 46
רְנָנִים 47
רִסִיסֵי לַיְלָה 34
רֶסֶן 50
רַע 101
רַע 64
רֵעָה 64
רֵעָה 64
רְעוּת 64
רֹעִי 106
רַעְיָה 64
רְעָלוֹת 86
רַעַם 32
רַעֲנָן 60
רְפָאִים 74, 98
רִפְסֹדֹת 115
רֶפֶשׁ 30
רֶפֶת 49
רַקָּה 65
רֶקַח 82
רַקָּחָה/רֹקַח 89, 105
רָקִיעַ 28, 38
רָקִיק 78
רִקְמָה 41
רֹקֶם 105
רִקְמָה/רֹקֵם 88
רַקַּע 137
רקשׁ 42
רָשָׁע 101
רִשְׁעָה/רֶשַׁע 101
רֶשֶׁף 32, 110
רֶשֶׁת 55
רִתּוּקוֹת 136
רֹתֶם 56, 59

שְׂאֹר 78
שִׁבְכָה 55
שָׂדֶה 29, 141
שְׁדֵרָה 129
שֶׂה 49
שׂוֹבֶךְ 59
שׂוֹדְ 59
שׂוֹדְ 127
שׂחק 119
שָׂטָן 107
שֵׂיבָה 63, 65
שֵׂיבָה טוֹבָה 63
שִׂיד 129
שִׂיחַ 59
שֵׂדְ 58
שָׂכְוִי 46
שַׂבּוֹת 55

שְׁלֹשׁ קְלִשׁוֹן 139
שְׁלֹשׁוֹם 43
שְׁלֹשִׁים 118
שִׁמָּה 31
שְׁמַיִם 28
שְׁמִינִת 117, 118
שָׁמִיר 40
שָׁמֶן 57, 73, 81, 89
שֶׁמֶן שְׁשׁוֹן 57
שָׁמָר 79
שְׁמֵרוֹת עֵינַיִם 66
שָׁמֹשׁ 29, 113
שֵׁן 30, 69
שָׁנָה 44
שָׁנִי 42
שַׁעֲטְנֵז 88
שְׁעָלִים 67
שַׁעַר 33, 126, 140
שִׁפּוֹת 80
שִׁפְחָה 64
שֵׁפֶט 101, 105
שָׁפָט 100
שִׁפִּי 30
שִׁפְיֹפֹן 53
שִׁפְכָה 69
שִׁפְלָה 31
שָׁפָן 53
שָׁקֵד 80
שִׁקּוּי 76, 79
שִׁקּוּץ 97
שָׁקָל 141, 142
שִׁקְמָה 57, 81
שִׁקַּפִּים 127
שָׁקָר 101
שֶׁקֶתוֹת הַמַּיִם 49
שָׁרָב 29
שַׁרְבִיט 104
שָׁרָה 113
שְׁרִיָה 109, 110
שִׁרְיוֹן 109
שִׁרִּים 117
שְׁרִיר 70
שָׁרָץ 46
שֹׁר 68, 69
שֹׁרֶשׁ 59
שְׁרֵת 96
שָׁשָׁר 42
שַׁתָּה/שָׁתוֹת/שַׁת 68
שְׁתִי 88

תָּא 113, 128
תְּאוֹ 48
תַּאֲלָה 100
תְּאֵנָה 73, 81
תְּאַשּׁוּר 57
תֵּבָה 115, 135
תֵּבֵל 29
תְּבֵלֵל 74
תֶּבֶן 78
תִּבְנִית 97
תִּדְהָר 57
תְּהוֹם 34
תְּהִלָּה 117
תּוֹדָה 96
תּוֹלַדוֹת 93
תּוֹלָע 54
תּוֹמֵם/תְּוֹמִים 92
תּוֹעֲפוֹת 48
תּוֹר 87
תּוֹרָה 100, 120
תּוֹשָׁב 64
תּוֹתָח 109
תַּחְמָס 47
תַּחֲרָא 109
תַּחַשׁ 54
תַּחְתִּיִּם 116
תַּחְתִּית 30
תֵּימָן 36
תֵּימָנָה 36
תִּירוֹשׁ 79
תִּישׁ 49
תְּכוּנָה 131
תַּכִּיִּם 46
תְּכֵלֶת 51
תֹּכֶן 140
תַּכְרִיךְ 85
תֵּל 29
תִּלְבֹּשֶׁת 84
תָּלוּל 141
תְּלִי 109, 110
תַּלְמִיד 120
תָּמִים 98
תָּמִים 74
תֹּמֶר/תִּמֹּרָה/תָּמָר 73, 81
תַּמְרוּר 112
תַּן/תַּנָּה 52
תְּנוּךְ 66
תְּנוּפָה 96
תָּנוּר 134
תַּנִּין 53
תְּנֻשֶׁמֶת 47, 53
תְּעָלָה 35, 71, 73
תֹּעַר 109, 135
תֹּעַר הַסַּפָּר 121
תֹּף 118
תַּפּוּחַ 81
תָּפֵל 76, 129
תְּפִלָּה 117
תֹּפְשֵׁי מָשׁוֹט 115
תַּקּוֹעַ 118
תְּקוּפָה 44
תְּקוּפַת הַשָּׁנָה 45
תֵּקַע 118
תֹּר/תּוֹר 46
תְּרוּמָה 97
תְּרוּמִיָּה 97
תְּרוּעָה 107
תִּרְזָה 57
תֹּרֶן 112, 116
תְּרָפִים 97
תַּרְשִׁישׁ 40
תִּרְשָׁתָא 104
תַּרְתָּן 108

SCRIPTURE INDEX

Genesis

1:1 44
1:3 28
1:5 43
1:6 46
1:9 29
1:11–12 57
1:26 62
1:30 57
2:5 ..... 29, 59
2:7 66
2:9 76
2:10 34
2:11 37
2:12 ..... 40, 58
2:22 ..... 62, 67
2:24 92
3:1 53
3:7 ..... 81, 85
3:14 67
3:15 70
3:16 ..... 73, 92
3:18 58
3:19 66
3:21 ..... 84, 85
3:22 67
4:4 92
4:7 126
4:11 100
4:17 124
4:20 ..... 31, 126
4:22 ..... 92, 137
5:1 93
5:4 44
5:7 43
6:9 64
6:14 ..... 56, 115
6:15–16 141
6:16 ..... 116, 127
6:17 28
7:9 28
7:11 ..... 28, 44, 127
7:19 141
7:21 46
8:5 30
8:6 127
8:11 ..... 46, 60
8:19 93
8:20 94
8:21 96
8:22 45
9:4 66
9:13 33
9:22 69
9:24 79
9:25 105
10:8 108
11:3 ..... 32, 38, 129, 134
11:6 ..... 64, 107
11:30 63
11:31 93
12:5 92
12:15 ..... 104, 124
13:2 142
13:7 101
13:10 ..... 29, 31
13:17 140
14:1 103
14:10 ..... 33, 40, 129
14:14 ..... 64, 92
14:15 ..... 36, 64
14:23 ..... 86, 136
15:2 109
15:9 46
15:12 29
15:13 64
15:15 63
15:17 ..... 32, 43
16:3 92
16:4 103
16:14 ..... 33, 34, 130
17:7 100
17:12 ..... 92, 105
17:14 62
18:6 ..... 77, 140
18:11 63
18:12 103
18:25 98
18:27 32
19:2 ..... 124, 140
19:3 31
19:6 126
19:8 129
19:15 43
19:26 40
19:28 ..... 38, 134
19:33 92
19:34 43
20:9 ..... 96, 101
20:12 92
21:8 62
21:12 63
21:14 ..... 33, 76, 134
21:16 110
21:23 92
21:33 56
22:2 30
22:3 51
22:6 135
22:13 58
22:24 ..... 64, 93
23:4 74
23:15–16 ..... 141, 142
24:14 ..... 63, 133
24:22 ..... 87, 141
24:25 ..... 76, 78
24:27 111
24:53 84
24:65 86
25:6 36
25:11 74
25:16 ..... 64, 124
25:24 92
25:25 85
25:29 ..... 76, 106
25:30 41
25:31 92
26:5 95
26:12 140
26:19 35
26:26 106
27:3 ..... 76, 109, 110
27:9 49
27:12 100
27:16 88
27:29 103
27:37 44
27:40 66
28:11 130
28:12 127
28:18 38
29:27 43
30:14–16 ..... 72, 82
30:32 ..... 41, 42, 49
30:33 43
30:35 42
30:37 ..... 56, 80
30:38 49
31:10 49
31:19 97
31:21 35
31:34 50
31:39 74
31:40 35
32:10 50
32:13 29
32:15 49
32:21 96
32:33 68
33:1 64
33:19 142

34:2 103
34:4 63
34:9 93
34:12 93
34:26 109
34:31 106
35:11 ..... 64, 69
35:14 31
35:18 66
35:20 74
36:6 105
36:15 ..... 62, 103
37:3 85
37:20 33
37:25 ..... 72, 83, 89
37:34 75
37:35 ..... 36, 74, 75
37:36 108
38:8, 13 93
38:14 84
38:18 ..... 87, 136, 138
38:21 106
38:25 87
40:3 125
40:10 ..... 60, 78
40:12 98
40:13 104
40:15 125
40:16 78
41:2 57
41:8 104
41:9 101
41:42 ..... 87, 88
41:43 111
42:19 125
42:27 134
43:11 ..... 80, 83
43:23 125
43:30 128
43:33 63
44:8 64
44:12 132
44:20 63
45:6 45
45:17 48
45:19 111
46:4 66
46:34 63
47:4 57
47:18 70
47:19 77
47:31 130
48:7 141
48:10 63
48:13 67
48:18 65
49:4 130
49:5 ..... 71, 99, 108, 109
49:9 52
49:10 104
49:11 ..... 79, 84
49:12 ..... 42, 80
49:13 ..... 34, 115
49:14 ..... 67, 135
49:16 64
49:17 ..... 53, 111
49:19 108
49:21 52
49:22 ..... 113, 127
49:23 110
49:26 95
49:27 52
50:9 ..... 108, 111
50:10 75
50:26 ..... 74, 132

Exodus

1:1 62
1:16 ..... 71, 131
1:17 63
2:2 44
2:3 ..... 57, 135
2:9 62
3:1 ..... 50, 93
3:2 59
3:8 140
4:10 65
4:25 93
4:26 99
5:6 108
5:9 101
5:14 43
6:12 66
6:20 92
6:26 107
7:19 ..... 34, 35, 130
8:3 128
8:5 53
8:9 130
8:20 54
9:3 48
9:9 29
9:11 97
9:31 ..... 57, 77, 88, 131
10:9 ..... 44, 99
10:14 54
10:26 46
11:2 64
11:5 39
12:7 126
12:8 72
12:9 69
12:11 ..... 44, 68, 99
12:13 71
12:15 78
12:19 64
12:22 ..... 58, 71, 128
12:34 ..... 68, 78
12:38 64
12:39 78
12:42 43
12:45 64
13:4 45
13:16 86
14:23 50
14:24 43
14:25 111
15:2 117
15:7 77
15:8 ..... 34, 66
15:13 50
15:17 125
15:25 56
15:27 ..... 34, 73, 81
16:3 133
16:13 47
16:15 ..... 58, 76
16:16 140
16:23 99
16:24 54
16:31 ..... 72, 82
16:33 133
16:36 ..... 77, 140
18:2 93
18:16 100
19:4 48
19:13 118
19:17 30
20:10 64
20:25 38
20:26 127
21:3 70
21:6 137
21:10 84
21:19 50
21:20 50
21:30 101
22:8 100
22:9 84
22:24 105
22:26 70
22:30 46
23:3, 6 102
23:11 72
23:15–16 ..... 44, 99
23:28 54
23:38 96
24:10 129
24:11 104
25:1, 4 42
25:5 57
25:6 ..... 69, 70, 82, 83, 88, 89
25:7 95
25:11 ..... 37, 94, 129
25:12 ..... 94, 130
25:13, 17 94
25:18 ..... 94, 137
25:25 141
25:29 ..... 94, 96, 132, 133
25:31–35 95
25:33 80
25:38 96
25:39 142

26:1 105
26:4 136
26:14 84
26:15 129
26:18 36
26:25 130
26:28 127
26:31 129
26:36 ..... 105, 129
27:2 94
27:3 96
27:4 94
27:5 94
27:6–7 94
27:8–9 129
27:19 ..... 126, 127
27:20 ..... 81, 131
27:21 94
28:4, 8 ..... 85, 95
28:11 105
28:13 38
28:14 136
28:16 141
28:17 40
28:18–19 39
28:20 ..... 39, 40
28:30 ..... 97, 98
28:32 109
28:33 ..... 73, 81, 85
28:33–34 95
28:34 118
28:36, 40 ..... 86, 95
28:42 ..... 69, 84, 87, 95
29:3 135
29:6 86
29:9 95
29:12 66
29:14 68
29:17 67
29:20 ..... 65, 66
29:22 48
29:25 96
29:33 64
29:40 140
29:42 96
30:1 ..... 94, 128
30:6 94
30:13 141
30:18 132
30:23 ..... 56, 82, 89
30:24 ..... 56, 72
30:25 89
30:34 ..... 54, 59, 72, 82, 83
30:35 83
31:2 64
32:4 137
34:7 96
34:13 97
34:15 96
34:22 ..... 45, 99
34:33–35 86
35:22 87
35:25 88
35:29 96
38:8 89
39:3 38
39:28 95
39:30 ..... 120, 137
39:40 136
40:15 95

Leviticus

1:2 96
2:4 78
2:5 133
2:14 77
3:4 68
3:9 67
4:10 48
4:28 49
4:32 48
5:1 101
5:12 96
5:15 101
6:2 ..... 94, 134
6:10 84
6:15 95
7:9 133
7:13 78
7:18 98
7:31 66
7:33 69
8:17 121
8:23 70
8:29 48
9:2 48
10:4 92
11:5–6 53
11:7 51
11:13 48
11:14, 16 47
11:17 46
11:18–19 ..... 47, 53
11:20 46
11:22 54
11:30 ..... 47, 53
11:34 79
11:35 ..... 133, 134
11:37 81
12:2 69
13:2 71
13:3 65
13:4, 19 41
13:23 71
13:29 65
13:30 42
13:39 41
13:41 ..... 65, 66
13:47–48 88
13:55 65
13:58 88
14:4 56
14:9 65
14:10 ..... 48, 140
14:37 42
15:25 98
16:21 44
18:12 ..... 62, 70
18:16 92
18:17 62
19:4 97
19:10 80
19:19 88
19:20 101
19:27 65
19:28 70
19:35 140
19:36 ..... 135, 142
21:13 63
21:18 ..... 73, 74
21:20 ..... 69, 71, 73, 74
22:12 98
22:13 93
22:22 71
22:23 74
23:14 77
23:17 ..... 76, 78, 140
23:18 48
23:27 98
23:27–28, 36 99
23:34 44
23:40 ..... 59, 81
24:5 78
24:11 100
25:10 101
25:15 64
25:19 81
25:22 43
25:24 101
25:25 102
25:47 92
25:49 ..... 92, 101
26:1 97
26:5 ..... 45, 60, 78
26:16 71
26:30 97
27:16 ..... 78, 140
28:42 69

Numbers

1:3 108
1:16 64
1:52 112
2:2 112
2:25 36
3:36 95
4:6 ..... 54, 96
4:10 94
4:12 96
5:2 74
5:3 62
5:15 77
5:17 ..... 126, 128

5:21 69
6:3–4 79
6:5 . . . . . 135, 137
6:9 44
7:3 111
7:9 66
7:17 96
8:2 131
8:11 96
8:16 62
9:15 94
10:9 107
10:10 29
11:4 64
11:5 . . . . 57, 71, 73, 80, 81, 82
11:7 40
11:8 . . . . . 78, 133, 139
11:32 43
14:29 108
14:33 97
15:19 97
15:20 138
15:38 . . . . . 65, 85
16:5 99
16:38 137
18:7–8 96
18:15 98
19:2 . . . . . 41, 48
19:9 98
19:15 132
19:18 74
20:19 111
21:6 53
21:18 . . . . . 102, 103, 104
21:20 29
21:28 141
22:4 99
22:11 100
22:22 107
22:24 . . . . . 80, 111, 130
23:3 30
23:21 . . . . . 107, 118
23:22 48
23:24 76
24:1, 4 98
24:5 126
24:6 . . . . . 56, 71, 82, 83
24:7 . . . . . 64, 133
24:8 107
24:20 74
25:7 110
25:8 . . . . . 68, 126
28:14 96
30:5 96
31:12 114
31:14 103
31:22 37
31:27 107
31:32 112
31:37 113
31:50 87
32:16 49
32:41 124
33:2 111
33:52 97
33:55 . . . . . 58, 70
34:11 30
35:19 100

Deuteronomy

1:1, 7 31
1:15 105
1:39 62
1:44 54
2:5 70
2:36 124
3:11, 17 130
4:6 120
4:45 100
6:2 100
7:5 97
7:13 81
7:14 74
8:9 102
8:15 . . . . . 31, 54
10:16 . . . . . 69, 99
11:10 . . . . . 42, 81
11:11, 14. 33
11:24 36
11:30 36
12:2 60
13:6 101
13:17 100
14:5 . . . . . 48, 49, 52
14:12 48
14:13 47
14:15 51
14:16, 18. 47
15:21 73
16:9 138
16:18 101
16:19 101
18:3 67
18:8 29
18:10 98
18:11 97
18:15 95
19:5 138
19:21 66
20:20 107
21:3 . . . . . 48, 50
21:12 67
22:6 46
22:8 . . . . . 112, 128, 129
22:12 85
23:2 . . . . . 69, 74
23:13 132
23:14 . . . . . 68, 138
23:18–19. 106
23:26 77
24:4 92
24:5 98
24:6 39
25:2 140
25:5 93
25:11 69
25:13 142
26:2 135
27:23 93
28:8 . . . . . 125, 126
28:26 46
28:28 74
28:35 65
28:42 54
28:52 112
28:57 62
29:4 84
29:16 97
29:17 . . . . . 57, 58, 72
29:19 100
30:3 114
30:6 99
30:20 141
32:2 . . . . . 33, 120
32:10 65
32:11 46
32:22 . . . . . 30, 128
32:24 71
32:25 63
32:26 62
32:31 . . . . . 101, 103
32:32 . . . . . 57, 82
32:33 52
32:34 . . . . . 53, 71
33:4 99
33:6 62
33:12 63
33:15 30
33:23 36
33:24 89

Joshua

1:4 43
2:19 111
4:19 36
5:2 99
5:2–3 135
5:11 106
5:11–12. 77
6:5 . . . . . 48, 118
6:16 118
6:19 125
7:5 . . . . . 30, 31
7:19 96
8:28 29
9:4 135
10:11 33
10:12–13. 29
10:24 103
10:40 30
11:10 103
12:8 35
13:3 103

15:1 97
15:7 30
15:19 34
17:11 30
22:8 114
23:13 50

Judges

1:6 67
1:7 131
3:16 141
3:20 131
3:22 70
3:23 127
3:24 69
3:25 127
3:27 107
3:31 50
4:4 101
4:18 131
4:21 137
5:2 65
5:4 32
5:6 111
5:7 102
5:8 107
5:9 105
5:10 ..... 42, 131
5:17 33
5:21 44
5:22 50
5:26 137
5:28 127
5:29 93
5:30 88
6:19 49
6:31 97
7:9 112
7:13 78
7:16 131
7:19 43
8:2 80
8:7 58
8:9 113
8:26 87
9:14 58
9:37 67
9:46 ..... 113, 125
9:48 138
9:49 59
9:51 127
9:53 ..... 39, 65
9:54 108
11:37 64
12:2 100
13:5 137
13:20 32
14:3 99
14:12 84
14:18 29
14:19 113
15:14 ..... 114, 136
15:15 65
15:25 133
16:5 107
16:7 ..... 110, 136
16:21 ..... 125, 136
16:25–26 130
17:4 97
18:16–17 126
19:12 64
19:16 63
20:11 63
20:16 110

1 Samuel

1:6 93
2:8 ..... 29, 130
2:10 101
2:13 135
2:13–14 96
2:14 133
2:22 63
2:36 142
3:1 98
4:18 66
5:4 67
5:4–5 126
5:6 71
6:4 96
6:11 132
6:20 98
7:9 48
8:13 ..... 89, 104, 105
8:23 102
9:3 51
9:9 95
9:22 128
10:1 ..... 104, 134
10:5 ..... 108, 113
13:6 ..... 29, 58, 74
13:19 110
13:20 135
13:20–21 138
13:21 ..... 50, 139, 141
14:12 112
14:14 ..... 29, 141
14:25 82
14:26 111
15:3 51
16:1 ..... 104, 132
16:13 134
16:16 118
17:4 108
17:5 109
17:6 ..... 86, 109
17:7 ..... 109, 110
17:18 80
17:21 112
17:40 ..... 50, 109, 135
17:43 100
17:46 70
17:51 109
17:56 63
18:6 118
20:5 99
20:18 131
21:8 ..... 48, 103
22:6 141
22:7 108
22:19 62
23:23 108
24:14 44
24:15 101
25:1 124
25:18 80
25:33 100
26:11 134
26:20 54
28:3 97
28:16 107
31:3 108

2 Samuel

1:10 ..... 67, 104
1:22 36
1:24 86
2:13 130
2:23 67
2:25 64
2:29 43
3:31 74
5:7 112
5:8 130
5:23–24 56
6:5 ..... 56, 118, 119
6:14 ..... 117, 119
6:19 ..... 79, 81
7:6 94
7:27 117
8:2 140
8:7 109
8:10 136
8:16 104
9:13 73
10:4 68
11:2 124
12:3 132
12:30 86
12:31 ..... 78, 138
13:6 ..... 78, 106
13:10 76
14:2 75
15:30 70
15:37 64
16:13 30
17:9 55
17:13 31
17:19 77
17:20 35
17:28 81
17:29 80
18:8 56

18:9 59
18:14 110
19:19 115
19:24 65
20:3 93
20:10 67
20:15 . . . . . 107, 113
21:10 39
21:16 110
22:3 . . . . . 109, 112, 125
22:16 34
22:30 30
22:37 70
22:46 . . . . . 112, 124
24:7 112
24:16 44
24:22 . . . . . 50, 78

1 Kings

1:38 51
1:40 . . . . . 117, 119
3:7 63
4:19 . . . . . 103, 107
4:22 140
5:2 140
5:3 . . . . . 46, 52
5:6 49
5:23 115
5:25 . . . . . 76, 77
6:1 45
6:3 130
6:4 127
6:5 128
6:6 127
6:7 . . . . . 31, 110
6:8 127
6:9 . . . . . 128, 129
6:15 129
6:16 128
6:18 . . . . . 60, 72, 81
6:19 . . . . . 94, 125
6:20 37
6:21 137
6:23 . . . . . 57, 81
6:31 . . . . . 126, 130
6:34 127
6:36 129
6:38 45
7:5 127
7:6 126
7:15 140
7:23–25. 96
7:25 48
7:26 140
7:27 96
7:30 . . . . . 96, 111
7:32–33. 111
7:50 . . . . . 96, 127, 133
8:2 45
8:12 32
8:31 100
8:37 . . . . . 54, 71, 77
9:15 112
9:19 . . . . . 124, 126
9:26–29. 115
10:1 103
10:9 104
10:11 56
10:12 130
10:14 141
10:15 108
10:22 . . . . . 46, 51
10:25 89
10:27 57
11:4 63
11:30 88
12:10 . . . . . 67, 69
12:11 109
14:3 . . . . . 133, 134
14:11 52
14:15 57
14:28 . . . . . 113, 128
16:18 . . . . . 112, 124
17:6 47
17:12 . . . . . 78, 126
17:17 62
18:29 43
18:45 33
19:4 . . . . . 56, 59
19:8 76
19:18 69
20:29 108
20:30 128
20:38 . . . . . 71, 85
20:42 107
21:1 . . . . . 60, 80, 124
21:8 103
21:23 124
22:27 125
22:34 111
22:49 115

2 Kings

2:20 133
3:15 117
3:16 33
3:25 108
4:1 105
4:2 . . . . . 133, 134
4:10 . . . . . 112, 131
4:39 . . . . . 57, 78, 82
4:42 . . . . . 77, 135
5:23 134
6:25 . . . . . 68, 140
7:11 127
8:15 88
9:11 74
9:30 88
9:37 68
10:2 109
10:7 . . . . . 133, 135
10:22 . . . . . 84, 131
11:2 128
12:6 . . . . . 64, 95, 105
16:18 112
17:25 52
18:16 . . . . . 125, 130
18:17 108
18:27 68
19:28 50
20:5 65
20:7 . . . . . 72, 73, 81
20:13 . . . . . 113, 126
21:13 . . . . . 133, 141
23:5 28
23:11 . . . . . 124, 126
23:17 111
25:1 113
25:30 76

Isaiah

1:6 73
1:8 81
1:10 100
1:11 48
1:25 37
1:29 56
1:30 60
1:31 32
2:16 115
2:20 . . . . . 53, 87
2:21 59
2:22 68
2:23 86
3:3 97
3:14 113
3:16 88
3:17 65
3:18–19. . . . . 86, 87
3:20 . . . . . 85, 86, 87, 88
3:21 87
3:22 . . . . . 84, 85
3:23 . . . . . 85, 86, 89
3:24 . . . . . 84, 135, 136
4:6 . . . . . 33, 126
5:1 30
5:2 . . . . . 78, 81, 124
5:5 80
5:6 58
5:10 141
5:12 . . . . . 117, 118
5:17 49
5:18 50
5:24 57
5:26 . . . . . 111, 112
5:28 . . . . . 31, 39, 135
5:30 28
6:4 126
7:14 63
7:19 . . . . . 35, 50, 58
7:24 40
7:25 138
8:1 120

8:7 35
8:16 120
9:4 . . . . . 86, 108, 109
9:9 81
9:17 39
10:6 29
10:15 . . . . . 59, 138
10:18 . . . . . 60, 70
11:1 59
11:4 101
11:6 51
11:8 62
11:12 28
13:1 98
13:8 42
13:21 . . . . . 49, 52
13:22 . . . . . 52, 113, 117
14:9 103
14:12 28
14:15 35
14:23 136
14:29 53
16:3 101
17:5 77
17:6 . . . . . 30, 59, 81
17:10 78
18:2 115
18:4 29
18:5 . . . . . 59, 60, 79
19:3 97
19:8 . . . . . 55, 106
19:9 105
20:4 114
21:2 98
21:5 . . . . . 108, 131
21:8 113
22:1 31
23:2 29
23:8 105
23:11 112
23:18 105
24:13 79
24:15 36
24:17 55
24:20 49
25:5 . . . . . 31, 117
25:10 68
26:14 98
27:9 129
27:12 35
28:2 33
28:4 . . . . . 60, 81
28:5 86
28:10 67
28:15 34
28:16 38
28:17 . . . . . 37, 140
28:20 130
28:25 . . . . . 72–73, 77, 82
28:27 . . . . . 82, 138
29:3 113
29:7 98
29:13 100
29:22 41
30:2 76
30:6 52
30:8 . . . . . 120, 121
30:14 . . . . . 32, 120, 134, 135
30:15 107
30:17 . . . . . 112, 116
30:20 120
30:24 . . 51, 77, 78, 81, 82, 138, 139
30:25 35
30:28 . . . . . 50, 138
30:30 33
30:32 118
31:9 32
32:14 113
33:2 107
33:7 108
33:12 129
33:14 32
33:21 . . . . . 115, 116
33:23 115
34:9 129
34:11 . . . . . 46, 47, 53
34:13 81
34:14 47
34:15 53
35:1 31
35:6 73
35:7 . . . . . 29, 31, 34
35:8 111
36:12 68
38:10 44
38:11 29
38:12 . . . . . 106, 126
38:17 36
40:2 66
40:4 . . . . . 29, 30, 31, 35
40:12 . . . . . 67, 140
40:14 120
40:19 105
40:20 81
40:22 . . . . . 28, 129
41:7 . . . . . 38, 137
41:18 34
41:19 57
41:29 97
42:8 117
42:18 73
42:22 114
44:7 44
44:12 . . . . . 96, 135, 138
44:13 137
44:14 . . . . . 56, 57
44:19 106
44:26 31
45:9 . . . . . 29, 134
45:16 97
46:6 142
47:2 84
47:13 120
48:4 . . . . . 65, 66
48:18 34
48:19 30
49:9 30
49:15 62
49:21 114
49:23 62
49:25 101
50:3 41
50:9 54
51:1 31
51:4 64
51:6, 8 54
51:10 34
51:17 132
51:19 43
51:20 55
53:8 125
54:4 63
54:11 41
54:12 . . . . . 38, 39, 113
55:10 106
55:13 58
56:10 . . . . . 52, 95
57:20 30
58:6 . . . . . 114, 136
59:5 53
59:17 84
60:6 51
61:3 84
63:1 42
63:2 80
63:3 . . . . . 66, 80
64:1 106
64:5 84
65:3 94
65:8 79
66:1 . . . . . 104, 131
66:11 66
66:14 100
66:17 53
66:20 51

Jeremiah

2:2 93
2:13 34
2:23 51
4:3 30
4:11, 28 41
4:29 . . . . . 31, 51, 58, 111
4:30 41
5:5 50
5:8 69
5:10 113
5:27 . . . . . 55, 135
5:28 101
5:31 69
6:7 101
6:20 . . . . . 56, 83
6:22 28

6:27, 29 . . . . . 38, 105
7:18 . . . . . 78, 97
8:7 . . . . . 44, 46, 47
8:8 104
8:20 . . . . . 45, 81
9:2 124
9:9 31
9:21 77
10:5 60
10:13 32
10:19 71
11:16 60
12:1 101
12:9 . . . . . 42, 46, 52
13:24 32
13:25 140
14:1 33
14:3 130
15:7 78
15:9 43
15:18 44
16:5 76
16:16 106
17:1 137
17:6 . . . . . 31, 59
17:8 60
17:11 47
17:12 141
18:15 111
18:18 120
19:2 134
20:1 105
20:2 136
20:17 68
22:28 134
23:1 50
23:15 98
24:1 . . . . . 104, 106
25:27 67
27:9 98
29:2 105
29:26 137
30:6 41
30:13 . . . . . 71, 73
31:12 62
31:21 112
31:22 62
36:18 120
36:22 133
36:23 . . . . . 120, 121
37:4, 15–16 125
38:11 84
38:12 . . . . . 66, 67
38:22 29
39:6 41
40:1 . . . . . 114, 136
43:9 129
46:20 54
47:5 65
48:17 104
50:15, 25 113
50:26 126
50:39 52
51:11 110
51:14 107
51:27 . . . . . 104, 107
51:30 125
51:32 112
51:34 67
51:43 31
51:57 107
52:11 125
52:15 64
52:21 141
52:22 130

Ezekiel

1:5 46
1:14 32
1:22–23 28
1:27 38
2:6 58
2:9 120
4:2 110
4:9 . . . . . 72, 77, 82
4:10 141
4:12 106
5:1 105
6:11 137
6:13 96
7:7 44
7:12 105
7:14 118
8:3 97
8:16 65
9:2 . . . . . 109, 121, 132
10:2 67
11:1 36
12:24 98
13:10–15 129
13:10 127
13:11 33
13:12 129
13:18 . . . . . 67, 85, 86
15:4 76
16:3 93
16:7 66
16:10 88
16:13 . . . . . 41, 84
16:16 42
16:24 128
17:3 141
17:5 56
17:7 60
17:22 . . . . . 59, 141
19:9 55
19:10 59
21:20 109
21:26 86
21:27 98
21:31 104
22:18 38
22:29 113
23:3 66
23:12 103
23:14 42
23:15 86
23:20 69
23:24 . . . . . 108, 109, 111
23:40 . . . . . 42, 88
24:5 106
24:6 . . . . . 38, 71
24:16 107
25:5 49
25:6 . . . . . 69, 70
26:9 110
26:20 35
27 56
27:5 115
27:7 115
27:9 . . . . . 62, 116
27:11 . . . . . 108, 115
27:12 116
27:15 56
27:17 76
27:18 41
27:19 . . . . . 56, 72
27:20 . . . . . 88, 111
27:22 38
27:24 . . . . . 84, 85, 88, 131
27:26 115
27:27 . . . . . 115, 116
27:29 115
28:13 39
29:3 53
30:4 73
30:21 71
31:3 . . . . . 56, 60
31:5 60
31:8 59
31:14 35
34:28 . . . . . 107, 113
36:17 98
38:6 112
38:7 108
38:12 28
38:20 30
39:9 109
40:2 124
40:3 140
40:5 124
40:12 127
40:13 68
41:8 140
41:13 124
41:16 129
43:3 98
43:7 111
43:15 . . . . . 94, 134
44:30 . . . . . 77, 78, 81
45:11 140
45:12 141
46:23 128

47:3 70
48:12 97
48:15 98

Hosea

2:7 ..... 76, 79
2:12 69
3:2 140
4:12 69
4:18 79
5:11 100
5:13 ..... 71, 73
6:4 32
7:8 78
7:9 ..... 63, 65
8:7 59
8:9 51
8:13 96
8:14 94
9:2 ..... 60, 78
9:10 80
9:14 74
10:5 97
10:8 58
10:14 124
12:9 101
13:8 66
13:13 67

Joel

1:4 54
1:5 ..... 76, 79
1:7 59
1:11 106
1:14 99
1:16 66
1:17 ..... 81, 126
1:18 50
2:6 42
2:16 128
2:23 33
3:13 138
4:10 ..... 135, 138
4:13 106
4:17 98

Amos

1:1 106
1:5 31
2:11 98
3:5 55
3:12 ..... 65, 88
4:2 55
4:3 124
4:10 65
5:8 ..... 28, 74
5:9 28
5:26 ..... 28, 97
6:4 49
6:6 132
6:10 74
6:12 31
7:1 54
7:4 34
7:8 37
7:14 106
9:1 ..... 126, 128, 130
9:3 34
9:6 28
9:9 ..... 39, 138
9:13 106

Obadiah

4. 46
7. 55

Jonah

1:3 106
1:6 115
2:2 54
4:6 ..... 72, 83

Micah

2:12 ..... 49, 50
4:8 112
5:12 98
6:11 101
7:19 34

Nahum

1:8 34
1:13 50
2:4 88
2:6 109
2:12–13 52
3:3 141
3:5 69

Habakkuk

1:15 55
2:1 112
2:11 129
3:9 110
3:14 103
3:17 ..... 49, 76
3:19 52

Zephaniah

1:16 113
1:17 70
2:5–6 29
2:14 47
3:8 114
3:10 95
3:19 73

Haggai

2:19 126

Zechariah

1:7 45
1:8 ..... 41, 42
1:62 41
2:12 65
3:5 95
4:7 128
4:10 37
5:9 47
6:3 ..... 41, 42
9:3 125
9:12 112
10:1 31
10:4 128
12:3 ..... 31, 38
12:12 133
14:20 118

Malachi

1:7 94
1:11 89
3:2 ..... 40, 105
3:10 125

Psalms

1:4 32
2:9 134
3:3 117
3:7 110
4:8 77
5:1 117
5:9 107
5:10 66
6:1 ..... 117, 118
8:1 117
9:1 117
11:6 32
12:7 ..... 29, 38, 132, 134
16:1 137
16:4 73
17:4 100
17:5 ..... 70, 111
18:15 ..... 32, 109
19:3 55
19:5 ..... 100, 117
19:6 126
19:7 29
19:9 100
19:11 82
21:12 110
21:13 126
22:13 48
22:16 65
22:30 35
23:1 106
24:8 107
26:12 ..... 64, 99
29:10 34
30:1 117
30:6 44
30:11 108
31:9 67
32:4 29
32:9 50

35:1 107
35:3 109
35:8 33
35:16 73
37:2 42
37:35 56
38:8 68
38:10 75
39:1 50
40:3 ..... 30, 35
44:23 74
45:8 57
45:9 ..... 56, 89, 118
45:10 103
46:10 109
48:3 141
48:8 36
48:11 28
51:9 35
51:15 101
55:9 32
55:14 63
55:22 ..... 107, 109
55:24 74
56:9 121
57:2 33
57:5 52
58:5 53
58:6 97
58:9 54
60:8 133
60:9 109
60:10 133
62:3 127
65:1 117
65:13 50
68:14 37
68:16 30
68:26 117
68:32 102
69:13 118
69:22 76
71:15 121
72:6 33
73:4 ..... 67, 73
74:6 138
75:7 36
76:3 110
76:13 107
77:5 66
77:18 33
77:19 32
78:14 32
78:26 36
78:31 70
78:47 32
78:48 32
78:70 49
79:2 70
79:11 53
81:3 118
83:14 57
84:4 47
84:6 81
87:7 119
88:12 ..... 35, 36
89:7 32
89:40 104
90:3 29
91:13 53
92:4 118
92:12 107
93:4 34
94:2 105
98:6 118
102:18 102
104:2 129
104:3 ..... 111, 129
104:5 128
104:14 48
104:15 42
104:18 49
104:21 76
104:26 53
105:18 ..... 114, 136
105:34 54
106:20 97
107:4 31
109:19 85
110:3 ..... 34, 43
112:3 101
114:8 39
118:22 128
119:91 28
119:99 120
119:103 65
119:147 43
129:3 68
133:2 95
137:2 ..... 56, 72
139:13 68
139:15 70
139:16 67
141:3 65
142:8 125
144:12 130
144:13 126
144:14 48
147:17 35
148:8 32
148:10 46
150:3 118
150:4 ..... 117, 118
150:5 118

Proverbs

1:6 ..... 104, 120
1:8 120
1:9 ..... 66, 86, 87
1:17 55
3:10 80
3:22 66
4:25 66
5:19 ..... 49, 66
6:6 54
6:11 102
7:8 111
7:10 84
7:16 ..... 87, 88
7:20 ..... 29, 44, 135
8:10 37
9:16 101
11:7 101
11:12 87
12:17 101
12:18 73
14:4 ..... 49, 77
15:19 ..... 58, 127
16:11 142
17:3 105
17:22 73
18:8 67
18:14 71
19:17 105
20:1 79
20:17 ..... 31, 39
20:20 43
20:30 73
21:16 74
22:14 ..... 35, 55
22:20 43
22:22 102
23:2 ..... 66, 135
23:18 44
23:21 84
23:27 69
23:29–30 42
23:30 79
23:31 58
23:34 115
24:13 ..... 77, 82
24:25 100
24:31 58
25:11 ..... 44, 81
25:12 86
25:20 40
26:8 110
26:14 127
26:18 110
26:23 132
27:15 ..... 33, 129
27:21 ..... 38, 132, 133
27:22 139
30:15, 28 54
30:31 ..... 46, 107
31:2 92
31:8 102
31:24 85
110:2 104

Job

1:10 127
1:14 54